SHOT IN THE DARK

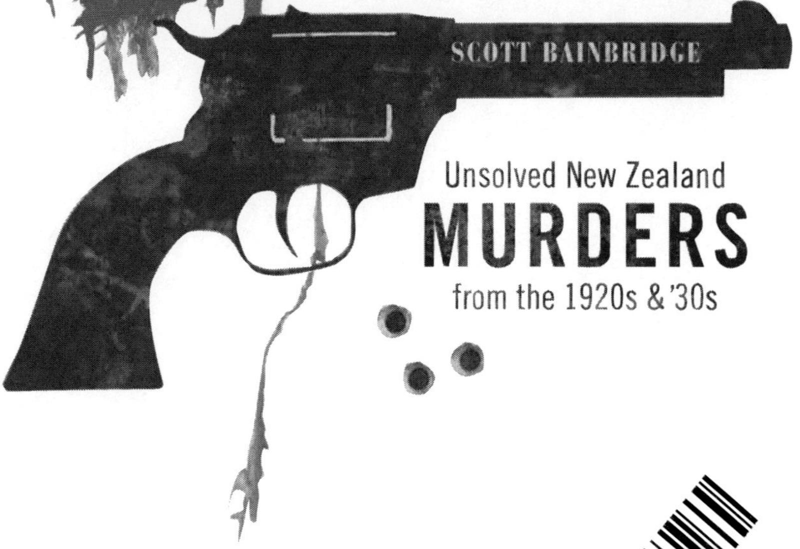

SCOTT BAINBRIDGE

Unsolved New Zealand
MURDERS
from the 1920s & '30s

A&U

For Noel and Ruby

First published in 2010

Allen & Unwin
83 Alexander Street
Crows Nest NSW 2065
Australia
Phone: (61 2) 8425 0100
Fax: (61 2) 9906 2218
Email: info@allenandunwin.com
Web: www.allenandunwin.com

National Library of New Zealand Cataloguing-in-Publication Data
Bainbridge, Scott, 1969-
Shot in the dark: unsolved New Zealand murders from the
1920s and '30s / Scott Bainbridge.
Includes bibliographical references.
ISBN 978-1-877505-02-7
1. Murder—Investigation—New Zealand.
2. Cold cases (Criminal investigation)—New Zealand. I. Title.
364.15230993—dc 22

Designed and typeset by Janet Hunt

10 9 8 7 6 5 4 3 2 1

SHOT IN THE DARK

Contents

Introduction

New Zealand embraced the dawn of the Roaring Twenties with hope. The country had endured the loss of some 18,000 soldiers during the Great War (1914–18) leaving very few families untouched by the conflict. Following the war, the Spanish influenza epidemic swept mercilessly throughout the dominion killing more than 8,500 people. Despite the massive effect these tragedies had on the country's 1.2 million people, the old adage 'the only way is up' prevailed.

In Europe and the United States the coming of the 1920s brought social, artistic and cultural change that saw the era become known as the Roaring Twenties and the Jazz Age. In the United States this new age was somewhat tempered by the advent of the Prohibition era. Change was not quite so rapid or all encompassing in New Zealand but the country was not left behind in the progress. The inter-war years were a significant period in the history of our country.

The 1920s began with the government spending £26 million to settle around 10,500 returned servicemen as farmers on one million hectares of Crown and private land. Farm production flourished with the advent of electrification in milking sheds, the availability of tractors and the application of artificial fertilisers. The economy experienced a post-war boom. Exports of dairy products and meat to England provided many farmers with a high standard of living. Millions of trees were planted in the central North Island in what was a visionary step towards prosperity. Despite this new prosperity, falling export prices led to severe recessions in 1921–2 and 1926–7 creating significant gaps between rich and poor.

The 1920s also saw significant urbanisation and at the end of the decade 60 per cent of the Pakeha population lived in urban areas. At the same time, 90 per cent of Maori still lived in rural areas.

During the 1920s, the self-proclaimed prophet Tahupotiki Ratana set out on a mission to preach the gospel to Maori and unite them under God. He attracted a huge following and his church soon held considerable political influence. In 1924, Ratana took a 30,000 signature petition to parliament calling for the ratification of the Treaty of Waitangi.

Reform Party leader, William Massey served as prime minister from 1912 until he died in office in 1925. His belief that farming was the key to a stable economy earned Massey the nickname 'Farmer Bill'. This dogged belief in the importance of farming meant that Massey regularly found himself off-side with other sectors of industry.

The 1920s saw two royal tours take place. The first, in 1920, was the highly anticipated visit of Edward, Prince of Wales (the future King Edward VIII), who toured to thank New Zealanders for their contribution to the war effort. In 1927, the Duke of York (the future King George V) and his wife spent a month travelling from Auckland to Bluff.

Other distinguished visitors included famed Russian ballerina, Anna Pavlova, in 1926. Her visit inspired a Wellington chef to make a dessert in her honour. Australian aviator Charles Kingsford-Smith became the first aeroplane pilot to fly across the Tasman in 1928 with thousands greeting him upon arrival at Christchurch's Wigram aerodrome.

This was an era of power and speed. Major hydroelectric projects were established bringing electricity to homes all round the country. Wagons and carts were still prevalent in rural areas but by 1925 private motor vehicles numbered 100,000. This number doubled within five years. Rail travel also improved and air travel began to be seen as a possibility.

Technological advancements made household appliances attractive. Shacklock introduced the Orion electric range and you could buy 'the world's best wireless'—a Radiola—for a £5 down payment at Farmers Trading Company.

The first radio stations began broadcasting in 1922 and the airwaves were rich with American jazz. The Charleston was the dance of the era and silent movies became a popular form of entertainment. In fashion, the 'flapper' look was in vogue with thoroughly modern young women wearing their hair in short bobs and donning sleeveless low-waisted dresses that could be scandalously raised to knee-level.

In the sporting arena, Gisborne boxer Tom Heeney became New Zealand's best known sportsman of the decade. His career highlight was his 1928 fight with world boxing champion Gene Tunney at Yankee Stadium in New York. Heeney took the fight to the eleventh round before losing on a technical knockout.

The All Black team known as the *Invincibles* toured the United Kingdom, France and Canada in 1924. The All Blacks played 32 games in total, winning them all including the Grand Slam over Ireland, England, France and Wales. Their 19–0 victory over Wales vindicated the controversial defeat suffered at the hands of the Welsh by the *Originals* in 1905. A young fullback, George Nepia played in all 32 games cementing his place in New Zealand rugby history.

The Roaring Twenties closed with the Wall Street stock market crash of 1929, which in turn led to the Great Depression. New Zealand export income dropped by 20 per cent in 1929 with a further 20 per cent decrease in 1930. Reform Prime Minister George Forbes reacted by drastically slashing state spending and cutting public servants' salaries by ten per cent.

In 1931, Forbes and his Reform Party formed a coalition with the United Party led by Gordon Coates. The coalition government made further cuts and many New Zealanders were forced to live below the poverty line. By 1933 the number of unemployed reached nearly 80,000. As part of the relief effort, the government established work projects to get unemployed men working. These work projects included bulding roads in remote areas, such as Haast Pass and Fiordland. The conditions in many of the relief camps were extremely primitive and the men were paid a pittance for long hours of hard physical labour.

After years of depression and deprivation, Michael Savage's Labour government swept into power in 1935. This new government promised economic stimulus, state housing and better conditions for those people working on relief programmes.

While the early 1930s were grim, New Zealanders had their share of victories to celebrate: the legendary race horse Phar Lap was at the height of his winning form, Jack Lovelock won gold in the 1500 metres at the Berlin Olympics, 'Hine-o-te-rangi—Daughter of the Skies' Jean Batten was setting aviation records across the globe. Despite the good times, the 'Golden Weather' was all too brief. Very soon, storm clouds brewing across Europe heralded the dawn of a new era.

While politics, the economy and society underwent massive change in the inter-war years so too did crime and policing. In the early 1920s, typical crimes included larrikinism, orchard raiding, bicycle theft and cattle rustling. More serious crimes like assault, vandalism, theft and burglary were principally put down to the unsettled social climate of the time and blamed on unskilled returned servicemen or swaggers as they were known. The swaggers travelled from town to town in the search of work, with many of them frequenting pubs, getting drunk and fighting. Many burglaries and nuisance crimes were blamed on swaggers, who would disappear as swiftly as they entered town.

As the 1920s wore on, guns began to replace daggers as the weapon of choice for New Zealand criminals. Despite the advancements in fingerprinting and forensics, for the first time ever a large number of murders during the 1920s and 1930s remained unsolved.

While I was researching my second book *Still Missing*, I discovered some intriguing mysteries from the inter-war years that seemed to have been forgotten over the passage of time. One of these cases was the disappearance of Nellie Mouat in Christchurch in 1925. Despite reports that Nellie was 'living it up' in Dunedin, her husband Fred was arrested and convicted for her murder. Sensational reporting of the case and his very public appeals did well to keep the case alive and provoke widespread interest at the time. The Mouat case should be remembered as one of the most controversial trials in the history of New Zealand crime. Yet Fred's release in 1937, after 12 years of hard labour, was not even afforded the briefest of mentions. I began to wonder how many similar cases existed that had been all but forgotten.

After the release of *Still Missing*, much of the feedback I received was about the older cases in the book. When families approached me about cases, they didn't have a lot of information because the death or disappearance of a family member was seen as a dark secret that was rarely spoken about. Only the barest of facts had been passed down through generations and fact had been surpassed by myth or gossip, which was rarely if ever substantiated. The more I delved into these forgotten cases, the more I began to wonder whether a fresh look at the cases might provide some conclusions.

1. The Murder of Constable Dorgan

The soldier in battle is often liable to be ambushed, but the police officer throughout his whole career is liable to fall into the ambushes which exist in the dark streets and alleys, the burglared dwelling or shop, in the unprepared encounter with the lunatic, the drunkard, the street rowdy, and the domestic disturber. At all time he literally carries his life in his hands. Our dead comrade here is a witness to the truth of what I say. He is the last of a long list of men of our force who have laid down their lives in the execution of duty, either in obedience to orders, in answer to requests for their protection, or in response to a still higher call to risk their own lives to save others.

New Zealand Police Commissioner John O'Donovan's address
at the funeral of Constable Dudding, 9 October 1919

The devastation of the First World War had a huge impact on New Zealand, and the memory of hard times and loss were far from distant. Communities became more socially cohesive, as people tended to look out for their neighbours. Violent crimes were at an all time low. But the country was changing.

On 6 October 1919, Constable Vivian Dudding was shot dead while attempting to intervene in a domestic dispute in Wellington. He was only the fourth officer in the history of the New Zealand Police to be killed in the line of duty.

The cold-blooded murder of Constable Dudding sent shock waves throughout New Zealand during a time when the country was finally beginning to enjoy some post-war peace and prosperity. But what caused further alarm was the fact Dudding had been killed with an automatic revolver, a weapon authorities had begun to see appearing in increased numbers over recent years.

Dudding's murder accelerated the need for some accountability and led directly to the passing of the Arms Act 1920, which sought to make permanent the wartime restrictions on the carriage, possession and importation of firearms. All private owners of firearms were required to register their firearms by 1 April 1921 and any owners who did not register their firearms were required to destroy them or hand them in.

Thousands of returned servicemen had brought back automatic pistols as trophies from the war and within the first 12 months of the act being in force 200,000 firearms were registered. Thousands more had not been declared.

The burden of enforcing the new legislation fell to the police, who were already overworked. Most police districts complained of a shortage of personnel and regularly asked for staffing increases. The low pay, long working hours and conditions were not a welcoming incentive for new recruits, as well as being a general source of disgruntlement for the rank and file.

During the post-war boom, the cost of living had increased by at least 60 per cent since 1914. In comparison, the basic police wage rose by only 33 per cent between 1914 and 1921. Housing for police officers was also a contentious issue. Renting was seen as a more practicable option due to the constant transfers of officers between stations. Most stations preferred single men for the simple reason it was easier to house them in the barracks or dormitories, as opposed to having to find housing for married officers with children, which was more difficult. But rent was at an all time high and housing was in short supply, particularly in smaller centres.

One officer who had canvassed the commissioner to provide more support for officers in need of decent accommodation was Constable James Dorgan of Timaru.

James Dorgan was born in County Kerry, Ireland on 26 January 1884. As a teenager, he emigrated to Christchurch with his parents and two brothers. After leaving school and working at a variety of menial jobs, Dorgan entered the police force and was appointed Officer 1764 Christchurch on 11 July 1912, at the age of 28.

While still living in Christchurch, Dorgan began courting Minnie Shine of Timaru. It was a requirement for all single policemen to apply through their superiors for permission to marry and, as the relationship progressed, Dorgan requested permission to marry Miss Shine. Dorgan's senior officers in Christchurch carried out character checks on Miss Shine and all her family. Fortunately for the young couple, Minnie's family were found to be 'of very sound moral character' and approval to marry was granted.

In preparation for their marriage, James Dorgan transferred to Timaru on 29 March 1915. People there soon came to know him as a friendly, approachable policeman and he was popular with his fellow officers. Minnie Shine became Minnie Dorgan when the couple married on 14 December 1915.

The couple soon settled into married life in Timaru and before long Minnie was pregnant with their first child. Minnie had always kept poor health and this was exacerbated by her pregnancy. Her health deteriorated so badly that she suffered from almost nightly epileptic seizures. After the birth of their first son, John, in 1916 James Dorgan decided to try and find a police position that would allow him to spend more time with his family.

On 16 April 1917, he applied for a transfer to Temuka, which was a smaller station and would mean that he could spend every night with Minnie and their child. His application was denied because the commanding officer in Temuka chose to appoint a single man to the post. Dorgan was disappointed but he continued his duties in Timaru.

Minnie and James had their second child, David, in 1919. Although delighted to have another child, Minnie's health was still a concern.

On 23 September 1919, with a third child on the way, Dorgan applied for a vacancy at the small police station in Waimate that would require no night shift duty. In his application, Dorgan wrote he wished to transfer because of his wife's ill health. His application was accompanied by a letter of support from his sergeant but even this didn't help. Dorgan was dismayed to learn his application was declined.

Meanwhile, the housing shortage in Timaru was so acute Dorgan struggled to keep a roof over his family's heads. The policeman could scarcely afford to pay rent on his wages even if he could find a place to rent. Property owners wanting to sell would often leave their houses empty rather than having to bother with tenants. Finding and keeping a home for his family was a constant worry for Dorgan.

Frustrated by his situation, he wrote to Commissioner O'Donovan. In his letter, Dorgan wrote of his desire to move as he was a married officer with a sick wife and young children. He said he could not secure a dwelling for them because the unstable economy saw a large number of New Zealand homeowners selling their houses.

During 1920 the Dorgans were forced to vacate three tenancies within a matter of months as the owners decided to sell their houses rather than rent them out. This was deeply unsettling for the young family. Minnie Dorgan required constant medical attention and had three young children to look after.

On 7 July 1920, Dorgan wrote to Commissioner O'Donovan again. He told the commissioner that his applications to transfer stations had been unsuccessful because he was married with a family. He also pointed out that he was being forced to consider moving to the suburbs, which would mean a 40-minute walk to the station, rendering him useless in case of an emergency.

In a memorandum dated 16 July 1920, Commissioner O'Donovan empathised with Dorgan's plight but said that the housing situation extended to all areas of the community, not just police. He also pointed out that the housing shortage was no more acute in Timaru than elsewhere in the country. He said he would not consider transferring officers to other localities purely because of the housing shortage. The commissioner's decision turned out to be a fateful one for Dorgan.

The night of 26 August 1921 was a cold one in Timaru. At 9pm, Constables Dorgan, Christopher and McCullough clocked in for their night-shift beat duty.

Being the senior officer of the three, Dorgan was assigned the number one beat, which extended half way along Stafford Street—Timaru's main shopping area. Constable Christopher was assigned the number two beat along the rest of Stafford Street. Constable McCullough was given the number three beat which ran along the back streets of the town centre.

The number two beat included the one of the town's larger department stores, T & J Thomson Drapers—the building still stands and is now home to the Farmers department store. The shop is a two-storied brick building with a large double-windowed front with panelled doors. On the upper level was a large balcony that overlooked Stafford Street.

Scotsman, Thomas Thomson had worked for his father's drapery business from an early age. In 1874, he sailed to New Zealand with big dreams. He worked with his brother James for some years before establishing his own shop in Stafford Street in 1888.

By 1921, Thomas Thomson was 66-years-old and struggling to keep up with the ever-changing pace of business. However, he insisted on being the first one to open up in the morning and the last person to leave. Over the past few years there had been several break-ins at Thomson's. Some people put this down to Thomas Thomson's carelessness with security and wondered whether it was time the old man handed the running of the store to his son. Each time a burglary took place, police were called out to investigate. What baffled police and Thomson was that many of the break-ins revealed no signs of forced entry.

On the night in question, Constable Christopher strolled past Thomson's between 11.30pm and 11.45pm. He shone his torch through the windows and was able to see right into the store as there were no blinds covering the windows along the shop front. There were no lights on. As a matter of course Christopher checked each door on the ground floor and found them to be secure.

For a Friday night it was unusually quiet. The cold probably kept people at home and there were no ships in port and only a few out-of-town guests staying in the hotels and boarding houses. There was a dance at the Empire Hotel, which finished around 11pm. A few groups of people leaving the dance milled around before eventually drifting home but other than that there was little activity.

At around 12.40am, Christopher returned along Stafford Street, when he glimpsed a sudden flash of light coming from inside T & J Thomson's. He walked towards the building but the light disappeared as quickly as he had seen it. From the street, the shop looked as empty as it had an hour earlier. But when Christopher shone his lamp on the front door he noticed that the glass panels on an inside door had been completely covered to obscure any view from the outside. What was happening behind those doors?

Christopher switched off his torch and quietly listened for a few moments but heard no movements. He quickly walked away from the shop and retreated into the doorway of the fruiterers next door. He flashed his torch on and off for a few moments—a pre-arranged signal to his colleagues. Seconds later, Constable Dorgan sprinted across the road and asked what was wrong.

Christopher told him what he had seen and Dorgan said that it was probably old man Thomson still at work. There had been several times in the past when police were alerted to a possible break-in only to find it was Thomson working late.

Christopher told Dorgan that the shop was definitely closed up and secure one hour earlier. He was certain there was something wrong.

Constable Christopher checked the windows along the alley and the door at the rear, while Dorgan waited at the front door. As he returned to inform his colleague that the building seemed secure, both officers saw another quick flash of light coming from inside the menswear department. There was definitely someone inside the shop. Dorgan hissed at Christopher, 'You better go up to Thomson's house and tell him to come at once with the keys. I will watch the back of the shop.'

Christopher took five minutes to reach Thomson's house. It was now 1.10am. Thomson agreed to come to the shop but Christopher did not wait for him. As the constable raced along the street adjacent to Stafford Street, he saw three people walking ahead of him. As the constable brushed past the party, they all heard what sounded like four gunshots in rapid succession coming from further along the street. Christopher ran towards Thomson's store with the three bystanders following close behind.

Arriving at the store, Constable Christopher saw that the shop front was clear. He pushed back the iron gates and walked slowly and carefully along the right-of-way leading to Thomson's back yard. By the light of the moon, he saw a figure staggering towards him. It was James Dorgan, who upon seeing his friend cried out, 'Christopher, I am done!'

'You're alright, don't be a fool,' Christopher replied, hoping like hell it was true.

Dorgan collapsed in his arms, knocking them both to the ground. Christopher struggled to move the injured officer into a comfortable position. He looked around. There was nobody else in the alley.

'Where is he?'

'He fired four shots and went up the back,' replied Dorgan, indicating a cliff face beyond the yard.

'I'm thirsty. Get me a drink of water, please. I know I'm done.'

The trio who had followed Christopher back to Thomson's soon arrived on the scene and offered their assistance. They were Eleanor Cloudesley and her friends Miss Stringer and Mr Jones.

Christopher asked Stringer and Jones to hurry to an address in nearby Sophia Street to summon Sergeant McGregor. He turned to Cloudesley and asked her to remain and comfort his injured friend. He then ran to a nearby telephone box and called the duty sergeant and local medic, Dr Ussher.

Meanwhile, Constable McCullough arrived on the scene to find Eleanor Cloudesley comforting the injured Dorgan. 'What is the matter Jim?'

'I have been shot, Mac. I don't know who it is and he got me in the backyard.'

McCullough looked down and noticed a bullet hole at the front of Dorgan's helmet, but noticed no sign of a head injury.

'It will be alright, Jim. The doctor is on his way,' said McCullough reassuringly.

'Well he is a long time coming. Please get me some water!' Dorgan then began writhing around in agony.

Christopher returned and was joined by Thomson, Dr Ussher and several other officers. By now Dorgan was barely coherent. Dr Ussher took the constable into his arms and tried to place him into a more comfortable position. Dorgan's breathing became more laboured. Within two minutes of the doctor's arrival, James Dorgan died.

The time of death was recorded as 1.30 on the morning of 27 August 1921.

37-year old Constable James Dorgan was the fifth New Zealand Police officer to be killed in the line of duty.

Senior Sergeant Fahey ordered constables McCullough and Taylor to remove Dorgan's body to the hospital morgue, while he secured the crime scene.

At the hospital, Dr Ussher carried out an examination of the deceased.

There was a small oval-shaped puncture wound made by a bullet about one inch below the right nipple. In addition, he had several small abrasions on the left side of his face. The puncture wound caused the fifth right rib to fracture, and there was a perforated wound in the lower lobe of the right lung. The cause of death was found to be internal haemorrhage.

Within hours of the murder, Commissioner O'Donovan had called an urgent meeting of senior police and declared that no expense or resources would be spared, vowing Dorgan's killer must be found and brought to justice.

The investigation into the murder of Constable Dorgan began in earnest. Senior Sergeant Fahey and Thomas Thomson walked around the exterior of the shop to check for any possible points of entry made by the killer. Constable Christopher had checked all doors on the ground floor at 11.40pm, and then again in the presence of Constable Dorgan one hour later. All doors were found to be securely locked.

Fahey and Thomson walked along the right-of-way, careful not to disturb any possible evidence. Around the back of the store they found the back door slightly ajar. The key was still in the inside lock. Thomson told Fahey he usually left the keys to all doors in the locks from the inside, and was adamant he had taken particular care to ensure the back door was locked when he left at 10.15pm.

As the two men walked through the door, Thomson found his way to the electricity meter box to switch on the lights.

Beneath the staircase just inside the back door were two large sacks filled with clothing or material. One bag looked like a large onion sack, and had the letters XEX, stencilled across the front, and the number 98 stencilled on the other side. The other appeared to be a sugar bag with no distinctive markings whatsoever. A quick look inside both bags found them to be crammed with an assortment of men's clothing taken from the store's menswear department. It was from within this department that Constable Christopher had seen the flash of light.

Strangely, the menswear department didn't look as if it had been disturbed at all. In fact it looked exactly as Thomson had left it when he locked up hours earlier. The only obvious difference was some sort of material covering the internal doors. The doors leading into the menswear department were made up of two panels of framed glass. Two pieces of thick brown paper made up of three sheets carefully gummed together were pinned neatly over the glass from the inside of the door, obscuring any view from the outside.

While nothing looked to be out of place in menswear, Thomson soon discovered some boxes of clothing had been emptied. In the department, there were numerous boxes and drawers containing clothing so the offender would have had to know exactly which boxes and drawers to check before making his selection. Could he have had some inside knowledge?

It seemed he had cleverly made his selection of items, and then carefully replaced the boxes back into position so it would not be immediately obvious the next day that a burglary had occurred. It could be a matter of days before anybody realised that a theft had taken place. How many times had this kind of burglary happened before? It could have been a regular occurrence and could easily have gone undetected as Thomson had no adequate stocktaking system.

The preparation of the screen to obscure the thief from the outside had been done carefully. If Christopher had not shone his torch inside then it would not have been noticed. The offender could have easily unpinned the paper and departed with his goods leaving no immediate sign of a burglary. This was a carefully premeditated theft.

By early Saturday morning, news of the death of Constable Dorgan quickly spread and people traipsed along to Stafford Street to pay their respects. While they did so, detectives moved in to complete a thorough scene examination. The investigation was led by Senior Detective Allan Cameron and Detective James Bickerdike of Christchurch. Both men were hard-nosed detectives with vast investigative experience. One of their own had been killed and they vowed to find the killer.

Thomas Thomson was interviewed at length. From him police learned that on the night of Friday 26 August, the shop was open until 9pm. It was not an overly busy night, but there had been a steady stream of customers through the store. At 9.10pm the last of the workers left while Thomson stayed to close up.

Thomson told police he left around 10.15pm after ensuring the doors were locked and the electricity meter was switched off. He headed straight home after leaving through the front door. He was adamant there was nobody else in the shop when he left.

Thomson said that the store had 14 employees, including his son who managed one of the departments. Apart from himself and his son, the only other workers to have keys to the main doors were James Sheehy, the sub-manager, and Stanley Shanks who was in charge of the Manchester department. Both of these men were long-term employees who Thomson regarded as trustworthy.

Thomson said he suspected some members of his staff of dishonesty and he told police that staff members would be fired if they were caught stealing. Thomson reluctantly conceded to police that it was possible a staff member could have had an extra set of keys cut.

Of the nine men employed in the store, Thomson was suspicious of two of them. Of these two, he had no proof that Mr Brown* was doing anything untoward. Conversely, Mr Styles* had occasionally been spotted carrying parcels home from the shop, but as nothing had been reported missing from the shop Thomson was unable to prove anything. Styles was also suspected of owning a gun.

The police investigators were keen to establish how the thief had entered the store. The only door Thomson claimed not to have locked was the outside door from the balcony into the workroom. There was no access from the road front to the second storey and there was nothing of value kept in the workroom. Detectives checked

* not real name

this door and found dust on the doorknob so clearly no one had used the door in some time. This door was ruled out as the point of entry. There did not appear to be any sign of forced entry through any of the doors.

That afternoon, Senior Detective Cameron found evidence of an attempt to force one of the store's back windows. It was possible the offender had gained entry this way, but it didn't match the method of the crime. An attempted forcing of the window seemed very amateur, whereas the execution of the burglary seemed professional in contrast.

There was a possibility the offender may have visited the store sometime prior to closing and had remained hidden inside waiting for the shop to be locked up. This seems unlikely as the offender would have been carrying the folded paper, two sacks, a torch and a gun. It seems more probable that he waited until the staff had all left and crept in the back door while Thomson went around locking the store. This would account for the fact there were no obvious signs of a break-in.

Constable Christopher had not noticed anything untoward at 11.40pm, but one hour later, he noticed a flash of light in the shop. In the 1920s, the timings of beats were always meticulous and the patrols were routine. It would not be difficult for any observant offender to know roughly what time the constable was due to pass a certain point.

In this case, the offender might have known the times Christopher was due to pass the store. One hour would be sufficient time for anybody with inside information of the layout of the store and location of specific items to make their selection and leave before the constable returned.

The brown paper, which concealed the burglary, was carefully removed from the doors by investigators. Thomson and his senior staff examined it and assured police that they had never used this type of paper in the shop. Thomson's clothes boxes all contained a thin type of brown tissue paper to cover their stock. The paper from the doors was thicker, similar to parcel paper.

The pasting together of the paper strips had been done carefully and neatly. It had been prepared sometime earlier and was completely dry. Samples were taken and sent to a government laboratory to try to identify the type of gum used.

While Thomson was given permission to open his store on Saturday morning, the menswear department remained off limits while detectives continued their examination. Senior Detective Cameron found clear fingerprint impressions on a small, glass showcase, and on one piece of glass, 22 centimetres square, from another showcase. These seemed to have been made very recently. Several boxes that had been emptied by the burglar still remained on top of this showcase. Police were confident these fingerprints had been made by the offender, even though no other fingerprints had been found at the scene.

On the afternoon of 27 August, police carried out an examination of the right-of-way and back section of the shop where Dorgan had died. Behind the shop was a yard described as a large and rough section. It contained vegetable allotments, owned by the fruiterer and other tenants, which were sectioned-off by high board fences. At the rear of the back section and beyond the gardens was a 1.2 metre-high iron fence and a 6 metre-high cliff which was overgrown with gorse. In the far corner by the fence was a hen house and it was here Constable Dorgan's torch was located. It was slightly dented.

The ground was dry and several footprints were found at the back near the fowl house. The marks indicated a scuffle had taken place. Having identified Dorgan's shoeprints, detectives took impressions of the other footprint.

Other footmarks matching this one were found on the loose garden soil at the top of the stairway at the head of the right-of-way. A person had walked over the soil to the top of the garden. They then walked down the right side of the garden before leaving around the end of the iron fence at the edge of the cliff. After killing Dorgan the offender must have escaped via an unintended route. The footprints indicated that he may not have a good knowledge of the outlay of the garden. Most of Thomson's employees past and present would have known the general outline of the rear section.

Upon analysis, the footprints appeared to have been made by a set of gumboots measuring 11 inches by 5 inches, which equates to a modern size 11. From this evidence, detectives concluded Dorgan had confronted the offender and grabbed hold of him near the back door of the shop. The confrontation must have happened quickly as Dorgan did not have any time to search the offender. The scuffle appeared to have started as Dorgan attempted to drag the offender to the corner of Thomson's building near the stairway at the side of the cliff. It was at this point the offender produced his gun and fired upon Dorgan twice at point blank range, although only one bullet found its mark. Another bullet missed and went through Dorgan's helmet.

A search was made in the grass and gorse for any discarded weapon or cartridge cases but nothing was found.

James Dorgan left behind a seriously ill wife and three children under the age of five. He had completed nine years service in the police so his wife was entitled to an annual pension of £18 plus 5s per week for each child. The citizens of Timaru quickly established the Dorgan Memorial Fund and the New Zealand public was so incensed at the callous killing of the gallant policeman that contributions flowed in from all over the country. In Wellington, the government unanimously decided that they would fund Constable Dorgan's funeral.

While the investigation continued apace, the funeral for James Dorgan was held on Tuesday 30 August 1921. The outpouring of grief was evident with thousands lining the streets and congregating outside the Church of the Sacred Heart hours before the requiem was due to start. Despite the cold, windy weather, the funeral procession was one of the largest ever seen in Timaru.

The church was packed and crowds gathered outside to hear Father Hurley praise Dorgan's good work and acknowledge the hard work of the police in general. Dorgan was remembered as a big and powerfully-built man who was a kind and doting father and husband. As a policeman, he was not one who would needlessly annoy people or go out of his way to make enemies.

The service was attended by a number of senior policemen from all around the country. Commissioner O'Donovan was unable to attend because the steamer he had travelled on had failed to link up to the train, leaving him stranded. At the end of the service, his address was read by Superintendent Henry instead.

He expressed his sadness at the loss of a comrade and reminded mourners that the risk of death on duty was 'a necessary incident of our calling. It requires men of exceptional calibre to stand up to these conditions'. He went on to praise all police officers. Superintendent Henry then turned to the senior police officers. 'Your first duty will be to endeavour to bring to justice, according to the law of the land, the perpetrator of this most foul deed against society and its executive organisation. No desire for retaliation, no feeling of vengeance against the culprit, no matter who he may be, must be allowed to have place in your thoughts or to affect your actions.'

And of Constable Dorgan, he said, 'While our life lasts, his memory will be forever cherished by his comrades in the police force as well as by those good citizens of Timaru who have honoured us today with their presence and their sympathy. And when life fails in due time the monument which I trust will be raised over his grave to perpetuate his memory will commemorate in everlasting marble the heroic deed whereby he sacrificed his life and passed onto future generations, the tradition of the valour and fidelity to duty of the men of the New Zealand Police force.'

Sixty police officers formed a guard of honour between the church and the gate on Craigie Avenue, before walking at the head of the procession from the church to the cemetery. They were described as 'such a fine body of men looking splendid in their crisp uniforms'.

Over the next few days, police interviewed all employees of Thomson's. All alibis were checked and found to be satisfactory. Fingerprinting of staff eliminated all but two of the prints found on the two glass panels.

The two unidentified fingerprint impressions appeared to have been made sometime within the past fortnight. The impressions were of the left fore and middle fingers and showed less than half of a complete impression. Although part of the impression was smudged, there was still sufficient detail to show 25 defined characteristics.

The Fingerprint Bureau had been established in 1903, and by 1921 retained around 22,000 sets of fingerprints. At that time, only those offenders arrested and sent to prison were legally compelled to provide a set of fingerprints. The unofficial word from police hierarchy was for detectives to try and gain fingerprints surreptitiously, or by any other means necessary, to find the killer of Constable Dorgan.

Police were optimistic the unidentified set of fingerprints belonged to the person who killed Constable Dorgan, but even if an arrest was made, the offender could quite easily claim he had been in the store and had asked to see an item. It was a believable defence. The prints alone were not going to be enough to secure an arrest.

Police then turned their attention to the possible murder weapon. Despite a painstaking search of the scene they failed to locate any spent cartridge casings so the bullet removed from Dorgan's body was critical to finding his killer. The bullet was sent to William Tisdall, a Wellington gunsmith and weapons expert. He carried out tests and concluded that the bullet weighed just under 85 grains and was likely to have been fired from a .32 revolver. Tisdall said that it was likely to have been a Smith and Wesson or similar American handgun.

Police began carrying out a check on all registered weapons in and around Timaru but believed the perpetrator was unlikely to have registered his gun. It was believed the murder weapon was most likely one of thousands of unregistered revolvers, which could prove impossible to trace.

Police attempted to form a profile of the offender from the items of clothing found in the sacks that had been left at the back door of the store. The bags were taken away for forensic identification and their contents accounted for:

Onion Bag:

8 gentlemen's ties
2 white starched collars size 15½
3 cotton collars size 15
6 shirts
2 swimming costumes
1 dozen black ribbed cashmere socks
1 pair boys' black socks
1 box suit, dark grey tweed

Sugar Bag:

8 assorted gentlemen's ties
2 starched collars size 12½
6 soft collars size 14½ and 15
3 shirts
2 swimming costumes (medium size)
1 packet (10 pairs) woollen tennis socks (size 10)
Collar studs and safety pins

Thomson calculated the total cost of clothing to be around £24 (the equivalent of about $2000 today). He worked with police in an attempt to determine the size and shape of the offender on the basis that the stolen clothing would fit that person.

The style of the clothing indicated the offender was young, stylish and athletic. Judging from the size of the clothing, the suit would have easily fitted a young man whose height was 5 ft 8½ inches in height (1.76 metres), medium in build, and whose chest measured 35½ inches (90 centimetres).

The socks were of a colour used at Timaru Main School and at the local tennis clubs. The sporting articles related to schools and clubs in the Timaru area so it was also deduced the offenders were probably local. The fact that there were two different sizes in the haul raised the possibility of there being two offenders or that the thief may have been stealing to order.

Police spent a great deal of time trying to trace the origins of the two sacks. They quickly realised that it was futile, as there were tens of thousands of them in circulation. There were no markings whatsoever and to positively identify its source was impossible.

However the onion sack featured specific markings, which should point to its origins. The sack was marked XEX on one side and 98 on the other. The process of tracking the sack's origin proved to be a lengthy one. It took police two months to check with all produce merchants and auction houses around the South Island. But the effort paid off when they found a Christchurch produce merchant had manufactured over a thousand bags with similar markings the previous year.

The produce merchant explained that XEX was the grower's season mark and 98 represented the weight of the bag when filled. He thought the bag had probably been filled and distributed around April 1921. Inadequate consignment records had been kept and the produce merchant was unable to confirm who had been sent that particular bag. He was able to verify that of the 600–700 bags of onions distributed around in April, 12 consignments were sent to Timaru, Fairlie and Waimate. Records showed that on 22 April 1921, four months before the murder, the following were dispatched from Christchurch:

Company	No. of Bags	Marking
R.Wilson & Co	48	XE
CF Cass Ltd	38	X
CF Cass	35	BXF
Manning & Dawson	10	XDX
Allchurch & Co	115	XLX

The manufacturer believed the marking XEX had been dispatched to a merchant in the Timaru district, but could not explain why the bags marked XEX were not on any consignment records.

Timaru police checked with every merchant in the district. The bag was extremely worn but it was shown to a number of grocers and produce merchants around the South Island. No one could identify it. Their promising lead suddenly dwindled away to nothing.

With no arrest and no suspects forthcoming, Commissioner O'Donovan placed pressure on senior detectives to secure an arrest. If the police could not solve the murder of one of their own men, what confidence would this give the public?

Police continued interviewing people known to have been in the vicinity of Stafford Street that Friday night. Fingerprints were taken from hotel workers, porters, night watchmen, cinema ushers and port personnel, but none matched the impressions taken from the glass panels in the store.

Early on in the investigation, and after an inventory of the stolen clothing, police considered the burglary may have been committed by two people because there were two distinct sizes in the articles. The possibility of there being multiple offenders was supported by various witness statements claiming there were two strange men seen in the area. Eleanor Cloudesley, Mr Jones and Miss Stringer were making their way to their respective homes after the dance at the Empire Hotel when Constable Christopher rushed past them along Stafford Street. When they arrived at Thomson's, Christopher asked Jones and Stringer to go and wake Sergeant McGregor in nearby Sophia Street. The couple ran to the address the officer had given them but Sergeant McGregor didn't live there. As they left, Jones and Stringer noticed two men directly across the road desperately trying to start a motorcycle. It was too dark to make out the features of the pair, but they appeared to be having a great deal of difficulty. In a few minutes they managed to start the bike and roar off in the direction of Washdyke. By now it was 2am.

Several kilometres away, Dr Ussher and the police also claimed hearing the sound of a loud motorcycle around the time they were removing Dorgan's body from the murder scene. This would also have been around 2am.

At 8am on Sunday morning 28 August, two men called into Smith's Garage at Pleasant Point—about 20 kilometres from Timaru—asking for petrol. The garage was closed on Sundays but the men seemed so anxious the owner agreed to open up the pumps. Yet when he returned to attend them, the men had disappeared. The garage owner said the motorbike was a BSA motorbike, whereas the description given of the motorbike seen and heard in town was of a larger, more powerful bike. It seemed there might have been two different motorbikes, each with driver and passenger, in the vicinity around the time Dorgan was murdered. Could one of these bikes have carried his killer away from the scene? Was this the key piece of evidence police were looking for?

Another line of police enquiry focused on the brown paper and gum used to block the store's windows. It wasn't until lab reports came back from Wellington that they made any headway with this evidence.

The Dominion Laboratory of the Department of Internal Affairs was able to ascertain that the gum was acacia gum (or gum arabic). This was no longer extensively used in 1921 and Walter Baxter's chemist shop was the only place in Timaru that still stocked it. Baxter told police he still sold this glue in small quantities to domestic buyers. However, the *Timaru Herald* frequently ordered large supplies of gum from him.

The origin of the brown paper used to cover the doors was more difficult to identify. Professional printers interviewed believed the paper to be cut so finely that it could only have been done at a newspaper or printing firm. Staff at the *Timaru Herald* did not have any of this kind of paper in stock but they could not be certain that they had never stocked it. Therefore there was a strong possibility that the paper and glue had been removed from the offices of the *Timaru Herald* some time earlier. This was not conclusive evidence but it was a lead the police were more than willing to follow. More importantly it now provided police with a prime suspect.

Albert Lamb had worked for Thomson's in the menswear department from December 1918 to November 1919 but was fired for theft. He was subsequently charged with stealing £200 worth of drapery from Thomson's over several months. The prosecution case was weak and Lamb was acquitted.

Despite his acquittal, Lamb was not reinstated and held a bitter grudge against Thomson's. He continued to socialise with many of his ex-colleagues, and was alleged to have said, he was 'going to do old Thomson over one day soon'.

When carrying out background checks on ex-employees, police found Lamb had secured employment as a storeman at the *Timaru Herald* after he had been sacked from Thomson's. In his capacity as storeman he would have had access to gum and brown paper. Furthermore, Lamb owned a motorcycle and was seen driving in town on the Friday morning of the murder. He was also reported to have left town suddenly several days after the murder.

Lamb became the prime suspect. Police moved quickly to locate him, but by then a number of weeks had passed since Dorgan's death. It was thought Lamb had left Timaru on the Saturday afternoon after the murder and had gone to Auckland to stay with relatives. Lamb would have had plenty of time to commit the murder and then catch the afternoon ferry from Picton to Wellington.

Detective Cameron, who was leading the investigation, headed to Auckland to find Lamb. By the time he got there Lamb had already left and was believed to be staying with a friend and looking for work in Taumarunui.

Cameron took the first train south to Taumarunui. On arrival he asked around for Lamb at local hotels and was directed to a boarding house in the small settlement of Horopito, 60 kilometres south of Taumarunui.

Horopito was only accessible by horse and was largely made up of various camps and workingmen's huts. The men living there worked on the railway or on neighbouring farms.

When Cameron found Lamb, the suspect agreed to give a statement. He told Cameron that he left Timaru on the Friday afternoon *before* the murder took place. He arrived in the North Island late on Friday afternoon and was able to provide a copy of his ferry ticket as evidence. Lamb explained he had travelled to Horopito and was there on Saturday 27 August, before going to Auckland and staying with relatives. Cameron was able to obtain corroborative statements from residents of the boarding house verifying Lamb's story.

Lamb denied carrying out the burglary and murder. He also denied ever threatening to rob the store but said he was sure he knew the identity of the offender. He believed an associate named Oswald Rooney was responsible. Rooney had allegedly boasted that Thomson's was an easy place to break into and, in 1917, he had been convicted of breaking into Thomson's and stealing several bags of clothes. He was sentenced to three years probation.

Police had already interviewed Rooney on 29 August, but he denied any involvement in Dorgan's murder saying he had been at the cinema on the night in question. Rooney had a 'less than salubrious' reputation and a history of petty crime. It was time to interview him again.

At the first interview, Rooney said that after the film ended he had met Pat Curtin outside Fuller's Theatre on Stafford Street at about 10pm. Curtin worked at Thomson's. Rooney said that he and Curtin had walked to the Balmoral Hotel and talked outside for a few moments until his bus arrived. He said he got on the bus and went straight home. His story was corroborated by Curtin.

Police carried out a search in the cellar of the boarding house where Rooney was living. They found ammunition for both a .32 automatic revolver—the type thought to have been used to kill Dorgan—and a .22 revolver. No weapons were located.

Investigators found that Rooney was still friends with a number of people working at Thomson's store, and that his aunt, Agnes Rooney, was in charge of the women's department at the store. The brother of one of his friends, Douglas Stevens*, also managed one of the departments in the store. Thomson assured police that Stevens' brother was one of his most trustworthy employees despite Douglas being the black sheep of the family.

Detective Cameron re-examined the initial interview with Rooney and recommended that police interview Douglas Stevens before re-interviewing Rooney. They located Stevens at Weraroa Boy's Training Farm—a prison-like institution for young offenders—in Levin where he was an inmate. He had been convicted for stealing clothing from his brother and stealing £12 from his mother the day after Dorgan's murder. Having committed the thefts, he swiftly left town. Stevens and Rooney were now squarely in the frame for killing Constable Dorgan.

Douglas Stevens had been interviewed by police the day after the murder. He said he had been at the pictures the night before and had gone directly home on the bus when the movie finished. Stevens also told police that his father had discouraged his friendship with Rooney. Stevens said he had taken his father's advice and did not associate with Rooney at the time of the policeman's murder.

On 13 December 1921, Stevens was re-interviewed at Weraroa Farm. This time, Stevens admitted he had been at the movies with Rooney on the night of 26 August. When the movie finished at 10pm, the pair walked to the bus but only Stevens boarded. Stevens felt he really needed to disassociate himself from the influence of Rooney once rumours started that he and Rooney had killed Dorgan.

A few weeks later, Stevens ran into Rooney outside a public toilet in Timaru. Rooney allegedly pleaded with Stevens, saying police had grilled him over the break-in and murder of Constable Dorgan and he asked Stevens to say that they had travelled home on the bus together. This was not true.

Stevens told police that it was a coincidence he left town the day after the murder. He felt he needed a holiday and admitted to stealing a sum of money from his mother. Cameron was sceptical about Stevens' story.

Senior Sergeant Fahey tracked Rooney to a boarding house and re-interviewed

* not real name

him on Christmas Day 1921. Rooney didn't know where Stevens was and therefore could not collude with him to make sure their statements matched. Rooney told Fahey he had been at the cinema, but had watched the movie by himself. When the pictures finished, he saw Stevens leaving the theatre and caught up with him outside. They talked for a few minutes before walking to the bus stop with Pat Curtin.

Rooney denied burgling Thomson's store and murdering Constable Dorgan. He said that he and Stevens caught the same bus to their respective homes. Rooney could not explain why he had not previously mentioned he had been with Stevens. He thought because they had not been together at the pictures, it was not relevant. Rooney admitted he had been intimidated by police when he made his first statement. He also told them that he had asked Douglas Stevens to tell police they had been together at the cinema and on the bus. Rooney knew police had not made an arrest and he did not want to be implicated in the case so tried to fabricate an alibi.

Rooney admitted he had stolen two revolvers in 1920, but said that when the Arms Act came into force, he had posted the guns back anonymously. He was surprised that police had found ammunition hidden in the cellar.

Fahey was convinced Rooney was the killer and Stevens was his accomplice. Both initially denied seeing each other at the cinema yet both admitted having an association at their second interview. The police also found that the stolen clothing would have fitted Rooney and Stevens.

While police hoped that they had their men, they couldn't ignore several factors. The stolen clothes were by and large sporting articles. Neither Rooney nor Stevens showed any interest in sports and were both thought to be quite lazy. Another factor in their defence was that neither Rooney nor Stevens had access to a motorcycle.

Just as police felt they were finally closing in on their men, the investigation suffered yet another setback. Two young men, Moore and O'Connor, came forward to police. They had been at the dance at the Empire Hotel on the night of 26 August. After the dance, they had escorted their girlfriends home and walked back to the Empire where they had parked Moore's motorcycle. On their way home, the motorcycle had stalled after driving over some loose metal and they spent some time attempting to start it on Sophia Street. These were undoubtedly the men seen by Mr Jones and Miss Stringer. Police checked their story with the men's girlfriends and they were soon cleared of any suspicion.

Shortly after Moore and O'Connor came forward, the mystery motorcyclists at Pleasant Point were also located. Two men admitted calling in at the garage at Pleasant Point on Sunday morning. They thought they were running low on petrol and begged the garage owner to open a pump for them. While he was opening it, the men managed to dislodge a block in the tank of the bike. Rather than wait for the garage owner, they left. Two more suspects in the case of Dorgan's murder were cleared.

Significantly, though, the fact that Rooney and Stevens didn't have a motorcycle became irrelevant. They remained likely suspects and another of their associates soon came to police attention. A man named Cornelius who worked as an usher at the cinema was friends with both Rooney and Stevens. Both Rooney and Stevens had claimed they had seen and spoken to Cornelius sometime during the course of the evening Dorgan was killed. Cornelius initially told police he hadn't been working on the night of 26 August but shift records confirmed that he had been at work that night.

A background check on Cornelius revealed that he had worked as a storeman for the *Timaru Herald*. Some months prior to the murder, a .32 cartridge was found inside the *Herald* building and Cornelius admitted to staff that he owned two guns. Cornelius was regularly seen dressed in fashionable and expensive attire that he could not afford on his wages. Were these clothes the ill-gotten gains of a burglar?

When interviewed by police for the second time, Cornelius said that when they first spoke to him he had muddled up the nights that he had been working even though the interview had taken place just days after the murder. He admitted he had been working and said he had gone directly home after the last show. He told police that he had owned two guns but several months before the murder he had found out they were stolen and he threw them into the sea. Police could find no further evidence to link Cornelius to the crime.

There was a further piece of evidence that seemed to rule out the involvement of most of these local men. Before he died, Dorgan said, "I have been shot, Mac. *I don't know who it is* and he got me in the backyard.'

Constable Dorgan had been a police officer in Timaru for six years and knew most of the larrikins and petty criminals. Unless the offender's face was completely covered, Dorgan would have had a clear view of him. Of the suspects, the policeman knew Cornelius, Stevens, Rooney and probably Lamb.

At the beginning of 1922, police had exhausted all avenues and were no closer to solving the crime. Commissioner O'Donovan was beginning to realise his greatest fear—that he would not be able to bring Constable James Dorgan's killer to justice.

The murder frustrated police and had a huge impact on the Timaru community but this was nothing to the pain felt by Dorgan's ailing widow and his three young children who would grow up never knowing their father.

The Dorgan Memorial Fund continued to grow and those who donated had their names and the amounts donated listed in the *Timaru Herald*. The fund raised £199.16s.2d—the equivalent of $16,000 today. Of this amount, £184 was used to erect a headstone and monument to Dorgan. The balance of £15.16s.2d (about $1200) was added to the trust fund established for Dorgan's family.

The Dorgan case has an unusual postscript. In 1925, the Commissioner received some information that led him to ask detectives to consider another possible suspect for the Dorgan murder. These enquiries were conducted extremely discreetly.

In May 1925, Mr Smith of C Smith Limited Drapers in Greymouth, complained to local police he suspected one of his staff was stealing rolls of sheeting and offloading it to his competitors or selling it on the black market.

An undercover operation was set up by Detective JB Young. On the evening of 16 May, he caught Thomas Christopher, the employee in charge of Smith's Manchester department, red-handed passing four dozen pairs of towels to Fred Thomas, who managed a rival drapery firm in another part of Greymouth.

A search of Christopher's boarding room located more stolen articles and a Webley .45 calibre revolver. It was quickly ascertained the revolver had been legitimately registered to him while he was a serving police officer in Timaru.

Christopher had been one of Dorgan's closest friends. Although they did not complete training together, they were posted to Timaru around the same time.

Christopher had discovered the break-in, and Dorgan sent him away to summon Thomson. When he returned, Dorgan had been shot and died in his arms Christopher struggled with the fact that it could have easily been he who was killed if Dorgan had not sent him away.

The incident plagued Christopher and he left the police force a year after Dorgan's death. He moved to Greymouth where he had a variety of jobs before finding stability at Smith's store. When caught by Detective Young, Christopher admitted the offence and pleaded guilty. He was given two years probation for theft and required to pay an additional penalty for not advising his change of address pursuant to the Arms Act. An order was made to confiscate his revolver.

Upon hearing this news, the Commissioner ordered the Dorgan murder reviewed on the suspicion Christopher might have been stealing the clothing from Thomson's and that he had shot Dorgan when apprehended.

Timaru detectives were quick to correct the assumption. The statements of Eleanor Cloudesley and her two friends corroborated the fact Christopher had rushed past them at the time the four shots were fired.

As he lay dying, Dorgan told Constable McCullough he did not know who shot him, and the footprints found did not match Christopher's boot or shoe size.

While no further suspects were found the case remained on the minds of Dorgan's colleagues and the police hierarchy for many years. There was a genuine feeling of failure they could not bring the killer to justice.

2. The Arch Hill Mystery

At around 11.15am on the morning of Sunday 17 July 1921, Albert Prosser, a professional wrestler, and his friend Stewart Smith, a professional boxer, were nearing the end of a gruelling training run. Prosser and Smith both lived with their families at 280 Great North Road, Grey Lynn, in Auckland, as they worked together to prepare Smith for an upcoming prize fight. They decided to take a shortcut home through a vacant section on Great North Road that ran between Kingsland and Grey Lynn.

The section had a dirt track cut along the side of Arch Hill that locals used as a makeshift footpath. The back of the section dropped away towards Kingsland into a steep gully that was covered in thick blackberry and assorted native bush. The gully, in turn, led to more tree-covered vacant sections.

The pair ran up the steep gully and at the top, when they spotted the figure of a young man, dressed in a smart suit, lying in a reclining position, just off the track at the rear of the section. As he lay among the rushes on the edge of the bank, he was out of sight of passersby on Great North Road.

At first glance he appeared to be asleep, with a long grey overcoat covering him from the waist down like a blanket. Lying on his back with his head inclined to the left, his left arm was outstretched and his right arm flexed on the right thigh.

Thinking he was probably a drunk sleeping it off, Smith called out to him in an attempt to rouse him. There was no response so Prosser walked over to check the man. He immediately noticed blood on the young man's head, shirt and tie, and what appeared to be vomit on the collar of the coat. Thinking it was a case of suicide Prosser sent Smith home and ran to the corner, where he flagged down a passing motorist and asked him to contact police. He then ran to fetch Dr Share who lived nearby.

Within minutes, the footpath along the edge of the section was covered with people leaving the morning service at Saint Joseph's Church two doors away on Great North Road. Word quickly spread of the dead body on the vacant section, and people huddled together in groups wondering whether if it was anybody they knew.

Constable Pollard from Newton Police and Dr Share were first to arrive on the scene. Dr Share very quickly determined it was a case of murder. Inspector Eales and Detective Sergeant James Cummings arrived soon after to assist in securing the scene. The crowd continued to grow.

Dr Murray arrived at 12.45pm and agreed with Dr Share's initial findings. Judging from the position of the body, it was unlikely to be a suicide—it appeared to have been a brutal and frenzied murder. Dr Murray assessed the deceased to be a young man aged about 20 years and 1.87 metres tall.

There was a graze on his forehead and his right eye was swollen shut. There was a bruise across his cheek and across the right ear lobe to the neck. There was a rectangular wound between the lip and nostril. His nose, upper and lower jaw appeared to be broken. There were two more wounds behind his right ear and over the occipital bone—later examination found his skull was broken in three places. Hair was grazed off the scalp. His upper lip was cut right through. He had probably worn a dental plate, but this appeared to be missing.

The body was lying on a hat, which had bloodstains under the rim and on the crown. His shirt, tie and singlet were saturated with blood, and his braces were bloodstained front and back. His coat was wet on the left sleeve, and had dirt and congealed blood from elbow to shoulder. The right sleeve was wet and had dirt marks and dry blood on the inside of the right sleeve to the cuff. His trousers were bloodstained at the front, and muddy and wet at the seat.

In addition to the head wounds, there was a deep graze over his right shoulder to the spine, and his right arm was broken. There were numerous bruises to the left arm and right hand. Dr Murray estimated time of death occurring between 4 pm and midnight the previous day.

Such horrific injuries could not have been self-inflicted, yet there did not appear to have been a struggle. The young man had been very savagely bashed to death. There were traces of blood from the deceased's mouth and nose on his trousers. There was blood on the overcoat, but it was surmised the coat had been placed over the body after the attack.

A few metres from the body, detectives found a single kauri fence paling, 15 centimetres by 2.5 centimetres, and 1.2 metres long. It weighed 2.27 kilograms. It matched the fence that ran between the vacant section and one of the adjoining properties. The paling had three rusty nails protruding from it. Both ends were covered in blood with human hairs sticking to it. This was most likely to be the murder weapon.

It was quickly established the deceased was Francis Edward Jew, aged 19 years. He lived with his parents and brother at 12 Arnold Street, Grey Lynn. Several young men among the church crowd claimed to know him well. Detective Sergeant Cummings checked Jew's pockets and found eight shillings and seven pence, three pencils, a set of keys and two tram tickets. There were no banknotes in his breast pocket.

Jew's older brother, John, was at home that morning when a worried William Shearer, who owned the local fruit shop, called to say that a dead body had been found on the vacant section and there were rumours it was his brother, Frank. John Jew did not think it could be because, as far as he knew, Frank had spent the night at his friend Alf Newdick's house at 248 Great North Road. He would still be there. They rushed to Newdick's and found Alf preparing to check on his horses. John Jew asked if Frank was there. Newdick was surprised, saying he had not seen Frank since yesterday. Jew turned to Shearer and said, 'It looks like it is Frank up on that section.'

Alf Newdick joined John Jew and William Shearer and they hurried back to Arnold Street to alert Mr and Mrs Jew. Then they raced to the vacant section. John Jew had the heartbreaking task of making the formal identification of the body.

He was in shock as he watched police secure the crime scene and doctors prepare to remove the body of his badly bashed brother. Two young men, Herbert McGregor and Tom McMahon, leapt to support him as he was about to collapse. They were friends of his brother and as they consoled him they offered to walk him home. McGregor and McMahon both appeared stunned and lost for words. Stammering, they eventually talked about speaking with Frank the previous night—they could not believe he was dead.

McMahon said he waited with Frank until the latter caught the tram into Auckland. McMahon said he then hung around in the vicinity of the terminus for a few hours, but could not recall seeing Frank return to Grey Lynn.

John Jew looked around at the huge crowd of people who had gathered. All looked sad and some sheepish. Some offered words of sorrow and comfort, but within weeks many of the men, friends and acquaintances of Frank Jew, were hauled into police stations around Auckland and grilled for hours. It was suspected some of these friends knew something about Frank Jew's murder, but that they were deliberately withholding details from police. They appeared to be stalling, lying and denying. Frank Jew had been well-liked by all who knew him—he was a timid and harmless fellow. He enjoyed the love and respect of many of his peers in life but, sadly and strangely, not in death.

Throughout the 1920s, the media unfairly labelled Frank Jew as an unremarkable and carefree youth-about-town who had kept company with unsavoury characters. Born in Auckland on 9 November 1901, Francis Edward Jew was the younger of two boys. Their father was a respected builder. Frank was remembered as being quiet and unassuming. In 1921, he was 19 years old and living at home with his parents and brother.

He left school at 16 and secured a job as a carter for Alfred Tracey's grocery store on Great North Road. He went about his job with great diligence. In the early 1920, he was promoted to grocery assistant—he was a good, reliable worker and seemed content with his lot in life. Naturally shy, his job brought him out of his shell and, as he gained confidence, he quickly became popular with many customers.

He didn't have a girlfriend, nor was he ever known to express an interest in the opposite sex. However, he was mad keen on sports and attending sporting events, such as football, boxing and horse racing. He had a large circle of male friends who often called him 'Putty'. They were mostly sporting types who liked to drink to excess. However, he could not tolerate alcohol well—when he socialised, he nursed one or two beers all night. His friends knew of his low tolerance to alcohol—he would become very sick if he had more than two drinks. They knew that, as the evenings progressed and his friends became drunk, Jew would act as if he was inebriated.

Another one of Frank's idiosyncrasies was to invent a more colourful and exciting life for himself. He often told people he ran a backstreet bookie operation. He boasted about knowing which horses were 'dead certs' and about making a lot of money for himself and his punters. Sometimes he flashed fistfuls of cash, saying he had had a good day on the track—other times he would be down in the dumps, confiding to anyone who would listen that he had lost big-time at the races.

Gambling was well-entrenched in early twentieth-century New Zealand, although it was frowned upon in many circles of society. In 1920, the Gambling Amendment Act was passed and the business of bookmaking became illegal. Overnight, literally hundreds of backstreet bookies opened shop.

Frank Jew told people he ran with the big players, but most people thought this unlikely. None of his friends ever met any of his punters and he probably bet a lot less than he actually professed. It did not suit his nature—he always shied away from anything confrontational. It was generally believed he created an exciting façade to escape his mundane life working in a grocery store, and to make up for not being as 'tough' as many of his friends.

On Saturday 16 July, Frank had finished work at lunchtime. He collected his weekly wages of £4.10s.6d from Mr Tracey then returned the £1 he had borrowed from his boss, before returning home as usual. When he went out later, John Jew said his brother had placed a number of coins in his trouser pocket and his notes in his breast pocket. He had about £5 when he left the house, intending to place bets on 'Mustard Pot' and 'No Bother' racing at Wellington that afternoon.

Frank Jew hadn't mentioned his plans for the rest of the day. John assumed he was going to watch rugby league at Carlaw Park and then have tea with the Newdick family, as was his weekly custom.

The Newdick family were butter merchants, and had their butter factory and stables on their property at 248 Great North Road, Grey Lynn. Most Saturdays, Frank helped his best friend Alf Newdick feed and brush the horses before joining the family for tea and the evening's entertainment at their home in Selbourne Street. John Jew was sure his brother had no alternative plans, and could not understand how and why Frank had ended up being beaten savagely to death on the vacant section.

Dr Murray carried out a post mortem in the presence of police and Dr Share. He concluded death was due to skull fractures combined with haemorrhage and laceration of the brain, caused by a blunt instrument used with force. The injuries were compatible with blows struck with the fence paling found nearby. The paling was checked for fingerprints—none were found.

The section was carefully and methodically searched. On the afternoon of 19 July, Detective O'Sullivan located what appeared to be an upper plate of dentures, approximately two metres away from where the body was found. It should have contained three teeth, but only one was in its fitting.

On 20 July, Constable Poll located a single human tooth with a piece of jawbone attached, also about 2 metres away from where the body was found. Police were certain Frank Jew had been murdered and dragged or carried to the position where he was found. Yet it was also feasible the force of the blows were so fierce they had knocked his teeth a considerable distance. But who would want to murder Frank Jew? He was a quiet and harmless individual who naturally shied away from aggression. He was not a threat to anybody.

When his body was found, his gold cameo ring was still on his finger. He had only a small amount of cash in his pockets. Robbery was not immediately considered as a motive. As police learned of his alleged 'other life' as a bookmaker they considered whether he could he have been killed as part of a bookmaking racket. Did he owe money to real bookies, many of whom had ties to the criminal fraternity and would not hesitate in roughing up a bad debtor? Was this simply a beating that went too far?

Jew's friends and associates did not believe his bookie status. All agreed he was naïve and certainly not street savvy. The bookie role was merely to impress people. Some had played along and admitted occasionally placing small, insignificant bets through him. It was unlikely Jew knew many actual bookies and, even if he owed money, he had around £80 in his bank account. He shied away from all violence and it was generally agreed he was the type who would very quickly clear his debts before things got out of hand.

Police continued searching the vacant section, but could not locate any more clues. They were going to have to rely on witness testimony from Jew's numerous friends and associates. This made it difficult for police to obtain a true picture of events, including Frank's last movements, on the night of the murder.

Detective Sergeant James Cummings, one of the first senior police officers on the scene, remained head of the investigation.

Frank Jew would always pick up the *8 O'clock* newspaper from Shearer's Fruit

Shop on the corner of Great North Road and Williamson Avenue. The fruit shop was a focal point for the residents of Grey Lynn. Next door to the fruit shop, the Shearers also ran a laundry. Next to that was Tracey's Greengrocer, where Jew worked, and a few other small businesses. A few blocks along, and on the other side of the road, were Saint Joseph's Catholic Church and the vacant section where the body was found.

Alfred Tracey was absolutely devastated his young protégé, whom he had seen mature into a confident but reserved young man, had been murdered. He was at a loss to explain it. He confirmed Frank had worked on Saturday morning and planned to spend the rest of the day going to Carlaw Park with a bunch of friends to watch rugby league—Newton was playing the City that afternoon. He offered to place a bet for Tracey, but the older man declined.

After lunch at home, Frank walked to Alf Newdick's home before heading to the rugby league. Newdick's two brothers were playing for Newton that afternoon, and around 12 people, including Jew, the Newdick family and various hangers-on, piled into the Newdick's van. After dropping two of the Newdick children at the cinema, they arrived at Carlaw Park in time for kick-off. Jew informed the other passengers he would bet six points in favour of City.

At half-time, the crowd sauntered over to one of the hotels outside the park. Frank and Alf went into the Strand Hotel where they each bought a beer. They bumped into Tom McMahon, who was at the game with another friend, but was inside drinking by himself. Frank Jew knew McMahon from school, although Tom was about a year older. McMahon had been living with relatives in the Bay of Plenty for a while and had only recently returned to the city. In the course of the conversation, McMahon produced a bottle of champagne he had hidden in his pocket and invited Frank and Alf to join him later to share it. When the game resumed, they went their separate ways. Inside the grounds, Frank and Alf ran into Jim Lipscombe, who also worked at Tracey's. Lipscombe gave Frank £1 from his brother, who had earlier agreed to place a bet with Jew on the outcome of the game.

At the end of the match, the group piled back into the Newdick's van and headed to the Thames Hotel for a beer. Frank offered to stay in the van to look after the two children. Later they drove to the Rob Roy Hotel, and onto the Star Hotel in Grey Lynn, where they arrived about 5.45pm. This time Frank joined the group inside and, it was believed, he had one beer. The group arrived back at the Newdicks soon after 6pm.

Once there, Frank told Alf he would help him bed the horses as usual. Alf went to get ready and returned to the kitchen a few minutes later, but Frank was not there. Mrs Newdick did not see him leave and they assumed he had already made his way down to the stables. He wasn't there either. Alf Newdick brought the horses in and returned to the house. There was still no sign of Frank.

After tea, Alf took one of the horses out riding, calling into Shearers' at about 6.50pm to purchase some fruit. Later, Alf Newdick walked to the terminus outside Stebbings' and took the 8.30pm tram into the city, where he met a friend at the Prince Arthur Hotel. He returned home by taxi at about 10pm. He told police he did not see Frank after he left his home around 6pm the previous evening.

William Shearer from the fruit shop confirmed that Frank used to come in every Saturday evening on his way home from Newdick's. At around 6.25pm that Saturday evening, Shearer noticed Jew talking to Herbert McGregor at the terminus outside his shop, before they came in and each bought a soft drink. Jew also ordered and paid for his newspaper, saying he would be back later to collect it. Shearer said Frank was staggering and boasting that he was flush with money from betting at the football and on the horses. Like others, Shearer believed Frank was feigning drunkenness in order to impress his friend.

As they left the shop, Tom McMahon arrived. McMahon was staggering as well, but he was most obviously drunk. The three young men were joking and laughing out loud, and Jew came back to borrow a cork screw, which he popped back a few seconds later to return. The lads lingered outside for another 15 minutes before dispersing.

The *8 O'clock* was delivered late—around 8.50pm. Shearer began closing his shop at about 9.30pm, when McMahon and two others he did not recognise came into the shop to buy soft drinks, which McMahon paid for in coins. Shearer thought McMahon looked well and truly sobered up. It was then he remembered Frank Jew had not been in to collect his newspaper—it was unlike the lad to forget to pick it up.

Mrs Shearer, who had been in the back of the shop when McGregor and Jew had called in at about 6.30pm, later heard some raised voices outside. She assumed it was the young men who had been in earlier. It didn't sound like a serious argument—more a loud discussion over the football result.

When Alf Newdick came into the shop at 6.50pm, she assumed he was part of the group who had been arguing outside a few minutes earlier. She asked where the others were and Newdick replied 'they' had gone to get cleaned up. Later, it was established Mrs Shearer and Alf had been talking about two different groups of people—Newdick thought Mrs Shearer was referring to his brothers, whereas Mrs Shearer meant Jew, McMahon and the unknown man who was later identified as Herbert McGregor.

Herbert McGregor confirmed he was in the Newton team that had played at Carlaw Park on Saturday afternoon. He was at Shearer's laundry, dropping off his dirty clothes, when he ran into Frank Jew standing outside. Frank excitedly ran up and shook his hand, congratulating him on the afternoon's win. McGregor thought this strange as Frank was naturally reserved and not the type to instigate the shaking of hands. McGregor felt he was 'acting it up'. Frank invited McGregor to have dinner with him, and mentioned Tom McMahon would be along shortly with some champagne. McGregor declined the invitation, but remained chatting for a few minutes. McGregor believed McMahon was sober when he arrived. The group continued talking for a few more minutes until McGregor's tram arrived. Tom's older brother William was already on the tram with a group of young men. McGregor joined them and they all headed to town for the evening. Returning at about 11.10pm, McGregor noticed Tom McMahon sitting on the seat outside Shearer's with two men named Fred Edmonds and Stanley Rogers. McGregor said he and the four others then headed home around 11.20pm.

After McGregor had left on the 6.40pm tram, Jew and McMahon remained sitting on the seat outside Shearer's. A number of people stated the pair began to sky-lark and act the fool. At one point, Jew leapt up and said, 'I bet you one pound I can walk straighter than you!' He asked some boys to draw a straight line on the footpath with chalk and to judge the outcome. McMahon accepted the challenge and produced his champagne bottle, which he placed on the seat. McMahon turned to Jew and said menacingly, 'I'll whack you on the head with that bottle if you take it from me!' Jew responded by laughing at him.

A middle-aged couple arrived and sat on the seat waiting for the tram. McMahon made a nuisance of himself and Jew dragged him away, saying he was drunk and that he should head home for a sleep. The pair walked down an alley beside Shearer's and then staggered back.

They caught the 6.45pm tram, McMahon saying he wanted to go to King's Theatre in Newton 'to buy a dozen eggs'. Jew laughed and paid for the tickets as McMahon staggered to his seat singing at the top of his voice. Jew was embarrassed and told McMahon he should go home to bed. As the tram slowed for the next stop at Ariki Street, McMahon suddenly decided he wanted to hop off. Both young men alighted and walked back to Shearer's.

At 7pm, the pair met up with John Corden, Arthur Dobbs and Matthew Brodie, who were planning to catch the tram to town. McMahon and Jew were staggering and singing loudly and appeared to be drunk, although all three believed Jew was just pretending. Outside Green's Home-made Pork Pie shop, McMahon asked the group to wait while he went and bought two pies—he gave one to Jew and devoured the other himself.

Turning into Elgin Street, the group bumped into two men named Palmer and McKeown—Jew recognised them as regular customers at Tracey's. McMahon immediately tried to entice Palmer into a fight for no particular reason. Corden and Brodie dragged McMahon away, while Jew apologised profusely for his friend's behaviour. Jew exclaimed loudly to McKeown that he had had a good day at the races, but lost on the football, and that he was broke. He then pulled a fistful of banknotes from his trouser pocket and exclaimed he was 'going to bet £5 to £2 on City to win'. McMahon whispered that Frank was 'full of it'. When they arrived at Harcourt Street, Jew announced he was going home as he felt sick. McMahon called him back and they walked to Gregory's grocery store, which was closed. As they huddled in the doorway McMahon produced a wine glass and his bottle of champagne. They took it in turns, having a glass of champagne each. Jew was the last to partake and got less than half a glass. He took a small sip and tipped the rest on the footpath. Before the others could protest about the waste, he suddenly vomited in the doorway and lay down, saying he wanted to go to sleep. Then he said, 'Come on Tom, we will go to Newdick's loft and have a sleep'.

McMahon replied with an emphatic, 'No you will not!' So, Jew suggested they got to the section below the church for a sleep. McMahon wasn't keen for that so Jew said he would just stay where he was. Corden, Brodie and Dobbs offered to walk Jew to Newdick's, and McMahon to his home, but McMahon became indignant saying he was going nowhere, and was going to stay with Putty. The three left Jew and McMahon at 7.15pm and caught the 7.30pm tram to Dobbs' house.

David Walker, a salesman who knew Jew, came forward stating he had seen Jew in the company of a group of men loitering outside the vacant section. The witness also knew McMahon and McGregor, but stated that neither of these men was present. So, it seems that soon after Corden, Brodie and Dobbs left, Jew and McMahon may have parted ways.

It took a while for police to confirm the next positive sighting of Frank Jew from a reluctant witness. When police first questioned William Dunn on the day Jew's body was discovered he said he had not noticed anything. Dunn was known as a liar and petty criminal. He had lived in Grey Lynn for two years and had frequented Tracey's Store, across the road from his home. He had caught the tram outside Shearer's every day. Yet, he claimed never to have met Jew.

Within a fortnight rumours were circulating that Dunn actually had a story to tell. He was eagerly telling anybody who would listen—unless they were police—that he had seen Frank Jew near the vacant section.

Dunn and his wife moved to Cambridge a week after the murder. Detective Sergeant Cummings demanded an explanation and, in the presence of Dunn's wife, threatened to prosecute him for withholding information. Dunn answered that he did not want to get involved nor did he want to get anyone into trouble. He then said he and his wife had left their house at about 7.30pm on the Saturday night in question to go to the theatre at Newton. As they were passing the vacant section their attention was drawn to two men. One was standing just inside the vacant section, and he was wearing a fawn overcoat, dark suit and felt hat. Another was sitting on the kerb dressed in a dark tweed overcoat with his hat in his hands, and he appeared to be vomiting.

Dunn said he did not know Jew personally but knew he was the local grocery boy. He thought the man standing inside the vacant section was Jew. He was certain the man sitting on the kerb was not Tom McMahon, but a much older, shorter, and stockier man. Dunn said the man he thought was Jew knelt down and felt the grass and remarked that it was wet. The man sitting on the kerb made no reply.

Although police were sceptical about anything Dunn said, his statement, if true, raised three important questions: Who was this older man? When did Jew and McMahon separate? Where did McMahon go?

Dunn's reported sighting of Jew and another man at the entrance to the vacant lot came to be treated with some truth as it fitted other facts that had come to light as other witnesses also placed Jew at the vacant section after 7.30pm.

Agnes Henderson, returning home from church around 7.45pm, passed Jew walking the other way—towards the vacant section. Jew was carrying his overcoat on his arm and said 'Good night, Mrs Henderson'. He did not appear to be drunk or sick. She did not see anybody else in the area.

Margaret Morris was walking to church around 7.45pm, arriving a few minutes later. She stood on the church steps talking to an elderly man for a few minutes. Her attention was drawn to a sound coming from the vacant section. It was dark, but she noticed a man standing beneath the telegraph pole which marked the tram stop. He was dressed in an ill-fitting suit, and did not have an overcoat. He had broad shoulders and strong facial features. Mrs Morris also noticed the figure of a man sitting nearby on a park bench just inside the vacant section, but she could not make out any features. It was dark and there were trees obscuring her view.

When she left the church 20 minutes later, she glanced over towards the park bench and saw a man lolling on the bench with his mouth open. She thought it was the same man she had seen sitting on the bench earlier. A hat and overcoat lay beside him. She believed he was drunk and in the process of passing out. A car slowed down to park outside the church, so the brief light allowed her a few seconds glance at the man's facial features. She firmly believed it was Thomas McMahon on the park bench. There was no sign of the other man who had earlier been standing under the telegraph pole.

The police decided to re-interview the fighters, Prosser and Smith, who found the body and alerted authorities. The Millingtons owned the house in front of where Prosser and Smith were staying, two houses along from the vacant section. Mr Millington contacted police on the Monday after the murder having discovered a brown sticky substance on his letterbox that he believed to be blood.

Both Smith and Prosser were strong, fit men, dedicated to their sport. They stood no nonsense from young and drunken larrikins. Police thought it possible they may have become annoyed by the drunken goings-on outside their home and given Jew a beating that had gone too far. Then, going home, they had inadvertently brushed blood against the letterbox. Then, next morning, they conveniently discovered the body and alerted police.

Smith and Prosser told police their respective families left Grey Lynn at 6.20pm on Saturday night to go to the cinema in town. They noticed two men sitting on a seat near the vacant section. When they returned around 8.20pm, they did not notice anybody around. Smith believed he heard someone groaning on the section and thought it sounded like someone, possibly a drunk, vomiting in the bushes, but did not think any more of it.

The brown substance was tested and was not blood. The testimonies of Smith and Prosser were believable—they were quickly discounted as suspects.

Police continued to attempt to piece together a picture of Jew's last night and whom he was with. Other witnesses saw him in the company of one or more men, but it seemed there were no further sightings of him alive after Mrs Henderson's sighting at 7.45pm.

Herbert Cole was a friend and neighbour of Tom McMahon. Two days before the murder, Cole and McMahon had arranged to meet at the Albert Hotel at 3pm on Saturday, after the league match. When McMahon failed to show, Cole went home. He spent the rest of the evening playing cards with his aunt and cousin.

Around 8.45pm, he left his aunt's house to walk to Shearer's to buy the paper. He noticed McMahon leaning against a tin fence just along from the shop diagonally opposite the vacant section. Cole asked him why he had failed to meet him as previously arranged. McMahon replied he had been to the league and had got drunk. He said McMahon told him he had earlier caught up with Frank Jew in the pie shop, and had seen him just five minutes earlier, standing outside the vacant section. Cole bought his newspaper and went home.

William Macky told police he was returning from the barber's at around 8.30pm and stopped to chat to bus driver Percy Lupton, who was parked in his bus near the terminus. Lupton complained it was a quiet night and he had no passengers. They continued chatting until around 9.15pm, when they were joined by Tom McMahon. He appeared to be happy, but under the influence. McMahon went into Shearer's and bought soft drinks for himself, Macky and Lupton. Lupton suggested the two join him for his 9.30pm run out to Point Chevalier and back. They did, and the bus was full on the return journey.

When they arrived back at the terminus outside Shearer's at 10.25pm, McMahon walked over to Green's pie shop and bought pies and a cup of tea each for himself, Macky and Lupton. By now McMahon appeared to have sobered up. Lupton left soon after, and Macky claimed he and McMahon had stayed outside Shearer's talking until 11.20pm, when they started walking in the direction of their respective homes. McMahon had not mentioned anything about being in the company of Jew earlier.

As helpful as Macky appeared to be, police did not trust him as he had several offences for theft, and was considered dishonest. Furthermore, his testimony had been contradicted by Herbert McGregor, Fred Edmonds and Stan Rogers.

Percy Lupton was more than happy to talk to police and relished the fact police regarded him as an 'important witness'. He enjoyed being part of the murder-mystery, which was the talk of Auckland, and milked the situation for all it was worth. Lupton more or less corroborated Macky's story, but continued to annoy police on an almost daily basis wanting to alter his statement. By the time of the inquest, his story barely resembled what he had originally told police. His testimony was not given much credence, except for the points which corresponded with Macky's statement.

So, Lupton confirmed he invited McMahon and Macky to join him for the 9.30pm run to Point Chevalier. He said he had spotted Jew and McMahon outside Shearer's about 6.25pm, with a third man he identified as Kelly. He felt absolutely certain the third man was not McGregor. The three men appeared to be having a disagreement about the football.

Mrs Morris also believed that the man standing under the telegraph pole at 7.45pm resembled Kelly.

Dunn was taken in and shown a line-up that included McMahon but failed to pick him out saying the man he had seen with Jew was older. Could it have been Kelly?

Police tended to believe the plausible Mrs Morris. Perhaps Lupton and Dunn were telling the truth about the presence of a third man? Kelly was brought in and intensively grilled as to his whereabouts on Saturday night. Kelly vigorously denied being anywhere near the scene, saying he had been in town most of the night. However, Kelly admitted having a 'beef' with Lupton, who, he was sure, was putting one over him. Police did not trust Kelly or Lupton, but Lupton was eager to appear helpful. With the independent sighting by Mrs Morris, they decided to take Kelly's suit for forensic testing.

Lupton remained faithful to his story, insisting Kelly had been present earlier in the evening, and he was drunk. As police gathered more information, it became evident Lupton had not even been in the area to witness what he claimed he had. Nobody had seen him there and records checked indicated he was actually driving his bus at 6.25pm. When questioned, Lupton conceded he may have been wrong about the times and it was more likely about 6.10pm, when he had been at Shearer's, and had seen Jew, McMahon and Kelly.

Several weeks later, Lupton contacted police having just recalled a vital comment he felt they should know—as he drove off at 9.30pm, McMahon allegedly commented, 'Is that Putty under Shearer's?' Lupton could not see anyone there.

Jew was not seen again after 7.45pm, when he passed Mrs Henderson on her way back home from church. Around the same time or a few minutes later, on her way to church, Mrs Morris noticed a man standing under the telegraph pole. It could have been either McGregor or Kelly, but both were denying being there at that time.

A man is sitting and then sleeping on the bench inside the vacant section, and this is believed to be McMahon. Where did Jew go? If the man standing under the telegraph pole was not Kelly or McGregor, who was he?

However, David Walker claimed he had seen Jew standing outside the vacant section with a group of men that did not include McMahon or McGregor five minutes earlier.

Therefore, after leaving Corden, Brodie and Dobbs at about 7.15pm, Jew and [probably] McMahon headed in the direction of the vacant section. The man seen vomiting in the gutter at 7.30pm was most probably McMahon, although Dunn strenuously refuted that.

Whether it was or not, McMahon must have walked to the vacant section, and proceeded to pass out on the bench just inside the section at around 7.45pm. He was still there at 8.10pm.

McMahon was next seen by Cole, leaning on a tin fence across from the vacant section at 8.45pm. What had he done in the interim? How long had he been asleep?

Henry Churchill operated a small drapery store adjacent to Shearer's that also sold the *8 O'clock* newspaper. He, too, remained open until 9.30pm. He stated he saw McMahon and Herbert Cole walk right past his shop at closing time. They were speaking in low and serious tones. McMahon was heard to remark, 'Well, he shouldn't have done it.' The pair walked over to Tracey's and sat under the verandah talking in hushed tones for ten more minutes. Churchill did not know what they were talking about. He also heard McMahon say, 'I'll get two to carry me over.' The pair then said goodnight and parted company.

Churchill was a well-respected man, and his statement made it clear that Cole had not told police the full story. Cole was re-interviewed again and stuck to his original story, but conceded it could have been closer to 9.30pm when he saw McMahon. Cole could not recall seeing Churchill, even though he and McMahon walked past his shop. Cole believed Churchill was mistaken. He said the conversation with McMahon had mainly been about beer and he could not recall

McMahon making the comment, 'Well, he shouldn't have done it.' He could not think what it could be in relation to.

The men Jew was seen with between 7.25pm and 7.30pm were never identified. It was known that Jew had spent the majority of the early evening in McMahon's company. They may have parted around 7.25pm, and McMahon remained very close to the area where Jew was murdered, at least until 9.15pm when he met up with Lupton and Macky and went with them to Point Chevalier.

It is entirely possible McMahon had absolutely nothing to do with the murder. Jew was his friend. Why would he want to kill him? However, his conflicting remarks to acquaintances caused police to think he knew more than he was letting on. On the Sunday morning after the murder, McMahon was attending Saint Joseph's church with his parents and was leaving when Jew's body had only just been discovered. He was one of the first to see Jew's body and to identify it for police. He was also one of the first to console John Jew when he arrived to make the formal identification.

Tom McMahon told Detective Sergeant Cummings he had talked to Jew outside Shearer's between 7.30pm and 8pm and then, he thought, Jew caught the city-bound tram around 8pm. That is what he said to John Jew, too. Yet, he told McGregor that Jew left 15 minutes after McGregor had, which would have been 6.55pm.

Corden heard Brodie ask McMahon at church—before the body was discovered—where he and Jew went after they had parted ways the previous evening. McMahon said he left Jew at Gregory's, soon after parting from Corden, Brodie and Dobbs. This would have been about 7.15pm.

Brodie stated McMahon had told him he walked with Jew to the terminus, and Jew boarded a tram, a few minutes after the three parted, which would have been between 7.15pm and 7.30pm.

To Macky, McMahon said he left Jew at the vacant section at 7.30pm and believed he had caught the tram into town.

To Herbert Cole he said he had seen Jew earlier that night in Green's Pie Shop and about five minutes prior on the vacant section. This would have been at approximately 9.30pm, as Churchill's account of the time he saw Cole and McMahon talking seemed more reasonable.

It was time to interview McMahon at length but this was never going to be straightforward. Thomas McMahon lived with his parents in Grey Lynn. His father, Chief Detective Peter McMahon headed Auckland's detective branch and was a popular and respected member of the Auckland police community. Peter McMahon was in an awkward position.

His son worked as an apprentice for National Electrical Company and was on a modest wage. Tom had attended the same school as Frank Jew but was a couple of years older. He was regarded as being addicted to drink and, when under the influence, of 'quarrelsome disposition'. He already had a history of convictions for petty crimes. On 6 December 1920, Tom McMahon was charged with breaching the peace and fined £1. On 4 July 1921, just two weeks before his friend's murder, he was charged with being drunk and disorderly and fined £2.

The Jew family thought young McMahon was a bad influence and discouraged the friendship, but Frank was attracted to McMahon's carefree attitude and daring lifestyle. Six months prior, McMahon's parents sent him to live in the country with relatives, hoping to change his ways.

When he returned to Auckland, he quickly slipped back into his old habits—frequently getting into scrapes usually fuelled by alcohol. His performance at work slipped, and he started frequenting the pub at lunchtime returning half-cut and unable to work. These hotel visits increased in frequency in the days following Jew's murder. He had been given many warnings, but his employer had enough and he was dismissed.

Usually, after a scrape, his dependable father would frog-march Tom back to apologise for whatever misdemeanour had occurred. And, usually out of great respect for McMahon senior, Tom would be given another chance or let off the hook. Young McMahon was always given more chances than he deserved and he always let himself, his family and employers down.

Police were in a quandary as evidence seemed to point towards Tom McMahon having some knowledge of or possibly even involvement in his friend's murder. They were aware from the outset that the investigation would be fraught—there would probably be many people opting to withhold evidence out of fear or respect for Chief Detective Peter McMahon.

On the other hand, Peter McMahon was in an awkward position as he found himself being excluded from the investigation by his junior detectives. McMahon initially tried to muscle in on proceedings and quiz his detectives for snippets of information.

The Police Commissioner was well aware of the situation and told Cummings to exclude McMahon from the investigation. He encouraged detectives to avoid the temptation of loyalty and to avoid leaking details of the investigation to the Chief Detective.

Although Peter McMahon eventually agreed it was in his best interests to isolate himself from the police investigation, it was extremely stressful for him to watch his peers carry out the high profile investigation. It was not really known whether he had any influence on the public of Grey Lynn, who openly provided friendship and support for the McMahon family. McMahon was an honest policeman with an exemplary record, but was he capable of intimidation tactics? It was something police had to consider.

Thomas McMahon was formally interviewed on 19 July, two days after his friend's body had been discovered. He stated on the afternoon of 16 July he had a few drinks in town, but was not drunk. He caught the tram to the corner of Karangahape Road and Pitt Street about 6.15pm, and then walked along Great North Road in the direction of his home. Soon after, he ran into Jew, and then Brodie, Corden and Dobbs, and the group continued walking to Gregory's, where they shared the champagne. The group then broke up when Brodie, Corden and Dobbs left, and Jew and McMahon remained talking outside Shearer's from about 7.30pm until 8pm, when Jew left to catch the tram.

McMahon continued sitting on the bench until Lupton arrived in his bus, and around 9.30pm, he went on the trip to Point Chevalier.

Several days later, police learned about several other sightings of McMahon and Jew together at different locations. McMahon had omitted a great deal of vital information. Cole and Churchill were interviewed and, although their testimonies differed, both corroborated the fact McMahon was standing almost across from the vacant section between 8.45 and 9pm.

McMahon was interviewed again on 24 July. When asked about his meeting with Cole, McMahon seemed genuinely surprised. He said he could not recall meeting Cole at all, but added someone had recently mentioned he had been with Cole, so it must have been true. Cummings cautioned McMahon to be careful as this was a serious matter. The young man innocently replied that whenever he drank liquor he suffered from a poor memory. Then he said he could not remember much about events that night. He recalled what little he could and relied on what his friends and acquaintances had told him since. He had good mates, so if they said they had seen him, then surely they must be right. He could not be absolutely certain of facts from his hazy recollection.

Once again McMahon was asked to account for his movements on Saturday 16 July, and answer only what he could remember and not rely on what he had been told by others. McMahon could not really recall how he arrived in Grey Lynn from Carlaw Park. He originally thought he walked from Pitt Street, but now vaguely recalled he had come via Ariki Street, but he couldn't be sure.

He recalled meeting Jew and McGregor outside Shearer's, but could not remember details of the conversation. He remembered boarding the tram with Jew, but denied saying he wanted to go to Kings—he knew nobody there and had no reason to go. He couldn't remember alighting after the first stop, and only found out he did after he was told later by someone whose name he did not remember. He did remember meeting Corden, Brodie and Dobbs, and drinking the champagne.

He had been given the champagne by a man in Karangahape Road a few weeks earlier. He did not know the man's name or why he gave him the champagne. He had seen the man in town a couple of times before and offered a vague description, but did not think he would recognise him again.

McMahon could not remember Jew being sick—he had heard that from others. Nor did he recall hearing Jew suggest they go to the vacant section for a sleep. He thought he had waited around with Jew, and figured his friend had caught the 9pm tram to the city because it wasn't long after this time he met up with Lupton and took the ride out to Point Chevalier. Even so, he couldn't really remember talking to Lupton.

He had a very faint recollection of meeting Cole, but thought this had been at 8.30pm simply because that was the time Cole told him he had seen him. McMahon thought maybe it was closer to 9pm because he had parted from Jew by then, having just been read Cole's statement which indicated McMahon had seen Jew five minutes earlier. McMahon could not say why Jew was heading to town, when it was not his normal custom to do so.

It was a long and frustrating interview. Cummings felt strongly McMahon was not telling the truth and had something to hide. His excuse for not being able to remember certain facts was the influence of alcohol, but there were certain minor facts McMahon was able to remember and was adamant about. Was he being groomed to answer questions by his father? The Chief Detective had years of experience in dealing with interviewing criminals and his expertise in this area had assisted his rapid rise through the police ranks. He also had years of experience cross-examining witnesses during inquest hearings and was skilled in assisting the Crown Prosecutor in court hearings.

Detectives executed a search warrant of Thomas McMahon's bedroom, and seized the clothes he said he had been wearing on that Saturday night. Professor Frederick Armitage, the government bacteriologist based in Auckland, examined McMahon's hat, coat, overcoat, waistcoat and trousers. Dried bloodstains were found in both left- and right-hand trouser pockets. Armitage could not determine the age of the stains because, at the time, there was no test to do this. However, he could determine it was human blood and it would not have required much blood to form the stains. They were undoubtedly from wounds to the hands of the wearer and, by their position, he deduced they would have come from the knuckles rather than the palms.

Later, McMahon testified at the inquest that he never wore that particular suit to work. He said it was the suit he wore when he went out on Saturdays, and to church. He could not say why these stains appeared in his weekend suit, when it was more reasonable to find such stains in his work suit.

McMahon was interviewed again on 6 August and he began by asking to correct his earlier statement, which he was now going to contradict. He now said it was more like 7.40pm when he left Jew, and he waited on the seat outside Shearer's until Lupton came along.

In regards to the bloodstains in his suit pocket, he could not say how or when they got there. He said his suit was about three years old, and over the last few years, he had suffered numerous cuts to his hands. His explanation about the bloodstains was reasonable and certainly insufficient to warrant an arrest.

The murder of his dear friend 'Putty' had a profound effect on McMahon. The murder caused a sensation around New Zealand and the fact the killer had not been brought to justice made headlines in most newspapers. Whether it was being the subject of Grey Lynn gossip, guilt, pressure, constant police presence, or witnessing the personal and professional toll the situation had taken on his father, Tom McMahon began drinking even more heavily.

When questioned about his drinking, McMahon admitted he was paid £1.16s per week wages and he gave £1.6s to his mother. He kept the balance plus any overtime he might have earned. From what was left over, McMahon estimated he spent approximately a shilling per day at the Albert Hotel. Police privately monitored McMahon's movements and barmen at the Albert told them that McMahon was spending as much as ten shillings a day, well and truly exceeding his weekly wage.

After he was dismissed from work for returning from his lunch drunk once too often, and his father intervened, his employer relented and agreed he could work the following week for no wages. At the end of that week, Tom McMahon took leave from his job and was sent to Te Puke for two weeks convalescence. His family felt it was important he escape Auckland and unwanted media attention in the lead up to the inquest. It was also, in part, to prevent him from falling foul of the law in the interim.

The inquest into the death of Francis Edward Jew opened in the Auckland Magistrates' Court on 12 September 1921, before the coroner, Mr WR McKean SM. The newly appointed Crown Solicitor, Vincent Meredith, appeared for the police. In an observation-only capacity, Mr R Prendergast appeared on behalf of Thomas McMahon.

The case had attracted a great deal of public attention so a number of media were present, and the public gallery of the courthouse was packed throughout the ten-day hearing.

The court heard how the police had made exhaustive enquiries—about 1500 people had been interviewed. It was hoped the inquest might shed some light on the matter that could assist police to further their investigation. Mr Meredith addressed the public gallery reminding people they had a moral responsibility to come forward if they knew anything. Sixty-six people were called to give evidence.

On the first day, the hearing proceeded quickly through 14 witnesses and it appeared to be running smoothly. Frustration set in on the second day when acquaintances of Jew and McMahon took the stand.

Corden was interviewed about his movements on 16 July. His answers didn't match his original statement to police and he was cautioned to carefully remember what he had told police. He could not remember what he had said in his original interview.

Matthew Brodie also stirred Meredith's ire when he could not remember details of what he had originally told police about drinking the champagne.

Mr Prendergast—in one of the rare occasions he was allowed to interject—

stated there was nothing extraordinary in remembering one part of a conversation and not recollecting another part, to which a frustrated Meredith replied, 'Lapses of memory appear to be epidemic in Grey Lynn!'

William Dunn never wavered from his original statement saying the man he had seen with Jew on the vacant section at 7.30pm was older and stout, and did not match the description of McMahon. Dunn also claimed he had never met McMahon before the inquest, but Cummings observed the pair regularly sitting or walking together during breaks.

Then, full of self-importance and with his chest puffed out, Percy Lupton took the stand. He did not expect the attack from Meredith, who, although new to the role of Crown Prosecutor, was a barrister of exceptional reputation.

Lupton confirmed his statement to police but under heavy cross-examination, he mixed up his times. Eventually, his credibility was torn to shreds when Meredith made him admit much of his story had been cobbled together from local gossip, but he refused to admit where he had heard the stories.

Lupton went on to say he and Macky had been approached by McMahon just after 9pm, and that they had all journeyed together to Point Chevalier, returning around 10.25pm. Lupton could not recall who bought the drinks and pies at the end of the journey.

The court heard how Lupton had been interviewed numerous times and made regular approaches to police to amend certain aspects to his statement each time he remembered something new. It was not until 31 August that Lupton approached police, telling them McMahon mentioned seeing 'Putty' as they left the terminus at 9.30pm.

Thomas McMahon took the stand on Monday 19 September. He was cross-examined for almost two days. Meredith later reported it as one of the most memorable and frustrating cross-examinations he had ever undertaken, and—some years later—the coroner described it as farcical.

When McMahon stood down it was clear that the coroner had come to the end of his tether. Yet it was not the end of the drama. Mrs Morris was next to give evidence and as she was stood down a booming voice from the rear of the Court interjected proceedings. Approaching the bench, a dishevelled, bohemian-looking man announced he had some importance evidence to give.

Mr McKean asked the man who he was. The man introduced himself as Edward

Portière, artist and psychoanalyst. He had approached police on an almost daily basis offering his 'supernatural skills' to the inquiry, but was always rejected. Never one to take rejection lightly, Portière had decided to carry out his own private investigation, following detectives around and annoying witnesses as soon as police had finished interviewing them. Neither Meredith nor Prendergast had any desire to question him. The coroner growled that he did not want to hear any 'psycho-analysing mumbo-jumbo'. Meredith quickly located a transcript of an interview between Portière and police, and offered to read out the summary to avoid handing Portière the opportunity to hijack proceedings. Portière's testimony was nothing more than the ramblings of a murder-fanatic who wanted to convey his own eccentric theories and his testimony was quickly dismissed.

In final summary, the coroner said it was disappointing some of the evidence heard was unsatisfactory, and there seemed to be a good deal of reluctance on the part of some witnesses to state what they really knew—only after they had been reminded, and often prompted, were they able to recollect the facts as originally told to police.

While there was a balance of probabilities Jew and McMahon were together from about 6.10pm to 7.30pm, there was a high likelihood they remained in each other's company after 7.30pm.

In particular, he felt Lupton's evidence was candid and the coroner was satisfied that Kelly had been nowhere near the scene. He felt the evidence of Dunn, Coles and, to a lesser extent, Corden was poor, and he was of the opinion they were withholding vital facts.

The evidence of McMahon was deemed unsatisfactory. He had told friends one story about Jew, but gave quite a different story to police. The various police interviews with McMahon offered definite answers, but it became abundantly clear most of what McMahon said was untrue. He had admitted making things up to save his skin and relying on second-hand information from friends. The coroner felt McMahon's manner in the stand indicated he was not telling the truth. Although McMahon had been under the influence of liquor that night, the coroner believed his recollection of that night was much more extensive than what he had originally stated.

At the conclusion of the hearing, Mr McKean stated, 'My duty is to find when, where and by what means the deceased Jew came by his death, and I propose to record a formal verdict. I do not think the evidence justifies me in saying anything more. I find that the deceased Francis Edward Jew died at Grey Lynn on July 16, 1921; the cause of his death being compounded comminuted fracture of the skull, with haemorrhage and laceration of the brain. The fracture of the skull and the laceration of the brain were apparently caused by heavy blows with a batten that had been removed from the fence of the property adjoining the section on which the body of the deceased was afterwards found; and these blows were wilfully inflicted before midnight and after 7.45pm on the night of July 16, 1921.'

Francis Jew's senseless murder was added to the growing number of murders in New Zealand committed by 'a person or persons unknown'.

Police were disappointed with the outcome. Senior detectives had hoped the inquest might yield new information, or at least cause one of the witnesses to be more forthcoming. Although Meredith did his best, the evidence heard was not strong enough to warrant an arrest. If police had arrested McMahon on what was presented, there was a strong likelihood he would be acquitted.

The advice from the commissioner to Cummings was to quietly pursue a renewed investigation and listen closely to murmurings within Grey Lynn. The public of Auckland were outraged police could not solve this hideous crime and they were beginning to lose confidence in the police. But it was not that simple.

The scene examination, the murder weapon and the body yielded no clues. Police were forced to rely on a witness or a confession. Unless there was a change in loyalties or witnesses decided to tell the truth the investigation was unlikely to progress.

Police believed McMahon killed Jew in a fit of drunken rage, but it seemed strange that a man as intoxicated as McMahon said he was, and as witnesses believed him to be, could carry out an attack with such ferocity and not leave any tell-tale sign, such as fingerprints.

The bashing was so ferocious it would have left numerous sprays of blood specks on the killer's clothes. McMahon's clothes were clean. Anyway, why would McMahon kill Jew, a man he considered a close friend?

McMahon was undoubtedly in the Arch Hill area and could have been asleep on the park bench until he was seen across the road from the section by Coles and Churchill, who said there was nothing suspicious in his demeanour. Besides, would a killer hang around the murder scene? Soon after, he was socialising with

Lupton and Macky, joining them on a bus ride to Point Chevalier and buying them a pie and a cup of tea. Is this the behaviour of a murderer?

The Crown tried to convey robbery as the motive behind the senseless murder. Meredith's questioning tried to elicit from witnesses how much McMahon was carrying on the night of the murder. Jew had openly flashed a fistful of notes, saying he had won some bets. It was thought he had about £2.9s when he left home to go to Carlaw Park. But when his body was found the next morning he had only 8s.7d in his pocket.

McMahon did not have much cash—he'd already told police he spent an average 1s per day on alcohol after handing most of his wages to his mother. As for the barmen at the Prince Albert, their statements that McMahon was spending an average of 10s per day at the bar were regarded as exaggerated or dubious. Drinking companions that night claimed McMahon bragged he was flush with cash, but it was never proven whether it was his or Jew's money.

If McMahon was the killer was robbery a serious enough motive, even if he was drunk and out of control? Jew was the kind of fellow who wanted people to like him. If McMahon had even hinted he was broke, Jew was the likeliest person to lend his friend some money, and not pressure him for it to be repaid. Although the amount of money missing seemed too trivial to provide a motive for murder, police thought the murder was probably motivated by robbery. As the years progressed, they did not sway from this belief. They were also keen to paint McMahon as the killer.

The movements of the victim and prime suspect need to be re-examined:

6.30–7pm Jew and McMahon are seen loitering together in the vicinity of Shearer's, and then catching the tram.

7pm Jew and McMahon meet up with Corden, Brodie and Dobbs, and the five walk to Gregory's shop and drink champagne. Jew is suddenly sick, and tries to encourage McMahon to go with him to have a sleep at the vacant section, or in Newdick's loft.

7.15pm Corden, Brodie and Dobbs leave the pair at Shearer's.

7.25pm Walker sees Jew outside the vacant section with several other men. He knows McMahon and McGregor and swears they were *not* part of the group.

7.30pm Dunn spots Jew feeling the grass on the vacant section and remarking it is wet, to a man sitting on the kerb and vomiting in the gutter.

	Although Dunn does not know McMahon, he swears the man is *not* McMahon, but an older and stockier man.
7.45pm	Jew is seen walking towards the vacant section alone. He bids Mrs Henderson goodnight.
7.45pm	Around this time, Mrs Morris spots a shabbily dressed man standing under a telegraph pole. She believes it to be McGregor or Kelly.
8.05	Mrs Morris returns from church and sees a man on the park bench. She identifies the man as McMahon. The man she saw earlier under the telegraph pole has gone.
9.30pm	McMahon is seen by Cole, Churchill, Macky and Lupton, who notice nothing odd in his behaviour. He certainly does not act as if he has just beaten a friend to death.

Although police did not trust Dunn or Lupton, their testimonies seem to corroborate those of David Walker, Mrs Henderson and Mrs Morris, who were regarded as more credible.

Dunn had said he did not want to become involved or get anyone (i.e. McMahon) into trouble. Lupton was obviously a friend of McMahon and was prepared to cover for him. These seem to be reasonable explanations.

If the testimonies of Dunn, Lupton, Walker, Mrs Morris and Mrs Henderson are correct, then it would appear McMahon and Jew parted company around 7.30pm, soon after leaving Corden, Brodie and Dobbs. McMahon and Jew headed to the vacant section where McMahon was sick and then lay down on the park bench to pass out.

Jew headed somewhere around 7.45pm, and this was the last positive sighting of him until his body was found the next morning.

One theory worth examining is that one month after the inquest Macky told police he had heard from an anonymous source that Jew had been gambling with some rough characters at Tracey's stables and had been killed there. His body had been removed in a horse cart. Tracey's stables and the Newdick's were carefully examined, but no evidence of murder was ever found. Police doubted that Jew had been murdered at either of the stables as they were too small and filthy to even be used as a gambling den.

Jew was so timid his friends and family doubted he had any involvement in gambling—he only offered to place bets for people he knew would reject him.

He had never strayed too far from Grey Lynn and probably would not even know where to find a backstreet bookie. Jew was frugal with his money, and the money he was seen flashing around was more likely to be from his own savings. He only gave a certain amount to his mother, and he had already built up an impressive savings balance.

On Saturday evening Jew pretended he was drunk but told people different stories. To Shearer he stated he was flush with money having won bets at football and on a couple of horses. Half an hour later, to Palmer and McKeown, he said he had had a good day at the races but was broke because he lost at the football. It is likely he was lying on both occasions. However, he also told them both he planned to make another bet later that night or the next day. Was this true or was he simply acting bigger than he was? He might have had just enough bravado to attempt to run with the big players. Maybe he did meet a bookie and maybe he bragged to the wrong person about having made a lot of money. Maybe he was involved in a betting circle, and had run up big losses, although he had enough in his savings account to cover fairly heavy losses. Maybe he was in over his head—gambling was illegal—and because of his bragging was considered a threat.

Another explanation never examined at the time is the possibility of a sexual attack. Why did Jew loiter in the vicinity of the vacant section alone? Who were the other unidentified men seen in the vicinity of the vacant section? There was much innuendo about Jew never associating with females—he preferred to hang out with his male friends. While this is not abnormal, police recorded that Frank Jew did not seem to have an attraction for any female—his friends could not recall Jew ever talking about a female. He was naturally shy, so it could simply be that he was overcome by shyness around women his age.

Corden, Dobbs and Brodie said Jew suggested to McMahon several times that they should 'have a sleep at Newdick's loft or on the vacant section', and McMahon aggressively refused each time. Could it be that McMahon had violently spurned Jew's sexual advances and bashed him to death?

At the time of the murder, the vacant section where Jew's body was found was a discreet nightly oasis for homosexual liaisons and prostitution. In recent years, there had been two still-unsolved sexually-related murders within kilometres of Arch Hill.

McMahon may have confided to Cole what had happened when he saw him an hour later. Could this be what McMahon meant when he was overheard saying,

'He should not have done it'? Had Cole, loyal to McMahon or fearful of being implicated, lied to police and the coroner?

McMahon was most probably the man Dunn had seen vomiting and, soon after, passed out on the park bench. Jew was very much alive when McMahon was vomiting, but Mrs Morris said she saw another man, who was not Jew, standing under the telegraph pole.

Jew had been seen wandering along Great North Road alone around 7.45pm, while McMahon was probably passed out. Could he have remained in the area seeking a liaison? The clandestine activities known to take place at the empty section would account for the number of strangers seen in the area, and for the reluctance of witnesses to come forward. Had Frank propositioned or been propositioned by his killer?

Several years later rumours surfaced in the media that Jew had been castrated. Police were quick to deny this—there was no evidence of Jew having a sexual liaison immediately prior to his murder and he was fully clothed when found.

The murder had a profound effect on the McMahon family and within months of the inquest Chief Detective Peter McMahon tendered his resignation. Many felt it was premature—he was destined to become Commissioner. However, many others felt the scandal made it untenable for him to continue in the police.

Within days of the coronial inquest Tom McMahon quietly and suddenly left Auckland. The morning after he skipped town, his employers at National Electrical Engineering Company discovered three cash-boxes emptied of a princely sum of £47.18s.9d, plus tram tickets worth £3.12s. Fingerprints taken proved conclusively the thief was young McMahon and a warrant was issued for his immediate arrest.

Tom McMahon quickly fell in with a group who burgled their way around the Waikato and King Country. At the beginning of June 1922, he was living at a boarding house with his friends in Te Awamutu. Between 10 and 12 June, McMahon broke into a drapery business owned by the town's mayor, and stole a large sum of cash, clothing and other assorted goods. Several days later, police executed a search warrant on McMahon's room and found the stolen goods plus booty from other assorted burglaries around the town. Among the items found was a camera that had been reported stolen in November 1921 from an auction mart. It was learned McMahon installed an electric light in this mart, and later that night an electrical fault had caused the building to go up in flames. It was suspected McMahon had returned at night to steal cash and other goods, including the camera, before burning the place to the ground and making it look like the fire started from an electrical fault.

McMahon denied starting the fire, but admitted to the string of recent burglaries. He had no money in his possession, and when asked, said he had spent the stolen money on grog.

A few nights prior to the burglary, a housemaid named Beryl Cooper was walking home after attending the pictures when she was suddenly grabbed from behind and viciously attacked and repeatedly hit on the head with an iron bar. She sustained serious head injuries and lost four teeth. For days she teetered on the brink of death, but recovered and named McMahon as her attacker. He was arrested and charged with causing grievous bodily harm. McMahon stated he could not remember committing the attack and pleaded not guilty. The case was heard at the Hamilton Supreme Court and McMahon was found guilty of all charges and sentenced to a lengthy term of imprisonment.

3. The Aramoho Murder

The first European traders arrived at the mouth of the Whanganui River in 1831, followed by missionaries in 1840. Around that time, the settlement of Wellington was becoming overcrowded so the New Zealand Company began to look for other areas suitable for settlement. Edward Jerningham Wakefield looked north to a Maori settlement on the banks of a river, which was wide enough to accommodate large ships. Wakefield negotiated to buy 40,000 acres of land on the river in 1841. The settlement was christened Petre but its name was officially changed to Wanganui in 1854.

Just north of Wanganui several canny businessmen bought a block of land and soon a hotel, racetrack and a variety of small businesses sprang up. The settlement took the name Aramoho. The town grew further when the government decided that the Wellington–New Plymouth railway line would pass through it.

In 1887, the Aramoho Junction railway station was opened. The railway had attracted huge number of workers to the community. Over the next few decades, Aramoho gradually became a suburb of Wanganui and alongside the railway workers came a new generation of entrepreneurs and innovators. Among the young entrepreneurs was William Reuben Martin Oates.

Oates was born in Wellington in 1886. During the first years of the twentieth century, his parents decided to leave New Zealand for Melbourne. Not wanting to follow, the teenage Oates moved to Wanganui having secured employment as a delivery boy for Kernohan's Grocers and Provision Merchants Limited, a well-established grocery store in the heart of the town.

For several years he toiled away learning the intricacies of the grocery trade and worked his way up from being a delivery boy to working on the shop floor and then taking over some of the store's administration work. In 1909, he left Kernohan's and went to work as a house steward at Wanganui Hospital. During his time there, William met his future wife.

Born in Palmerston North in 1891, Margaret Henry came from a well-to-do family. She met William when her sister married one of his cousins. The pair soon fell in love and married in Palmerston North in 1915. The marriage disappointed some Wanganui locals who had seen Oates as a potential suitor for their daughters.

It didn't take long before William's friends warmed to his new wife. Margaret was quiet, humble and attractive and she was quickly accepted into the community, attending all civic events that might help further her husband's standing.

Although his job at Wanganui Hospital was secure and well paid, Oates desperately wanted to manage his own business. He pluckily approached an old family friend and successful businessman named Walter Hedges, and asked him for financial assistance. Oates quickly convinced his old friend to help finance him into a small grocery store in the up-and-coming suburb of Aramoho. Hedges could see the economic potential of the venture, but had no interest in working as he only recently retired. It was agreed Oates would manage the day-to-day running of the store while Hedges would be principal shareholder and accountant.

The store opened as WR Oates and Company on 1 June 1920. Oates employed three assistants and one delivery boy. His small shop was the only grocery store in Aramoho so it was consistently busy and he enjoyed a loyal patronage. William Oates knew the names of nearly all of his customers and took a genuine interest in their lives and well-being.

Oates was popular and was regarded as one of the borough's leading lights—not only was he the local store owner but he was also captain of the local cricket club. Handsome, energetic, friendly and always smiling, William Oates loved his life in Wanganui.

While keeping normal trading hours during the week, Oates kept the store open until 8.30 on Friday nights. Fridays were always the busiest days for trading as it was pay day and many of the locals shopped for the weekend or the week ahead. It was also the day when people would come in and pay off their accounts. Oates, like many shopkeepers at the time, allowed many of his customers to book up items during the week and repay him at the end of the week.

At the end of each day's trade, the three shop assistants would cash up their respective tills and hand the takings over to Oates before leaving for the night. Oates then put the cash in a brown canvas bag and finished locking up the store. Then, taking the bag with him, he would cycle the 800 metres to his house in Somme Parade, which Margaret's parents had helped the couple buy in 1921.

At home he would have supper with his wife and tally up the day's takings before going to bed. In the morning, he would take the money bag back to the shop before giving it to old man Hedges, who would come in each day to do the banking.

Like any other Friday, 26 October 1923 was busy in the store. From midday onwards, the railway workers began coming in to make their purchases and settle their accounts. The store remained busy until about 5pm and then quietened down until the last minute shoppers arrived between 7pm and 8pm. These were usually late shift workers or families finishing shopping after having attended the late afternoon session at the cinema.

On nights the store was open late, Margaret Oates would walk from their home on Somme Parade to bring dinner to her husband. They would then sit in the rear of the store and dine together. Occasionally William would have to go and attend to customers in the shop and Margaret would wait patiently for her husband to return.

At about 6pm, on 26 October, Margaret Oates arrived at the shop with her Sydney Silky terrier, to deliver a picnic basket containing dinner for her husband. She walked through the store towards the back room, stopping briefly to exchange pleasantries with shop staff. Out the back, she laid the food out on a fresh tablecloth and arranged two plates and tea mugs. The shop was still quite busy but Oates was able to slip away and enjoy some quiet time with his wife only having to return to the shop floor twice. This gave Margaret the chance to read the day's newspaper and, upon William's return, the pair giggled at the day's comic supplement.

Margaret was extremely happy. Her mother was due to arrive from Palmerston North the next day for a week's holiday. The couple talked about what they were going to do with Mrs Henry and they discussed what to have for tea the next night.

Margaret was slightly anxious because she had not yet made up the spare bedroom as she had only just washed the sheets that day and they weren't fully dry on account of the rain. William reassured her that she would be able to sort this out first thing next morning and said he was confident the house would be spick-and-span when Mrs Henry arrived.

Delivery boy Albert Trangmar finished up at 7.15pm. As he walked out, he bade Margaret Oates goodnight and she smiled at him but made no reply. Around 8pm, the shop started to fill with customers and William Oates returned to the shop floor. Margaret spent ten minutes tidying up then walked out of the store closely followed by her small dog. As she left called out, 'Goodbye dear and don't be long coming home!'

By 8.15pm, most customers had left the store so Oates began tidying up in preparation for closure. The tills were closed off and orders were filled ready delivery the next morning.

The assistants, Leslie Rush and William Franklin, left at different times between 8.30pm and 9pm with James Louisson being the last to leave. Louisson was a loyal employee and friend of Oates who had been employed at the store since it opened.

William Oates was the last to leave the shop. He collected the day's takings and carefully bundled them into his bag along with the latest copy of the *Sydney Referee* and two grocery journals. Oates locked the door to the store and walked out around 9.25pm. He placed the canvas bag in the basket on the front of his bicycle and cycled home.

Around 9.30pm, Oates passed the Aramoho Post Office and noticed the tram slowly approaching the tram stop in Field Street. Oates tipped his hat in greeting to Tom Rufford, who was seated in the rear of the tram, and called out 'Good night Tom,' as he cycled past. Rufford did not acknowledge him but later said he heard someone on a bike call out to him, but he couldn't see who it was as it was dark.

Oates arrived at his home at 232 Somme Parade around 9.40pm. The house was modest and well kept. It was situated 13 metres from the street. The back verandah was covered in creepers and there were large shrubs separating it from the house next door. Behind the house was a large well-kept section complete with vegetable garden. On the lower side was a belt of high pine trees which made the section private and not able to be viewed from the road.

Oates opened his front gate and whistled as he walked his bike around to the back of the house. It was dark and strangely quiet. Usually the dog would bark upon hearing his whistle, but Oates heard nothing. He hoisted his bike up onto the verandah, carefully leaning it against the outside wall of the washhouse. It was his usual custom to bring the canary in when he arrived home but the canary cage was not out on the verandah.

Oates opened the kitchen door and walked inside. The gas light was burning. He heard a slight shuffle and thought it was the dog coming to greet him. Just as he opened his mouth to greet his wife, he was suddenly struck on the back of his head with a heavy weapon. The force of the blow made Oates' knees buckle and he slammed into the wall. He managed to turn around while putting his hands up in defence, but was quickly struck again, this time above the right eye. The force of this second blow completely knocked Oates off his feet and he hit the floor. The sudden attack left him dazed but he had to defend himself.

The room was dark and his eyes were welling up with blood, but Oates could just make out the form but not the face of his attacker. As he tried to get up, Oates' head took another blow. He desperately lashed out and kicked the attacker in his chest knocking him back against the wall. The offender was quick to recover and rained blow upon blow on Oates' arms and legs. Oates continued kicking wildly and fought to remain conscious. Then, all of a sudden, he heard the back door close and realised that his attacker had fled. The attack was over as quickly as it started.

Oates could barely believe what had just happened. His head throbbed. His whole body was soaked with sweat and blood was pouring from his wounds. As he attempted to steady himself on the kitchen sink he slipped in a large pool of blood, which he assumed was from his own wounds.

Disorientated and unable to find the light switch in the dark, Oates staggered out the back door to ensure his assailant was gone. While standing there he noticed that his canvas bag with the day's takings had been taken.

Certain that the attacker was gone, Oates went in search of his wife. He staggered through the kitchen, calling out, 'Margaret! Margaret! Everything will be all right!'

As he opened the door from the kitchen to the hall, he noticed the door was off its runner. He could not hear the dog. Immediately panic set in. Striking a match, he noticed a trail of blood on the passage floor leading to the second bedroom. Then he noticed his wife lying on the floor in a large pool of blood.

Oates raced outside and bounded over the fence to his neighbour, Arthur

Pepper. But the Pepper family were not home.

Sydney Dobbins, who lived across the road at 229 Somme Parade, was preparing for bed when he heard persistent knocking at his door. He opened it and saw William Oates holding a blood soaked towel to his head and his face covered in open wounds.

'Oh, Mr Dobbins! I've been knocked out and robbed and my poor girl is murdered! I'm sure she's murdered.'

Dobbins sat Oates down on his front doorstep and rushed inside to call the police. He then returned to his injured neighbour who was desperate to return to his wife's side. Dobbins helped Oates along the street and the pair went inside the house. Striking a match, Dobbins noticed trails of blood on the kitchen floor leading to the passage way. A chair next to the dining table had been knocked over.

On the floor of the spare bedroom they found Margaret Oates. She was still alive but breathing laboriously. Her head was covered in a towel that appeared to have been forced into her mouth as a gag. Dobbins attempted to remove the towel then, upon noticing the extent of her injuries, changed his mind.

As Dobbins was about to go home and call a doctor, Oates walked back into the room holding a loaded double-barrel shotgun. Dobbins attempted to persuade Oates to hand it over, but he refused. Dobbins thought better of trying to force it off him. He followed Oates outside, where the distraught man sat down, nursing the gun and mumbling incoherently.

Dobbins raced home and telephoned the local doctor.

At 9.55pm, Dobbins' call was put through to Constable Bob Sims at the Dublin Street police station. Satisfied a doctor had been called, Sims picked up Oates' business partner, Walter Hedges, and the pair drove to Somme Parade. There they found Sydney Dobbins trying to calm the bloodstained Oates who, upon seeing them, cried 'My God constable, this is cruel. My wife has been murdered and he has got away!'

Hedges ran up to console the distraught man while Sims gently prised the shotgun from his grasp.

Having secured the firearm, the policeman made his way inside. When Sims got to her, Margaret Oates was still alive. A thick trail of blood showed she had been dragged from the kitchen, along the passage way into the room where she now lay. The bedroom was dark so the constable tried to locate a light but it appeared the gas jet had been dismantled.

Dr Wilson was the next to arrive. He had worked with William Oates at Wanganui Hospital and he knew the couple well. Seeing his friend arrive, Oates cried out hysterically for Wilson to help his wife.

When Dr Wilson got to Margaret, her breathing was shallow and her right arm and leg were in spasms. Her left arm appeared to be paralysed. Her body was fully extended and the towel covering her head was completely soaked with blood. Wilson smelt the towel for traces of chloroform, but there was none. Alongside Margaret lay her little Sydney Silky terrier, which had also been viciously beaten. He had probably leapt to the defence of his mistress and been bashed.

Arthur Pepper was Oates' immediate neighbour. He arrived home around 10.15pm and walked up the front steps to his home. As Pepper unlocked the door, he noticed blood on the door knob leading to a trail down the door to the ground. Panicking, he ran inside and checked all the rooms. Nothing. He raced along the road in time to see the ambulance arrive at the Oates household. He asked what he could do to help. Walter Hedges replied that everything was under control. Pepper said that Margaret Oates' mother was due to arrive the next morning. Hedges suggested Pepper telephone Mrs Henry as soon as they knew the extent of Margaret's injuries.

As Margaret's beaten body was removed from the house to the waiting ambulance, the injured terrier sat up and attempted to follow his mistress. Once outside the house, he awkwardly bounded towards the ambulance but collapsed at the roadside and died.

Margaret Oates was admitted to Wanganui Hospital at 11.10pm, and was treated by Dr Allen and hospital staff. She was unconscious and her breathing was laboured. She was pallid with a very weak pulse. Her head and chest were heavily bloodstained. Doctors Hutson and Allen carried out a full examination on the injuries she sustained and at the same time tried to keep her alive.

The doctors' notes described Margaret Oates as having a lacerated irregular wound to the frontal bone. Her brain had been punctured and lacerated and was protruding. A small piece of bone was completely separated and was lying on the brain substance. There were also another three star-shaped wounds on her head. It was believed the injuries were caused by a heavy blunt instrument.

Walter Hedges drove William Oates to the hospital. He was examined by Dr

Allen and found to have a wound in the top of his head. He had been struck with considerable force by a blunt instrument. Surprisingly, his skull was not fractured. There was no question of the injuries being self-inflicted.

The doctor believed that if Oates had not been wearing his hat when he was first struck, the initial blow would have probably killed him. Drifting in and out of consciousness, Oates continued sobbing hysterically, begging the medical staff to do everything to save his wife. His pleas were in vain. Margaret Oates died at 12.40am. She was 32 years old.

In the early hours, Walter Hedges telephoned Arthur Pepper to inform him that Margaret Oates had died. Pepper then rang Mrs Henry to tell her the bad news. In shock and disbelief, Mrs Henry rang her other daughter and the pair drove through the night to Wanganui.

A full post mortem was carried out the following afternoon. Doctors confirmed that as a result of her head injuries, a large haematoma in the mid-occipital region of her brain had developed, and the blood vessels in her brain had congested.

A body inspection showed her thorax, abdomen and pelvis had not sustained injury. There was no blood or marks on her hands, which indicated there had been no struggle. Additionally, her under-clothing had not been disarranged and there was no sign of any sexual attack. The post mortem concluded that Margaret Oates probably died from the effect of her first injury compounded by shock.

Police sealed the crime scene. A call was placed through to Wellington Police Detective branch to inform them a serious attack had taken place. Detective Sergeant Donald Cameron of Wellington Police was already in Wanganui so was dispatched take charge of the scene.

Chief Detective Kemp and Detective Walsh, along with fingerprint expert Senior Sergeant Dinnie were ordered to travel immediately from Wellington to Wanganui. They arrived in Wanganui before dawn on Saturday 27 October and immediately set to work. When they arrived they found they were dealing with a murder investigation.

A room-by-room inspection of the Oates' house was undertaken and it was confirmed no money or jewellery had been taken from any of the rooms. In fact, the amount of 13s.3d was sitting on the mantelpiece and Margaret Oates' jewellery was found in a bedroom drawer.

The main bedroom Margaret Oates shared with her husband had not been tidied and it appeared the beds had not been made since that morning. The bed in the spare room didn't have sheets on it and the blankets were in a pile at the foot of the bed, probably because Margaret Oates was preparing the room for her mother.

The police attempted to reconstruct what happened based on the state of the house and the evidence before them. There were several sheets hanging on the clothesline outside. There was a pile of dry washing in a heap on the washhouse floor.

The canary—which William Oates would usually bring inside when he came home—was in a cage in the kitchen. Margaret Oates probably brought it inside when she returned home from the store around 9pm.

On nights when her husband worked late, Margaret would prepare supper for him. On the dining table there was half a loaf of bread, some butter, two plates and two mugs. There was also a small box of chocolates. The *Truth* newspaper was open with another magazine underneath it. Margaret Oates had probably been sitting at the kitchen table with her back to the door when her attacker had sneaked into the kitchen.

Judging from her injuries, he must have struck while she was still seated. A kitchen chair had been knocked over and a scuffle ensued. There was a large pool of blood on the floor by the pantry door where she must have initially fallen. From this pool a trail of blood led through the door into the passage way, where there was another pool of blood. There were also blood spatters up the wall. She was struck again here and then dragged into the bedroom, where she was struck again.

This was the darkest room in the house—there was a gas light in the room but it was not working. The attacker must have felt confident that he wouldn't be seen from the street while he was carrying out his crime. At some point, the killer wrapped a towel around Margaret Oates' head either in an attempt to gag her or in order to drag her from the kitchen. The carpet runner in the passage was disarranged, a telltale sign of a body being dragged.

Police believed that after carrying out his brutal attack on Margaret Oates, the assailant had waited in the washhouse until he heard William Oates arrive home. He then followed Oates into the kitchen before carrying out his brutal attack. The assailant is then thought to have rushed out the back door, snatching the canvas bag containing the day's takings as he went. Where could he have gone?

Both Oates' and Dobbins' properties backed onto the property of William Webb at 5 Field Street. Webb told police that it would take a very active man to bound over the six-foot high fence that separated the properties. He also said he had heard nothing unusual all evening. If this was true, the assailant must have walked out the front gate and along Somme Parade without attracting any attention.

Police checked the ground for any telltale signs of someone leaving in a hurry, but found no marks.

By the time most residents woke the next morning, police were carrying out their scene examination. Word of what had happened spread quickly, and by mid-morning on Saturday, Somme Parade had attracted a huge number of curious sightseers.

Detectives went door-to-door talking to neighbours. Arthur Pepper, whose house had been William Oates' first port of call, Pepper told police that he had already been living in Somme Parade when the Oates moved in two years earlier and relations were cordial. He also said that whenever he had his kitchen and living room lights on they threw a strong light right into Oates' kitchen and spare bedroom, as well as a good part of the backyard. Pepper said that when these lights were on, he could see right into the house.

In the past there had been minor disagreements between Pepper and Oates because Pepper was prone to staying up late with the lights on, or having late parties, which annoyed his neighbours as they were trying to sleep. He assured police that the arguments were not serious and the pair bore no grudges.

Arthur Pepper and his family had gone out to do their weekly shopping at about 6.50pm. Once they'd finished their shopping, they went to the pictures. It was highly unusual for the whole family to be out in the evening. Pepper said that had he been home, he would have heard the dog bark or heard any movement as the two houses were so close together. He also thought he would have been able to see the attack as the Oates didn't have curtains on the side or rear windows of their house and his lights would have lit the kitchen and bedroom.

Pepper was devastated that on the rare evening that he decided to go out, his neighbour was viciously attacked and killed. He couldn't help but wonder if the attack would have happened if he'd stayed home.

About 60 metres from the Oates' house, there was a tram stop, which was lit by an electric street light that lit an area of about 90 metres, including the front yard of 232 Somme Parade. This had not deterred the killer.

The owner of a confectionary store on the corner of Somme Parade and Glasgow

Street told police that on the afternoon of the murder, a strange man called in to the shop to borrow a pencil, which she duly lent him. One hour later he returned with £1 cash to pay for it. At around 8pm, she had been in the sitting room at the rear of her store, when she saw the man she had served earlier leave the shop and walk quickly along the street carrying something in his arms. She called out to him, but he did not answer. She returned to her shop and noticed the money from the till had gone. Was this in any way connected to the killing? The woman provided a description, but police were unable to link it to a suspect.

A number of people were interviewed and asked what they knew of Oates' business. Arthur Pepper told police he had been at a euchre party some months back and heard someone mention that Oates took the takings home with him each night. Pepper could not remember who had said it or who else had been at the party. He said he thought at the time that, if the rumour was true, Oates was a target to be robbed.

There were a few people that actually knew Oates' habits and it appears he did nothing to conceal the fact he took home the takings each night. Oates was always the last to leave the shop. Therefore anybody could have easily observed his habits and movements without arousing suspicion.

When police interviewed Walter Hedges, another more sinister factor came into play. He told them that he had been on holiday for a week and while he was away no one was banking the takings. Oates took the money home each night and took it back to the shop the following morning amassing quite a sum. At the last minute, Hedges had decided to return a day early, and dropped by Friday morning to bank the four-day backlog of takings. If Hedges had stayed away the extra night as he had planned, then Oates would have had much more in his bag the night his wife was killed. Perhaps the killer knew of Hedges' holiday and his original date of return?

The murder sent shockwaves through Wanganui. Residents recalled the unsolved murder of an elderly Chinese market gardener named Chow Yat, who had been shot dead a year earlier in nearby Long Acre.

There were no similarities between the murders, but townsfolk quickly began comparing the two, and rumours quickly spread that there was a brutal killer on the loose. Newspaper reports told of women afraid to leave their homes, and men neglecting evening meetings to stay home and guard their families.

While this may have been exaggerated reporting, there was real fear on the streets of Wanganui and a lack of confidence in the police. They had not brought Chow's killer to justice, and it looked like Margaret Oates' killer was also going to remain free. Police tried to allay fears by stating publicly that the killings were in no way related, and that they were confident of finding both killers. Despite their assurances, townsfolk were sceptical.

The attack on William Oates and the murder of his wife drew a great deal of sympathy from the Wanganui public. Margaret's funeral was held on 28 October in Palmerston North. There was a large crowd in attendance but her husband—who was still in a serious condition in hospital—was unable to attend. All cricket matches in Wanganui were cancelled that day as a mark of respect and each of the borough's cricket clubs sent wreaths.

William Oates was released from hospital on 2 November 1923. He received plenty of support from the community, who rallied around to assist in providing housekeeping, meals and company. But there was also a cruel element spreading malicious gossip. Police received anonymous letters saying that William Oates had murdered his wife in order to collect insurance money. In various letters, Oates was said to have a mistress and was planning on sailing to Australia with her; that his business was failing and that he would profit from his wife's death.

Despite having expert evidence that Oates' injuries could not have been self-inflicted, police had to grudgingly put the accusations to the grieving widower. Oates emphatically denied having any involvement in his wife's murder. Margaret Oates' life was not insured, the business was thriving in spite of the recession and he had already paid two thirds off the mortgage so they were financially secure.

Oates was astounded at the heartless accusations and could not believe the cruelty of people, some of whom could have even been his own customers. Over the years he had given his time and energy to the people of Wanganui and loved the borough. He grew extremely bitter and could not bear to return to his store. He viewed every male customer as a possible killer and women as suspected gossip-mongers.

Police received numerous anonymous letters suggesting far-fetched theories and naming unlikely suspects. One letter led police to interview a man in Turakina, some twenty kilometres from Wanganui, who was flashing money around, and had drunkenly boasted he killed a woman. After an intensive grilling, the man was able to confirm he had not left Turakina on the night in question.

His movements were corroborated by workmates who also said the man often mouthed-off whenever he was on the booze.

Wellington police followed up on all known violent offenders. A ship's captain informed them of a sailor who had handed over the sum of £100 for safe-keeping. This sailor had never had this kind of money before, and it was reported that he had been seen carrying a bloodstained handkerchief. But when interviewed, the sailor was able to prove that he had been on a train when the murder was committed. He also had proof of the withdrawal of £100 from his savings account a few days before the murder. The bloodstained handkerchief was explained as a tourniquet following an accident on board ship. He was cleared of any involvement.

Police interviewed hundreds of people but could not progress the investigation. Public sentiment towards Wanganui police was at an all time low. *Truth* published a cynical response to Wanganui grumblings, praising police for doing their 'level best and working all hours under the sun in the relentless pursuit of the killer'. However reporters continued to publish incorrect information. The following article was published in *Truth* in mid-November.

> *The story goes that two small boys were engaged on the night of the tragedy in catching moths that were hovering around the lights in the street near the home of the victims of the murder.*
>
> *A stranger passed under the lights. Indeed the boys, intent on the pursuit of the moths, collided with the man. They got a good look at him and were observant enough to pick his picture when the Album of the Rogue's Gallery was shown to them for the purposes of identification.*
>
> *For the story of the small boys was one of the things the police of Wanganui traced, with the results recorded.*
>
> *The police in a southern centre were communicated with for this rogue and vagabond was known to be loose footed. Yes he had been seen in that town, but he had moved north. Probably to Wanganui.*
>
> *The two boys saw him following the woman who was afterwards murdered, but they were not near enough or they were too intent on their sport to hear a scream—if the woman had a chance to give such a warning or call.*
>
> *But inquire and search they, never so skilfully or painstakingly, the police have not been able to get a trace of this rogue. But they will get him yet.*

Little of this was factual. The boys had seen a woman walk past them and then they had bumped into a man. But the timing of these events ruled out the possibility that it was Mrs Oates they had seen. Despite this, reporters seized on the information and sensationalised it to the extreme.

The article did raise some questions that had baffled police: Did the killer deliberately follow Margaret Oates home, or was he already waiting for her there? Had he attacked her mistakenly thinking it was her husband?

Police were certain the attack was motivated by robbery. Staff of W Oates and Co told them it was common knowledge that Oates carried the takings home each night. Oates was robbed on a Friday which was a naturally busy night. Why did he choose this particular night to strike? Was it a coincidence Oates was robbed during the week Hedges was away? Did the assailant plan the robbery thinking Oates would clear a substantial sum on Friday night to add to his already full balance?

He must have been quite familiar with procedures to know the banking was not going to be done. Nobody—not even Oates—was aware of Hedges' decision to return early from holiday. Had Hedges not returned, the assailant would have got away with a much larger sum.

Did the assailant have prior knowledge of the layout of the Oates' house? He entered through the back door, which was Oates' normal habit when he arrived home from work. He avoided the rooms that would have been lit up if the neighbours turned their lights on. Did he know that the light was broken in the bedroom where he left Margaret?

This leads to another question: Did the assailant also know Arthur Pepper was going to be away from home that night? Pepper told police he rarely left home at night, but on the night of the murder relented to family pressure to take them to the pictures. Evidently his decision to go out was made spontaneously.

Had Pepper been home, he would normally be sitting at his kitchen table at the time the murder occurred. His lights would have illuminated the Oates' home and he would have seen the attack on Mrs Oates unfold. Pepper was never regarded as a suspect in the murder as he had been with his family for the whole evening.

Was Margaret Oates' killing a case of mistaken identity, or was it part of the plan for her to be attacked? Margaret Oates had no control over the grocery business and never handled the cash. When she left the store that night, the tills had not been cashed up and the store remained open for another half hour.

Police assumed the assailant had followed her home, killed her and lain in wait to attack her husband. Police thought it unlikely that he had broken in as there were no telltale signs of forced entry.

It seems more reasonable that the killer thought that William Oates was already home. He may have known it was Oates' custom to bring the canary in from the verandah each night. On the night of the murder had Margaret brought it in on account of the bad weather? Upon seeing that the canary was not outside, the killer may have thought Oates was already home.

When Margaret left the shop she was wearing her hat and coat. After the murder, these items were found in her closet. If the killer had lain in wait at home, it is likely he would have attacked her as she walked in the door. It is unlikely he would have allowed her to hang up her coat, fold some sheets, and then spend time in the kitchen preparing supper. Police continued their investigations but yielded no answers to these questions.

The Member of Parliament for Wanganui, Mr Veitch wrote to the Minister of Justice urging him to increase the reward for information leading to the identity of the murderer from £250 to £1000, but the government were reluctant, preferring to leave it to police to find the killer. When the minister learned that police were struggling to make headway in the case, a compromise was reached, and the reward was increased to £500. It made no difference.

The inquest into the murder of Margaret Emily Oates began at Wanganui District Court on Thursday 23 November 1923, presided over by Mr JS Barton SM.

Albert Trangmar, James Louisson, Leslie Rush and William Franklin all testified that it had been an ordinary Friday night, and that Margaret Oates brought in dinner as was her custom, leaving at about 8.15pm. They told how they assisted Oates in tidying up before leaving the store between 8.30pm and 9.10pm. They all knew Oates would have taken the day's takings home with him.

Dobbins, Hedges and Pepper also gave testimony about their respective relationships with Oates and of their recollections of the night of the murder.

Dr Allen described in detail how Margaret Oates' skull had been broken in four places.

Dr Hutson said it was his belief that the weapon was a heavy wooden instrument rather than an iron bar because the bruising to William Oates' body was not consistent with those caused by blows of an iron bar.

Still swathed in bandages and badly bruised, William Oates took the stand and emotionally recounted how he had met Margaret and how they had been very happily married. He recounted his movements the night of the attacks and told of finding his wife injured.

Detective Sergeant Cameron represented the police and testified that, despite an intensive investigation, they had been unable to secure an arrest. At the time of the inquest there was no firm suspect in mind.

The coroner found that the deceased, Margaret Emily Oates, had been murdered by some person unknown between 8pm and 10pm, on the night of Friday, October 26 1923, at her residence, with the actual death occurring at the Wanganui Hospital shortly after midnight. The cause of death was from shock following a fracture of the skull and laceration of the brain.

After the inquest, information trickled in but most of it lacked substance. Chief Detective James Cummings visited Auckland's Mt Eden Prison where it had been alleged a prisoner described in detail how he killed Mrs Oates. When Cummings interviewed the prisoner, it soon became clear that the man had been nowhere near Wanganui at the time.

Police eventually narrowed down the list of prime suspects in the murder to three men:

1) Frederick Phillips was the first police suspect. He was the manager of the local Goldfinch Timber Mill. The shop staff had heard Phillips and Oates arguing over an unpaid account on the day of the murder. Phillips was interviewed and was mortified at being considered a suspect. He admitted he was suffering hard economic times and the public confrontation had been highly embarrassing. Desperate as he was, Phillips was a just a hard-working businessman down on his luck—not a vicious killer.

2) Clarence White was a local ne'er do well who had notched up a number of nuisance crimes and burglaries in his young life. He had been seen hanging around Oates' store on the night of the murder. Robbery was the motive, and it was assumed he would be foolish enough to lavishly spend the proceeds. Police watched him closely but he did not act suspiciously. White was interviewed several times by Cummings—who felt confident enough to break him—but White held

fast. At the end Cummings doubted White was the killer. He was the type to have cunningly committed the burglary but was unlikely to kill in order to get money.

3) Dick Mitchell was a known local burglar. He had been seen loitering around Somme Parade on the evening of the murder. He had no firm alibi for his whereabouts later that night. Like White, he was considered capable of burglary, but not violence. Police certainly suspected he was the offender who had robbed the confectionary store on the corner of Somme Parade and Glasgow Street on the afternoon before the murder, but this was never proven.

William Oates' recovery from his injuries was slow. He returned to work, but his heart was no longer in it. Hedges came out of retirement to manage the shop with the assistance of Louisson and Rush.

James Louisson never forgave himself for not paying closer attention to the people he had seen as he walked home the night of Margaret Oates' death. For years he would continue to rack his brain to try and remember if there had been anybody he recognised.

Eventually, Oates sold his business, sailed to Melbourne in July 1924 and never returned to New Zealand.

Thirty-five years after the killing, Wanganui Police received a letter which had been posted on 5 March 1958 at Mooroopna Base Hospital in Shepparton, Australia. It read:

To the Sergeant of Police
Wanganui

Dear Sir,
It often enters my head wondering if you ever found a sequel to the killing of Mrs Oats of Oramako [sic], round about the year 1924, or 23. It so happens, a chap said to me at the time, that I know the man who did it, but he would not tell me his name. That man's name was SUMMERS but further than telling me that I knew the person, he would not give me any information other than to say he worked at the Pipe Works, Castle Cliff.

Well, I happened to be speaking to Tom Mills, who had the hotel about opposite to Police Station. There was a man in the bar who heard the conversation who proved to be a detective. He asked me to repeat what I had told Mr Mills then told me to drive him to the hotel where he might contact Summers, which I did, namely to the Metropolitan. When we arrived there I pointed the man out but he simply denied ever mentioning anything to me which made me look like a liar.

Well, a while later I left NZ for Australia, as I used to follow shearing. Some months after being here, I was shearing at a shed, namely Columbine, and it is always the usual thing if there are any travellers (namely, swagman, as called in NZ) to ask them in for a meal, and to my surprise one of the travellers was the man that Summers had spoke about. I did not wake up to the fact until the next night. I was thinking what had gone wrong that he should be carrying the swag and especially over here. I asked him to my room the night I recognised him. I talked to him for awhile, and gave him some tobacco and also a few bob and told him to go to a certain place in the town of Hay, get a room there and wait a few days until I come in when I would get him a job and take him with me, but needless to say he was not there and I have not seem him since. Probably he went back to NZ. They used to be comfortable, well-off, when I knew him and his brothers in a small town of Ormondville. They had a grocery store there together with other things and when I put it together it seems to point that he was the person responsible. Further after thinking about it quite a lot, I began to wonder if Mrs Oats [sic] was the woman he married. She and her sister used to look after the Norsewood Post Office that is if my assumption is correct. I often wondered when in the shop at Aramako where I had seen her before. Of course I could be making a mistake about her being the person he married together with her being a sister to the one who looked after the Post Office, but from my memory she resembled that person. You see I used to serve them with bread when I was little more than a lad or young youth. My old Dad used to be a baker in Ormondville and I often drove the cart on the Norsewood Round. However the man's name was Percy Sugden and should this be of any use it may give you a lead to put things together.

Remaining respectfully, JJ Skinner.
Strathbogie via Euroa, Victoria

When this letter arrived on the desk of Wanganui detectives, nobody had any in depth knowledge about the case. All police who had worked on the original inquiry had retired, moved away or were dead. The Oates file had been stored in archives gathering dust. There were some confusing and conflicting elements in Skinner's letter.

First, there were no established timelines in the letter so police were not sure when Skinner had run into Sugden.

They found the name Percy Sugden in old police records. His last known address had been Riverview Boarding House, Taupo Quay, Wanganui. In 1958, Sugden would have been 78 years old. At this age, it was unlikely he was travelling looking for work so it was assumed the encounter between Sugden and Skinner had occurred many years earlier. But why would Skinner raise this now?

Skinner's brother Jim still lived in Ohakune. When interviewed, he confirmed his brother John left New Zealand around 1924, but he had not heard from him since. John Skinner had lived in Aramoho at the time of the murder and had talked about it incessantly to his brother, believing Margaret Oates had been murdered by her husband. Jim Skinner was also able to confirm that they had known Sugden from Ormondville.

Records showed there was an active warrant to arrest Sugden for failing to provide for his wife and children, and failing to comply with a maintenance order from 16 October 1923.

Sugden had worked in the grocery store in Ormondville which he ran with his brother until the early 1920s when he had left his wife and his job and left Wanganui. A short time later, he reappeared and moved into the Riverview Boarding House and secured employment at Spiral and Lock Bar Pipeworks.

By 1958, the boarding house had been demolished. The Spiral and Lock Bar Pipeworks was still operating. Staff records showed Sugden had been a keen and diligent worker whose speciality was construction jobs. The only staff member to remember Sugden was an elderly man named William Webb. Webb said Sugden had been quiet and sullen, keeping mostly to himself.

Records showed Sugden last worked on 10 April 1922 when he vanished midway through the day. He never returned to his job and was never seen in the area again. Post Office savings records confirmed his account was closed at Wanganui on the same day. There was no other record of him being in the area after 10 April 1922 so it was unlikely he was there when Margaret Oates was murdered.

If the name William Webb sounds familiar, it's because he lived over the back fence from Oates in 1923. At the inquest into the murder, Webb testified that he had eaten dinner with his family, and then gone out walking returning home soon after 8pm. His daughter retired to bed around 8.30pm, and he at 9pm. They heard no sound from Oates' place that night.

Webb told the coroner it would take a very active man to bound over the fence because of its height, thereby negating this as an escape route. Furthermore he had heard nothing nor had he seen anyone suspicious in the area while he was out walking.

Webb had been considered an important witness because of the location of his home. Like Skinner, he became somewhat fixated with the murder. To the annoyance of police, Webb had carried out his own private investigations and regularly approached police naming individuals who he suspected of having killed Margaret Oates. More often than not, the names he gave to police were people who he disliked or held grudges against. Webb was cautioned many times against making false and misleading accusations. Had he made these allegations to take the heat off himself? Was he the assailant?

John Skinner's letter to police had said that Summers identified an employee of the pipe works as Margaret Oates' killer. At the time of the murder, Sugden was not working there—but William Webb was. Webb could have known Oates took the shop takings home each night. From his house, he would have been able to see that the Peppers were out for the evening.

In any case, Webb was not interviewed as a suspect in connection with the murder in 1958. Too much time had elapsed for them to be able to re-investigate. Police believed that whoever killed Margaret Oates and bashed her husband would have disposed of the satchel and murder weapon in the Whanganui River before quickly and quietly leaving town. William Webb made no effort to evade police and didn't seem to have anything to hide.

Webb's financial affairs were also taken into consideration. The killer would have made off with a great deal of cash and would likely have drawn attention to himself splashing money around. No one could remember Webb ever coming into a large sum of money and he had no convictions for assault or violence. Wanganui police didn't suspect him of the murder in 1923 and this belief did not waver 35 years later.

4. The Tragic Tale of Gwen Scarff

Derisley Wood, descendant of the Canterbury pioneering family, his wife Amy and their family lived in a palatial house in McMillan Avenue in the affluent Christchurch suburb of Cashmere. In January 1927, Mrs Wood employed two live-in domestic staff—20-year-old Gwen Scarff and Jessie McClure, a married woman in her forties.

On Friday 14 January, Gwen moved into an upstairs bedroom and began work as a housemaid the following day. She had one day a week off. Jessie McClure moved in on the following Monday morning and began work as a general domestic. Jessie was allowed one day off during the week and had Saturdays to spend with her husband and children.

The pair hit it off and quickly became close. Jessie grew fond of Gwen and developed an almost maternal instinct towards the chatty, naïve young woman with a head full of romantic dreams.

At first, Mrs Wood was happy with her selection of staff and ensured they worked hard. Jessie McClure worked quietly and diligently, but Mrs Wood quickly realised the same could not be said for young Gwen. Her flights of fancy and sneaking off to have long private telephone conversations during work time quickly became intolerable. Still, Gwen was bright and jolly and did not take offence at Mrs Wood's scolding.

On Thursday 20 May, Gwen suddenly became unwell—so sick she thought she was going to die. Mrs Wood had to look after her as she was vomiting and delirious. Gwen recovered but was frail, emotional and irritable, and she could not be comforted. Mrs Wood knew Gwen confided in Jessie McClure, but did not want to upset the social order by involving herself in the happenings of her servants. Slowly, Gwen's mental condition improved and she seemed more cheerful, if a bit absent minded.

On Tuesday 7 June, Gwen was working slowly and whenever Mrs Wood was out of sight she would slip away to use the telephone. She looked nervous and upset if her calls were unanswered—it was clear she had something on her mind. Mrs Wood had to remind her several times to pull her socks up, but this seemed to fall on deaf ears.

Around 2.20pm, a gentleman phoned asking for Gwen. Mrs Wood discouraged calls during work time but allowed her take the call—it might be the call the girl was expecting and, hopefully, she would be able to concentrate on her job for the rest of the day. Certainly, she seemed perkier after taking the call.

Mrs Wood heard Gwen leave the house at around 8pm, returning about an hour later. She did not tell anyone where she had been. Next morning, Mrs Wood was surprised to see Gwen up early, cheerfully attending to her chores. Normally, Gwen was hard to shift in the mornings. When asked, Gwen said she wanted to finish early—it was her usual half day and she wanted to get away as soon as she could after lunch, which she did.

She usually returned home early on Wednesday evenings, but did not do so that day. Next morning, when Jessie McClure took in a cup of tea it appeared Gwen's bed had not been slept in and her suitcase, bags and personal effects were missing. Nobody in the house could recall seeing Gwen remove her belongings.

A week later, Derisley Wood looked up from the newspaper he was reading and mentioned to his wife a woman had been found murdered—brutally bashed—near Burwood. She had no identification and the newspaper described the victim's clothes in the hope someone might be able to help identify her.

The national newspapers jumped on the story of the girl, later identified as Gwen Scarff—a young, sweet, naïve girl, taken advantage of. The story unfolded as a tale of sex, drugs, scandalous affairs, perjury and a very public murder trial. In the aftermath there was a national controversy around public trust in the police.

Born in Christchurch in 1906, Ellen Gwendoline Isobel Scarff was the eldest of three children born to Walter William Prideaux Scarff and his wife Ellen. The family lived at 11 Thorrington Avenue, Cashmere. Walter Scarff was a carrier by trade—he had his own truck. Highly respected by many, he was generally regarded as rough and taciturn. Although he ruled his family with an iron rod, he was fiercely loyal and protective of all his children.

In her early years, Gwen was a bit of a tomboy—solidly built with a boyish complexion—but she grew into a very handsome young woman. People remembered her as sweet and full of life, although simple natured and trusting. She had romantic dreams typical of many girls her age. She was a below average student, and clearly had no desire to stay at school—she simply wanted to be married, live in a lovely home and bear many children.

She left school at 15 and, with her father's help, got a job at the Carriers' Office in Tuam Street. She worked on reception, but she also dispatched trucks and helped with the wages. There, Walter reasoned, he could keep an eye on his artless daughter.

Not long after she began work, she struck up a friendship with Charlie Boakes—a casual relief driver. He was married with two small children and 18 years older than her. Boakes and Walter Scarff had been acquainted through their work since 1911. They were never friends, but there was a mutual respect and occasionally Scarff would pass work Boakes' way.

Popping into the Tuam Street Carriers' Office to pick up his pay packet he thought he recognised the office girl but couldn't quite place her. She introduced herself as Gwen Scarff. Boakes commented on how she had blossomed into a very attractive girl. Gwen giggled shyly—it was most probably the first time any man had noticed her in that way and she was smitten. Boakes made regular trips into the office and always took the time to chat to Gwen, making her laugh, teasing her and heaping attention on her. This quickly led to open flirting.

In 1922, Walter Scarff asked Boakes if he could fill in for him while he and his wife went away on holiday. Boakes readily agreed—he needed the income and it would allow him to spend some private time with young Gwen. Every morning Boakes would turn up at Thorrington Street to pick up the lorry. He would find it clean and tidy, with a cushion and blanket for his comfort. It is surmised Boakes and Gwen Scarff began a sexual relationship at this time.

During his holiday, Walter Scarff injured his hand and could not return to driving so he asked Boakes to continue working for at least four more months, while his hand healed. Eager for the work and the opportunity to prolong his relationship with Gwen, Boakes agreed.

He was leading a double life. With Gwen he talked lovingly to her, planning their future together. He told Gwen he was unhappy in his marriage and that he was going to leave his wife when the time was right. He begged Gwen to wait, and she promised to. They referred to Mrs Boakes as 'the evil witch'.

Yet to many in Sydenham, where Boakes lived, he was regarded as a loving husband and devoted father. He was in no hurry to change his domestic situation. If Gwen asked when he was going to leave his wife, he would have a reason why they needed to wait. Gwen was so infatuated she believed his every word.

When Walter Scarff returned to work Boakes was unable to see as much of Gwen. One day, he popped into the Tuam Street Carriers' Office and Gwen wasn't there. She had been strangely absent from work and when he asked around there was much speculation about her sudden departure. The story was that she had demanded a pay rise and been rejected, so she walked out and had not returned.

A few weeks later, Boakes was loading up his lorry when a red-faced Walter Scarff stormed up and grabbed him by the collar and threw him against the wall.

'What the bloody hell have you been doing to my Gwen?' he shouted.

'What do you mean?'

'She had a kiddie, and you're the father!' spat Scarff.

'No! That is a lie. I never touched her.'

By then, a number of men had gathered around. Not wanting to create any more of a scene, Scarff backed down. Boakes looked pleadingly at the other men and denied the accusation, adding it was common knowledge Gwen had 'put it about'. Scarff was furious and revealed that the baby had died.

Several weeks later, Gwen Scarff returned to work. No questions were asked, but word had spread—Gwen had become pregnant and she had been allowed to leave work for the duration of the pregnancy. Over the latter months of the pregnancy, Gwen had stayed at home in seclusion—she was not allowed to go out. She was unwell and refused to tell her parents the name of the man responsible for her condition.

The baby boy was born prematurely at home. Unfortunately, he was sickly and died three days later. After that, Gwen, who was weak, broke down and admitted she had been having an affair with Charlie Boakes. After she returned to work, her father forbade her to·have anything to do with him, but Gwen was stubborn, believing her man was unhappy in his marriage. She saw a future for them together.

Meanwhile, Boakes put his head down, kept quiet and did his best to avoid her.

He quit cartage work and began driving for Summers Bus Company, which took him away from Christchurch on a regular basis, hoping time would allow the scandal to be forgotten. In late 1926, he began driving for White Diamond Taxis from the Clock Tower stand in central Christchurch and it was not long before he began receiving regular visits there from Gwen Scarff.

In January 1927, Scarff noticed his daughter was acting funny—she was a bit moody. He decided she was bored and needed a change to take her mind off whatever she was brooding about. At his suggestion, Gwen applied for and gained the position as housemaid in the Derisley Wood household.

One day in March, Gwen's friend and workmate, Jessie McClure, noticed Gwen was not herself. She looked pale and sickly, and had no energy. When Jessie sat Gwen down with a cup of tea and asked what was wrong Gwen broke down and confessed that she was pregnant. She did not know what to do—nobody should know. She said she could not go home because her father was cold and unkind.

Jessie tried to calm her and asked about the baby's father. Gwen replied that she would not understand, but Jessie was wise and asked if the father of the child was already married. Gwen fought back tears and nodded.

The story tumbled out—she said she had known him ever since she was a child, he worked as a taxi driver, he was married with two children, and she visited him every Wednesday on her day off. But, she was at pains to add, he was very unhappy in his marriage and was planning to leave his evil and manipulative wife—not yet, but as soon as he could. Gwen sobbed uncontrollably.

When asked, Gwen said she thought she was about six weeks pregnant, but 'Charlie' was going to get her stuff that would help her out of trouble. McClure thought she meant pills that might procure an abortion—Gwen seemed determined she didn't want the baby. A few days after this conversation a package addressed to Gwen arrived in the post. It was a small, round cardboard box containing black pills. The handwritten instructions were to take two pills three times daily. Jessie later said Gwen was diligent about this. However, nothing seemed to happen and after she finished the pills she told Jessie she was going to have to tell her man they were no good.

The following Wednesday night, Gwen returned home late and went straight to Jessie's room. She sat at the end of her bed and told her that Charlie was agitated because nothing could be done until the end of the following month. He would get her some more pills then—much stronger pills that were guaranteed to work.

Jessie was dubious. By the time Gwen received the next lot of pills, she would be more than three months gone and procuring an abortion at that stage would endanger her health. Jessie expressed her doubt, but Gwen did not seem to care—she seemed happy to believe everything her Charlie told her.

A few more weeks passed. Again, Gwen returned from her night out and told Jessie that Charlie was getting hold of some much stronger stuff that was guaranteed to work. The catch was it would cost £5, which Charlie did not have. Cheekily, he asked Gwen to pay, promising to refund her when insurance money from his mother's estate was released.

On Thursday 12 May, Mrs Wood gave the women an hour off to go into town. They went to the post office and Gwen withdrew £4. She put the money in her purse with the £1 she already had. From there, they walked to the Grand Taxi stand, then to the Liberty stand, looking for Charlie. Gwen told Jessie to wait while she talked to a driver for about 10 minutes. She saw Gwen reach into her purse and hand the driver the money and when she got back she said, 'Well, I can do no more.'

On Monday 16 May, Gwen told Jessie she was going to meet Charlie at the top of the driveway that night. At 8pm she quietly slipped out of the house, returning about an hour later. She went straight to Jessie's room and said 'Would you like to see my £5 worth?'

Jessie agreed and Gwen held out a tiny bottle that was about half-full with what appeared to be reddish-brown liquid. She said Charlie had given it to her and instructed her to take it on Wednesday night after dinner. The following Thursday morning, Jessie rose and took a cup of tea to Gwen's room, but there was no response to her gentle tapping at the door. Jessie went inside and set the cup down. Gwen was asleep and breathing deeply, but to Jessie's horror her young friend was frothing at the mouth and there was vomit over the bedspread. Jessie eventually managed to shake Gwen awake but she was incoherent.

Jessie ran to fetch Mrs Wood. When they returned, Gwen was sitting staring out the window in a daze. Mrs Wood thought Gwen had food poisoning or had picked up a virus. Jessie was sure her symptoms related to the medicine but couldn't say anything. The two older women helped Gwen back into bed and nursed her through the day.

The next morning Gwen was still weak but able to sip her tea and have some dry toast. Although unsteady on her feet, she insisted to Mrs Wood she could work and tend to her tasks. To Jessie she expressed disappointment that Charlie had not called as he promised to see how she was.

That afternoon she went to her room and wrote a letter to Charlie, which she showed to Jessie. Jessie read it two or three times and was confident she could recite it word-for-word:

Dear Charlie,

Seeing that you forgot to ring I am writing you this letter. You will be surprised to know that the stuff has not done any good. All that I can suggest now is that you make a clean breast of everything to your wife. Stick by me and help all you can, as you know, when this becomes known, I will be barred from my home and I, the mother of your second child, will be stranded. Write to me darling and tell me what to do!

Jessie watched Gwen fold the letter into an envelope addressed to:

Mr. Charles Boakes,
Grand Taxi Stand,
Christchurch.

Afterwards Gwen became upset and inconsolable. The next morning at around 11am the phone rang at the Wood's house. Gwen answered it and, although still weak, she seemed to perk up slightly. She told Jessie she was going to meet Charlie at 2.30pm that afternoon. Returning at 10pm she went into Jessie's room to fill her in on the afternoon's development.

She and Charlie had gone to New Brighton by taxi and lay together on Brighton Beach. Gwen's eyes widened with excitement saying that Charlie had told her that it was the end of everything between him and his wife. He said he would divorce his wife and asked if Gwen would marry him. She had happily accepted, but then Charlie sat up and said she would still need to hold on a bit longer so he could sort her out, and wait for his mother's insurance money. Gwen replied she could only really hold off for six months.

Gwen said after that something strange happened. They were silent for a moment and then Charlie lay on top of her and said, 'What about choking you?' When Jessie asked what she thought he had meant by that, Gwen replied that he was joking—he couldn't mean it because he loved her too much. However, the women agreed it was a very odd thing for him to say. Charlie reassured her everything would be fine.

For the next week, Gwen seemed to be her old self. After her next day off Gwen returned wide-eyed and excited saying that this would be her last night as Charlie was taking her away the next day. Jessie asked where they were going and Gwen said they were going to Wellington and then to Hastings where Charlie had a friend with a farm—the pair were to go into partnership. She said she and Charlie were to live as man and wife until his divorce came through and then they would marry.

Charlie told her not to pack too much. He said they could replace things in Wellington—he was going to collect £54 from his mother's insurance policy in Wellington on the following Friday. He also told Gwen to withdraw all her money from her savings account and to start destroying papers and things with her name on. Gwen did not think this strange. She reasoned that he probably didn't want any trace in case her parents tried to track them down.

Jessie asked if Charlie had repaid her the £6 for the medicine and taxi fares, but Gwen shook her head and replied that he said he would pay her back before they boarded the ferry. Jessie asked about Charlie's wife. Gwen snarled and replied that she only felt sorry for the boy. The wife deserved everything she was getting.

Gwen did not leave the next day, but in between her duties, she discreetly burned her books and papers in the fireplace and discarded some of her clothes. She packed the rest of clothes in her suitcase and she wrote a letter to an old friend of her mother's, Annie Lok, saying she would pop in for tea the following day.

On Tuesday 7 June, Charlie rang at 2.30pm, and Gwen went out that night, but only for an hour between 8pm and 9pm. She did not say too much to Jessie who felt she was holding something back. Gwen found it hard to keep secrets and she seemed as if she was ready to burst. All she did say was that she and Charlie had met with Charlie's cousin, Arthur, who had wished them both well and offered to give Gwen £20 in a few weeks' time.

At about 6.30 the next morning, Robert Rickerby walked up the Woods' path to the kitchen to deliver the milk when he noticed a suitcase and some smaller bags and packages placed on the footpath. He was surprised to pass the young maid walking hurriedly down the path carrying a heavy suitcase. She was looking all around and seemed anxious. He bade her good morning, but she responded by asking if he had seen a man in a White Diamond taxi.

He replied he had not, and she asked if it was 6.30 yet. He replied it was not yet 6.30 by his reckoning. The girl said it must be about 6.35, and mentioned her boy was off to Wellington that night and this was the only chance she had to see him.

Just then a White Diamond taxi pulled up and the maid ran towards it.

As he walked back down the driveway he passed the maid returning to the house and the taxi had gone. A few minutes later, he saw the taxi make a u-turn and go past, but it was too dark to make out the features of the driver. He did, however, notice the luggage on the back seat as the car went past.

Mrs Wood was surprised to see Gwen up and about so early, but it meant Gwen was able to leave a little earlier than usual for her half-day off. When it was clear the next morning that Gwen's bed had not been slept in, Mrs Wood phoned Ellen Scarff to let her know Gwen had not returned from her outing the previous afternoon. Ellen Scarff was surprised—her daughter had not mentioned she was going away. Mrs Scarff said she would phone around Gwen's friends to see if they knew anything.

Jessie McClure was mystified. She had no idea about Gwen's intentions and had expected her back as usual the night before. She felt Gwen had been acting funny, but did not think she would run off with Charlie—she believed he was stringing her young friend along and would never leave his wife.

Investigations established Gwen Scarff had headed straight to town, arriving at the City Council luggage room at the Tramway shelter at approximately 1.45pm. She put her suitcases and bags into storage and as she was leaving she ran into a driver she knew from the Carriers' Office. She told Johnstone she was leaving town with her boyfriend and they were heading to Wellington that night. She said she was about to pick up their tickets for the ferry and that he had picked up her luggage the previous night. She produced her savings book, and said that they had £70 between them. As she rushed off she said she was meeting her man at the bank at 3pm.

Gwen headed back to Cashmere and called into her parents' home at about 2pm. She had afternoon tea with her mother as was usual on her day off. Ellen Scarff noticed nothing different or unusual about her daughter, although Gwen seemed to be in a hurry because she had some business in town and a hair appointment—she didn't say anything about leaving her job or Christchurch.

Gwen returned to town and picked up a blue raincoat she had on lay-by. She then travelled back to Cashmere, arriving for tea at Annie Lok's at around 5.10pm. Over tea, she told Annie she and Charlie were leaving Christchurch that night, and that she was not to tell anyone. She left Annie's an hour later, saying she had to meet up with another friend.

Tom Morten was the duty porter at the Federal Hotel in central Christchurch that night. At 11.30pm, the bell rang—it was strange for anyone to ring so late at night. He opened it to see a middle-aged taxi driver, whom he did not recognise, and an anxious, tired-looking young woman. The driver stayed in the shadows and asked if Tom could fix her up. The young woman looked relieved when he replied that there were rooms available and she shuffled past the taxi driver, who said he'd be back at 10 the next morning. She registered as 'Miss Armstrong' and was shown to Room 51.

At 9am on Thursday, the hotel maid took Miss Armstrong a cup of tea and some breakfast. Miss Armstrong told the maid she wanted all her meals delivered to her room. Around 10am a White Diamond taxi arrived at the Federal. The driver carried two suitcases to reception and asked the hotel clerk to deliver them to Room 51 and to tell the young lady to meet her friend at the corner of Colombo Street and Chester Street at 2pm. The porter thought the girl looked disappointed when he gave her the message, but she didn't say anything.

At about 2pm, Amelia Watts was sitting on a park bench beside the Avon River watching her grandchildren play in the park when she noticed an anxious young woman standing by the river. Returning her gaze, the young woman wandered over and sat down beside her. The girl said she was expecting a White Diamond taxi at 2.30pm, and asked the woman if she had seen it. When Mrs Watts said no, the young woman began to tell her story. Her boyfriend was a taxi driver and had left a message for her at the Federal Hotel. They were supposed to be in Wellington on Wednesday night but someone rang and told her boyfriend that the boat was an old tub and they would be too late for the train they planned to catch in Wellington the next day. So, now she was waiting for him to pick her up so they could go to Lyttelton by car.

She also told Mrs Watts that she and her boyfriend had been to Burwood the previous night to meet a friend she was planning to stay with that night. They waited at the monument from 7.30pm until 10pm and the friend did not turn up, so she had stayed at the Federal Hotel. She laughed as she told Mrs Watts she registered under a false name.

She said she was running away from home, she was scared of her father and she was turning 21 in August. She also mentioned that her boyfriend was 17 years older than her and drove White Diamond taxi number 22.

At 3pm, they were still talking, when taxi number 22 pulled up and, after talking to the driver for a few minutes, the young woman stepped into the taxi and they drove off.

The maid who delivered Miss Armstrong's dinner that evening told 'Miss Armstrong' she looked like someone she had been to school with a few years earlier. Miss Armstrong blushed, giggled and confirmed her real name was Gwen Scarff. She also told the maid she was waiting until her boyfriend was ready to take her to the North Island to be married and that she was staying there so her parents wouldn't find out. The maid agreed to keep her secret.

The next morning, Friday 10 June, Gwen drafted another letter to Annie Lok.

> *Dear Mrs Lok,*
>
> *Just a line to let you know that we could not get away last night as we got a wire to stop us at 4.45. Don't let dad or mum know anything especially where I am staying as you know what will happen. As far as I know now we are going up on Friday night, but I won't know until I see Charlie tomorrow. If you would like to see me tomorrow morning, come up and ask for Miss Armstrong, room 51.*

When Annie Lok received the letter she became anxious for her young friend and decided to ring the Scarffs. As a result, Ellen Scarff went to the Federal Hotel and asked to be shown to Miss Armstrong's room. Gwen Scarff immediately burst into tears and so did her mother.

Mrs Scarff had mixed emotions—relief at finding her daughter, bewilderment at her secrecy and anger for the trouble she was causing. Gwen sobbed that she could not come home because she pregnant. Ellen Scarff was stunned but remained calm as she asked who was responsible this time. Gwen turned away and said nothing. Ellen Scarff asked if it was the same person as before.

Until the previous morning, Ellen had thought everything was all right with her eldest daughter. After Mrs Wood's call, she knew something was up, but this news was completely unexpected. She did not know what to say. Gwen looked defiant as she told her mother she and Charlie were going to live on a farm near Hastings and he was going to get a divorce and marry her. Her dignity intact, Ellen left saying, 'Ring me up tomorrow and tell me what you're doing.'

A few minutes after Ellen Scarff left the hotel a visibly distressed Gwen raced downstairs and asked Miss Ussher to send an urgent message to Mr Boakes at the taxi stand. Eight minutes later Charles Boakes arrived and approached Miss Ussher saying he had a message that a lady at the hotel wished to see him.

Miss Ussher later recalled that Boakes arrived dressed in a muffler and military khaki coat that had been shortened as it only came to his knees. He seemed surprised to have been summoned and appeared anxious to know who had asked for him. Porter Connolly led Boakes to Room 51. Connolly clearly remembered Boakes' response when the door opened. He appeared to feign surprise for the porter's benefit and Connolly felt sure Boakes knew 'Miss Armstrong'. Miss Ussher saw Boakes leave the hotel about 20 minutes later and a few minutes later, a still-upset Gwen raced out of the Federal Hotel too.

At 5.50pm, Gwen turned up at Annie Lok's and she was crying as she asked if Annie had told her mother about her circumstances. Mrs Lok didn't answer. Instead, she led the girl inside, sat her down and made a cup of tea. Over the next four hours Gwen poured out her whole sorry tale. As she left Mrs Lok at about 9.50pm she said she and Charlie were now planning to head away on either Saturday or Monday.

By Saturday Gwen had been resident at the Federal Hotel for two days and the staff had warmed to the sad, pleasant-but-mysterious girl who seemed to be hiding a secret. She spent most of Saturday in her room knitting, telling the maids it was for her baby. The maid asked where the baby's father was. Gwen replied her boyfriend was obtaining a divorce and they were to marry in August, but they were leaving for Wellington in a few days to begin a new life together. The maid asked if it was the taxi driver. Gwen looked sadly out of the window and answered, 'Yes'.

Gwen told hotel reception that she would be checking out on Tuesday to meet her girlfriend who was arriving in Christchurch by train, and together they were going to Kaikoura. Then, some time between 10am and 11am, Gwen returned to reception and placed a call to her mother to say she and Charlie were going north on Wednesday 15 June. It was the last conversation she was to have with her mother.

That afternoon she ventured out for some fresh air. Outside the Gloucester Street garage of White Diamond Taxis she asked one of the drivers, a chap called Prisk, to fetch Charlie. He later said he assumed she meant Boakes, who went and talked to her for a few minutes before going back inside. Before she left, Gwen told Prisk she was moving to the North Island and she was not going home.

Around 10am on Sunday 12 June, Gwen visited Annie Lok again. This time she appeared to be calmer, and said that everything was going to be all right. The new plan was for her and her boyfriend to go to a house in Woolston on Monday night. Next, she visited Alice Parr and told Alice a very different story—Charlie had just received a telegram saying the farm work was not available for another week, so here was no choice but to postpone their departure for at least another week. She also told Alice about booking into the Federal Hotel under an assumed name.

As Alice Parr later told a newspaper reporter, Gwen was trying to deceive her family. She told them she was leaving on Wednesday, but the real intention from what she told Alice, was to drive over the hills to Lyttelton in another man's car, to avoid being seen by anybody they knew in Christchurch. When Alice asked about money, Gwen said it was expensive as all the fares and travel expenses totalled about £17 but Charlie had it all under control.

Alice Parr did not know who Charlie was, but it was clear that the girl was infatuated with him. She never said much about him, only that he was married but unhappy at home. Mrs Parr suggested strongly many times that Gwen should give him up for a younger, available suitor, but she was smitten.

Gwen returned to the Federal Hotel and had dinner in her room. Later in the evening, she went out for a few hours. She spent Monday 13 June in her room, knitting and gazing out the window. She had all of her meals in her room and chatted happily with the staff.

On Tuesday, Gwen asked the receptionist to summon a taxi driver named Neate. Sydney Neate arrived at 11am and put Gwen's suitcases in his taxi. They appeared to know each other, and they went to the City Council luggage room.

When Gwen returned to the hotel, she passed one of the maids on the stairs who asked if she was leaving. Gwen replied her boyfriend was shouting her and a girlfriend a night in Kaikoura, and then they were all travelling to Blenheim and Picton. She and her boyfriend were going to sail to Wellington, and then take the train to Hastings, where they had guaranteed employment until August.

George Lewis, the hotel manager, noted that 'Miss Armstrong' came to the reception at 12.30pm to settle her account, which amounted to £5. She told him she would be back later to collect the rest of her belongings and then she left. Sydney Neate said he saw Gwen talking to a tall, slim man he did not recognise on Colombo Street at about 2pm.

Soon after, Gwen returned to the hotel where she sat in her room. At 5.45pm, carrying her umbrella, attaché and a brown paper parcel, she left the Federal

Hotel for the last time and wandered towards Cathedral Square. At 6pm she came across a taxi driver named Leslie Arps. She told Arps she was leaving Christchurch that night with Charlie, and they were going to the North Island to live. She told him she had two suitcases—one, she was going to take with her and Charlie was taking the other. They planned to leave Christchurch separately, meeting up in Lyttelton.

When Arps asked her why she was leaving, she replied she was four months in the family way, and Charlie was responsible. Arps suggested she should go home to her mother, but she replied defiantly that she wouldn't do that—even though her mother was encouraging her to. Arps watched as she walked towards the tram shelter. He was sure the 'Charlie' she meant was Charlie Boakes, as he had seen her give Boakes a bunch of flowers at the taxi stand some time ago. But he had been with Boakes recently and Charlie had not mentioned leaving Christchurch.

At 1.30pm on Wednesday 15 June, 15-year-old Eric Mugford was driving a herd of cows along Lake Terrace Road, Burwood, about 200 metres from the main road to New Brighton North. Some of the herd broke away and wandered onto a private road that was unused—it had become overgrown with gorse and broom. When Mugford rode his horse a short distance along the rough road to turn them back he noticed a body lying on a bare patch of ground surrounded by high lupins. He was overcome with fright and rushed away.

He forgot about the cows and galloped to Delamain's Store. There, he told Mrs Delamain he had seen 'a man with his throat cut'. Mrs Delamain sent him to inform Reverend Tobin. Mugford rushed to the church and located Reverend Tobin, telling him he had seen the body of a man with his throat cut, adding that as he came upon the scene he noticed the figure of a man in a dark suit leaning over the body. He said the man took fright and ran into the scrub.

When they returned to the scene, there was indeed a body, but it was that of a young woman and it was covered in blood. Reverend Tobin did not know what to make of it. He instinctively felt for a pulse, but it was clear the person was dead. Mugford and Tobin backtracked to Delamain's and telephoned police. Ten minutes later, Constable Henderson from New Brighton police arrived at the scene, followed closely by Chief Detective Lewis and Detective Sergeant Young from Christchurch Criminal Branch.

Dr Davis was summoned and made careful observation. The deceased was fully covered with only her face and head exposed to the weather. There appeared to be swelling in both upper eyelids, especially over the right eye. Both hands were clenched, with thumbs turned inwards, and her gloves were soaked with blood. The deceased appeared to be trying to shield her head with her hands and it looked as if death had not been instantaneous.

Her skirt was raised slightly above the knees and her bloomers were exposed. Otherwise, the clothing was not disturbed. The name *GWEN* was stitched on a handkerchief found on the deceased. About two metres away from the body there was a black hat with red floral trim lying on the ground beside a small attaché case, a brown paper parcel and an umbrella. They did not appear to have been dropped there—it was assumed the deceased had placed them there before the murder. Spread out about two metres from the body, there was a blue raincoat. Blood from the head wound had pooled on the coat. Nearby, searchers found a small piece of skull bone and a piece of scalp with hair still attached was found close to the attaché case.

It appeared that the deceased had been sitting down peaceably on the raincoat when she was attacked—there was no indication of a struggle. Probably, she was preparing a picnic when she was savagely attacked. There was nothing to indicate she had been murdered elsewhere and dragged to this position. She had been viciously attacked and died right there. Dr Davis concluded the body had been lying there during the night because the area was shaded for most of the day and was still covered in frost, yet the grass beneath the body was fresh.

The body was removed to the morgue and Dr Arthur Pearson, pathologist at Christchurch Public Hospital, carried out a thorough examination at 4.30pm. There were a total of 15 blows struck, and the woman would have taken two to three minutes to die. The autopsy confirmed Gwen was four months pregnant. It was also confirmed that the body contained no digested poisons.

Dr Pearson initially estimated the time of death to be about six hours prior—about 10.30am. However, an expert watchmaker named Matson examined the victim's watch and found the watch dented and the stem bent, but the watch had been in good working order until it was hit. The glass was shattered and Matson deemed that the watch had been stopped by a severe blow. It was stopped at 12.27. From its mechanics, the watchmaker estimated the watch appeared to have last been wound 14 hours before it stopped. It is likely that the watch was wound at ten o'clock the previous morning which led Dr Pearson later to conclude the attack probably occurred at 12.27am.

Detective Sergeant Young took young Mugford aside and asked him to describe exactly what he had seen. The excitable boy recalled that he had seen a short man wearing a dark suit and hat darting into the broom.

By then it was nightfall, so police planned to return to the scene at first light to check for clues and to see where the trail led. There were large puddles of blood—the killer would have been covered in blood. Hopefully, the trail would yield some clues.

There was nothing on the body to identify the deceased apart from the handkerchief. The story in the *Christchurch Star* was read with great interest by a number of Christchurch residents, including staff at the Federal Hotel who remarked that the recently departed 'Miss Armstrong' wore clothes matching the description. The maid Gwen Scarff had gone to school with confessed she knew the true identity of Miss Armstrong. When this was reported to George Lewis, he immediately made his way to the Christchurch Police Station. Detectives accompanied Lewis to the mortuary and he identified the body as Miss Armstrong, whose real name was probably Gwen Scarff. Staff of Federal Hotel told police what they knew.

At around 10am detectives called Thorrington Avenue to inform Walter and Ellen Scarff their daughter may have been murdered. They made the painful trip to the mortuary to confirm it was, indeed, their Gwen. When detectives asked who they thought could have done this they did not have an answer. However, Mrs Scarff told police the last time she had seen Gwen she told her mother she was pregnant to Charlie—and they believed it was Charles Boakes. Walter Scarff was seething and went on to tell police Boakes was responsible for putting Gwen in the family way three years earlier, when she was just seventeen.

At first light a contingent of police under the command of veteran detectives Eade and Studholme returned to the scene of the murder. Once again, the ground was heavily frosted so any footprints leading away from the scene should still be evident in the ground—there were none. Nor was there any sign of broken foliage in the area near the body.

Detective Young felt that Eric Mugford's sighting of a man may have been as a result of shock. If a man had escaped through the lupins there would be an obvious trail. When Mugford returned to the scene with a police officer he pointed out where he had seen the man run, but there was no broken vegetation. Mugford's sighting of a man running from the scene was ruled out as pure fantasy.

Word of the murder spread quickly and as the morning progressed hordes of onlookers flocked to Burwood to stand at the edge of the road watching for signs of a breakthrough. David Davidson and two mates had arrived for a day's entertainment out of morbid curiosity. As they lined up along Lake Terrace Road about 22 metres from the murder scene Davidson leaned over to peer into a gorse bush. He noticed a double-ended spanner hanging from an inner branch and said to his mates, 'Funny place to leave a spanner'. As he reached in and removed it, he noticed it felt sticky and was smeared with blood. He carefully took it to Detective Eade and Dr Pearson, who checked it for blood and fingerprints and agreed it was probably the murder weapon.

Meanwhile, in town, detectives accompanied Ellen Scarff to the City Council luggage room, but there were a number of suitcases there and she could not identify Gwen's.

As police continued with their inquiries with family, her employers, work colleagues and hotel staff, eight people told police Gwen had recently admitted details of her circumstances to them. It seemed she was in the habit of telling people half-stories, exaggerations and outright lies. However, the consistent thread that ran through all the stories was that she was pregnant to a married man named Charlie who drove a taxi for the White Diamond Taxi Company, and they were going to leave Christchurch to live together in the North Island.

Her parents said they were of the firm belief the man concerned was Charles Boakes, who they also alleged was responsible for getting Gwen pregnant three years earlier. Even if it was proven Boakes had a sexual relationship with Gwen Scarff, there was no solid proof he murdered her or had even been associating with her around the time of her murder.

Amelia Watts provided an early breakthrough for police. She read the initial report in the newspapers and immediately realised the description of the murdered woman was remarkably similar to the sad girl she had talked to on the banks of the Avon a week earlier. A respected grandmother, police regarded her statement as one of vital importance—she was a stranger, yet the murdered girl had felt comfortable enough to confide in her. Mrs Watts told police the story Gwen had told her and confirmed she had departed in White Diamond taxi number 22.

Detectives Young and Thompson found Charles Boakes sitting in his taxi beside Cathedral Square and asked him to accompany them to the Central Police Station.

He seemed surprised but went without fuss. He remained cool and calm throughout the initial interview—he was not nervous nor was he excited. He gave a careful statement, confirming he was 38 years old, happily married with two children, living at 38 Windsor Road, Richmond, and was the driver of White Diamond Taxi number 22.

He also admitted having known Gwen Scarff for about 15 years—since she was a child. He had met her through his working association with her father. His said his relationship with Walter Scarff was on friendly terms but was work related—they were not close enough to associate with each other socially.

He admitted giving Gwen harmless, good-natured ribbing that might look like flirting, but he said he had paid her no more attention than the other women at the carriers' office. He told the police the story about the rug and cushion on the floor of Walter Scarff's truck when he had worked for him as a relief driver.

Boakes went so far as to say Gwen had a reputation among a lot of the drivers for being of loose moral character. To his knowledge, she had on ongoing sexual relationship with Reg Watkins, and he also believed she was having a sexual relationship with Leslie Arps, who was another driver for White Diamond Taxis.

He denied being the father of Gwen's first baby, saying the first he heard about it was when her father accosted him at the depot. He claimed that he wanted nothing more to do with her because he was worried her father would get the wrong idea—he claimed Walter Scarff was an extremely violent man and suggested to police they should turn their attention to him.

He admitted having seen Gwen around town over the last few years, but denied ever seeing her on a social basis and emphatically denied taking her on rides in his car. He said he was surprised to be summoned to the Federal Hotel to see Gwen, saying the poor girl looked as if she had been howling and begged him not to tell her mother that she was leaving. He claimed he had told her she should really go home and he had offered to call her mother. He said he had last seen Gwen the previous Saturday afternoon between 3.30 and 4.30pm, when she called at the Coliseum Garage to see him.

Boakes denied procuring any drugs for her and holding any money on her behalf, but later remembered she had asked him to hold £5 for her and he had refused.

In regards to his movements on Tuesday night, he said he was at home with his wife. He denied being in the Burwood area, saying he had last been in Burwood about a fortnight earlier. He did not know how he got the scratches on his forehead.

He conceded that Gwen had on occasion called him 'Charlie'. He denied telling her things were not right at home and restated that he was happily married. He clearly had no intention of leaving his wife. He denied meeting Gwen beside the Avon in White Diamond taxi number 22 on 9 June. He also confirmed he carried tools in his taxi—a jack, starting handle, rim tool, and two or three small spanners.

At the conclusion of the interview, Boakes seemed to hesitate before he signed his name to the statement. He asked if he could go over his movements again and remembered he had been out late on Tuesday 7 June. He said he had taken a party to Kaiapoi, later taking each passenger home one at a time. He said he had arrived home at about 1.30am, so started late on Wednesday morning, at about 7.30am. He could not have been in Cashmere at 6.30am as claimed. He was not out late on Monday 13 June or Tuesday 14 June, although he had been late home on Monday night after buying tobacco at Fullers' Store.

Detective Young showed Boakes the blood-stained spanner, but he denied it was his. He was quite happy to provide his fingerprints. When asked who he thought had committed the murder, Boakes believed Gwen's father had killed her on account of his violent temper. Boakes was free to leave but was asked to bring his logbook in for checking. The shopkeeper at Fullers' confirmed Boakes had been in on Monday evening and purchased a tin of Havelock Mixture tobacco.

Mrs Boakes was interviewed at the same time as Boakes and this slowed the process. She was described as being extremely unhelpful. She gave very different accounts for her husband's movements over the previous two weeks. If Boakes said one thing, Detective Thompson had to travel to Sydenham to see if Mrs Boakes would substantiate or refute the point. If refuted, Thompson would question her and have to return to Christchurch Police Station to put it to Boakes. Then he would do the same with Boakes. Because Mr and Mrs Boakes stories differed so much, it took a great deal of time.

On 17 June, detectives accompanied Ellen Scarff and the taxi driver known as Neate to the baggage area and Neate recognised Gwen's luggage from the labels. Inside the suitcase they found some clothes, knitting wool and needles. It seemed Gwen had been knitting baby clothes, which were not yet finished. There were two photos of a man identified as Charles Boakes. Everything in the cases was clean, neatly folded and packed. There was a wet face cloth, and the toothbrush had been recently used.

There was no money found on the body or at the scene of the murder. Gwen's small leather bag which contained her purse was missing. Her account showed she had withdrawn £4 on 12 May and £11 on 8 June, leaving a balance of 13 shillings. The investigation established she had given Boakes money for abortifacients and she had paid £5 for her accommodation at the Federal Hotel, so she should have been carrying about £6 in cash.

Police quickly ruled out Walter Scarff as being Gwen's killer. He may have been a hard man, but a killer he was not. The grieving father was obviously devastated by his daughter's murder. On the night of 14 June, Scarff was at a social evening at the Veterans' Association in Oxford Street until 12.30am.

Police believed Gwen was taken to Burwood to be murdered late on Tuesday, and was killed at around 12.27am. However, they could not account for where she had spent the evening after leaving the Federal. They assumed she spent the evening in somebody's car and they were keen to trace the girlfriend she said she was going to meet in Kaiapoi.

One of Gwen's closest female friends, Winifred Capes, was brought in and interviewed. She denied meeting Gwen or even making plans to meet her that night. However, during the interview she burst into tears and made a frank admission that would have a strong bearing on the case. She said in the summer of 1927—about six months earlier—she was at Gwen's house when Les Arps and Charlie Boakes arrived in a taxi and invited the girls on an excursion to the seaside. Win admitted going for a walk with Boakes and having sex with him in the sandhills, leaving Gwen in the car with Arps. She assumed Gwen had sex with Arps in the car.

Over the following months, Win regularly visited Gwen and whenever Gwen's parents were out, Boakes would turn up. She would look after Gwen's younger siblings in another room, leaving Gwen and Boakes in the sitting room. Win's statement corroborated all the other statements of open association and a relationship of sorts between Boakes and Gwen.

Police were satisfied evidence against Boakes was swiftly building. However, their investigation was set back as public attention was diverted towards alleged harsh methods used by police to achieve a result, when the following letter appeared in the *Christchurch Star* on 18 June:

THE TAXI DRIVER WHO WAS QUESTIONED

Sir

I read with interest the statement re the Burwood Mystery made by the taxi-driver when questioned by a 'Star' reporter yesterday. In the statement the taxi driver says that the police kept him at the station from 2 o'clock in the afternoon, until 10 at night, and that he was going back there that morning. If this is true then it calls for very serious investigation indeed.

The police have a right to examine and ask questions of any person who is suspected of a crime, but it is incredible that legitimate questioning could last over a period of eight hours. One could hardly believe that this could occur in any country in the world other than America. Doubtless the answer of the police will be the usual; that the taxi driver was under no compulsion to answer and could have left the station at any time he wished. This is true if the man knew his legal rights, but surely it is obvious that he did not know the position, because it is impossible to believe that a man would stay at the station for 8 hours because he liked it.

In recent years there have been 2 cases in particular, one of alleged attempted murder, and the other of alleged murder in which suspects were held at the station for six hours or more without food and whilst they have been questioned and cross questioned by police officers. It would be well if those who are interrogated as the taxi driver evidently has been should know that they can refuse to any questions asked by the police, that they can refuse to go to the police station when called upon, and if they do go until arrest, they may leave the station at any time notwithstanding anything the police may say to the contrary. The taxi driver would be well advised to see his solicitor so as to know what his rights are. I am, etc,
'British Fair Play'

Police firmly believed 'British Fair Play' was actually their main suspect in the case—Charles Boakes. The letter infuriated senior police who were critical of the newspaper for publishing it. The Commissioner wrote to the Minister concerned the public would refrain from volunteering statements in this case and others. There was an inference people need not co-operate when making statements to police—this could potentially hamper an investigation. He need not have worried—most people were sensible and realised police had a job to do. There was a murderer still at large who might strike again.

Boakes returned to see detectives on the morning of 17 June to amend his statement—he said he had his weeks mixed up and that he was out late on the night of 13 June not 7 June as he had stated earlier. He said his wife had been incorrect in some of the things she had said in regards to his movements and, once again, he emphatically denied being in the Burwood area at any time over the two weeks before the murder.

He also suggested police should interview Cunningham, the driver of White Diamond taxi number 23—he implied he could have been mistaken for Cunningham, who would also be able to verify Boakes been to Kaiapoi. Police interviewed Cunningham and he was ruled out of having anything to do with the case.

Later that afternoon, a tram conductor named Lilley came forward saying he had seen Boakes, whom he knew, enter the tram from the Burwood shelter at 10.31pm on Wednesday 8 June, and then alight at Tweed Street—this was when Boakes had said he was at home.

Sydney Neate, who had taken Gwen's suitcase and bags to the Tramway shelter, happened to be at the Bottle Lake Hospital in Burwood on the afternoon after the murder. He said he had seen a man cross the road and walk into the bush about 400 metres from the scene of the murder—a much heavier man than the one he had seen talking to Gwen in town the previous day.

On Sunday 19 June, 22 police returned to Burwood and carried out a more detailed search of the area. Again, they found nothing and the official search for clues was called off. Police had already carried out a thorough scene examination. They already had the probable murder weapon—the spanner. About 1500 engineers and vehicle mechanics around Canterbury were shown the spanner. It was a double-headed, metric spanner with serrated jaws specially shaped for hexagonal nuts—not a stock tool. It was most likely part of a set of spanners commonly supplied with new European vehicles at the time.

The spanner was shown to George Millar, who had sold his Mercedes, including a spanner set, to Charles Boakes in 1921. Millar could not say with any certainty that the spanner was from the same set, but he remembered the spanners had serrated jaws, like the murder weapon and there were six in the set.

The larger end of the murder weapon fitted AC sparkplugs and the taxi Boakes was now driving had AC sparkplugs. Police felt that, at last, they had a piece of evidence that could tie Boakes to the murder, but it was not enough. Nobody could positively identify the spanner as coming from the car Boakes had owned and forensic testing failed to find any fingerprints.

A petrol-station attendant came forward saying he had been discussing the murder with Boakes who admitted Gwen often told him her problems, although he took care to say he did not know who had put her in the family way.

Boakes was feeling the heat from both police and the public, but he boldly turned up for work in his taxi every day, acting as if he had nothing to worry about. Police made no effort to hide the fact he was their prime suspect and detectives spent time openly talking to his fellow taxi drivers.

On 22 June, a taxi driver came forward to say that a day earlier a group of taxi drivers, including Boakes, had been discussing the murder when the conversation turned to how Boakes was holding up. Boakes allegedly remarked, 'I'm all right. I have my time sheets fixed. The buggers cannot get anything on me.'

Dickinson, the proprietor of White Diamond Taxis, told police it was possible for running sheets to be faked, even if the petrol supply was measured and the speedometer checked. He said it was common practice among drivers whenever they wanted an afternoon off or to run an errand during work time. Boakes' running sheets for the week in question, showed some interesting entries.

On 8 June, Boakes recorded taking a fare from 'Cashmere' to 'Square' although the word 'Cashmere' was just legible—it appeared to have been overwritten—and, interestingly, the time of the fare was recorded as 6.35am. That was when a White Diamond taxi had pulled up outside the Woods' residence in Cashmere and removed Gwen Scarff's luggage and when Boakes had denied being anywhere near Cashmere. Nine other drivers' running sheets were checked and no other driver had been in Cashmere that day.

Boakes' running sheet for 9 June recorded a return journey from Mount Magdala to Paparua lasting from 1.30 to 3.15pm, but the '3.15' appeared to have been altered.

The running sheet for 14 June showed the meter had broken down at 2.30pm, and the car was running on the speedometer, so it was impossible to check his movements.

Every week *Truth* ran large stories airing details of the tragic girl and her brutal murder. Although much of what was published was based on fact, the features disproportionately covered the more lurid and sexual elements of the case to keep readers enthralled.

The Commissioner worried such reporting could endanger Boakes' right to a fair trial and decided to keep press releases to an absolute minimum. Reporters resorted to shadowing police and if police spent more than a few minutes speaking to someone the waiting reporters swooped in and carried out an interview. The likes of young Mugford and Mrs Watts were interviewed minutes after finishing with police and were happy to tell their respective stories to the press. Criticism in the press upset police, who were increasingly frustrated by their lack of progress.

On Saturday 25 June, a gang of workers clearing scrub from council land in the Burwood area discovered a khaki-tweed, Defence-issue overcoat. It was folded inside out and had been placed under lupins, about seven metres from the road—about 1.6 kilometres away from the murder scene heading towards the city. When they unfolded the coat it had obviously been smeared with blood.

Detective Sergeant Young arrived and took the coat for forensic testing. There was nothing in the pockets to identify the owner. However, it had been shortened and hemmed very roughly with black thread and the original brass buttons had been removed and replaced with plain black buttons. The nap was worn at the back as would occur with a person wearing the coat in a sitting position constantly. Muriel Ussher, John Connolly and the porters at the Federal Hotel had said Boakes was wearing a shortened, khaki army coat.

Boakes was kept under observation and he was never seen wearing a coat until Monday 27 June, two days after the *Christchurch Star* announced the finding of the coat. Then, he was seen at work wearing a too-long, army-style, khaki overcoat. When questioned, he said he could not remember where he had purchased the coat, but he had owned it for a number of years. Miss Ussher told police she firmly believed this coat was much longer than the one he was wearing when he visited Gwen Scarff at the hotel on 10 June.

On 30 June *Truth* reported for the first time that Gwen was going to run off with a married man named Charlie—Boakes must have felt the net closing in. On 1 July, he called in to see detectives and he went over everything again. He did not deviate from the story he had told Young and Thompson on 16 June. However, this time he was talking to Detective James Bickerdike, an experienced, hard-nosed detective whose particular speciality was obtaining confessions. While Young was a super-sleuth and Eade was adept at finding clues in unusual circumstances, Bickerdike was a master interrogator who relished the challenge of pitting his wits against criminals. He had already made up his mind Boakes was lying about a number of things.

All Boakes wanted to do that afternoon was verify his whereabouts at the time of the murder. When Bickerdike raised the fact taxi records showed he was the only driver to have a fare from Cashmere on the morning Gwen left the Woods', Boakes admitted he had picked up a passenger in the general Cashmere area and drove him to the Square. A number of other taxi drivers witnessed this. When asked to describe his appearance and address, Boakes could not remember specifics. Boakes denied trying to alter his running sheet, on which the word 'Cashmere' looked to have been over-written with another word rendering the entry illegible.

Of the alleged sighting of him near Burwood War Memorial at 10pm on 9 June, he again denied being anywhere near Burwood that night. He admitted purchasing a Mercedes from Millar, but said the car was repossessed soon after. As far as he was aware the spanner set was seized along with the car and he said he never used it anyway.

The trip to the beach with Arps, Gwen and Win was raised. Boakes said that his wife's health was bad and she could not have sex, but he denied having sex with anybody else, despite rumours his young housemaid had left her job a year earlier after he pestered her for sex

Bickerdike asked if he had anything else he wanted to get off his chest. Boakes looked at the floor and said that in 1910 he had some girl-trouble in Auckland—she had an illegitimate child, but he stressed the child was not his. Nevertheless, he had been charged and imprisoned for six months for perjury and failing to pay maintenance. In fact, the girl had a child to Boakes and he had forced her to have an abortion when she became pregnant a second time. On the day of the trial, he had dyed his hair to look as different as possible from his child.

Bickerdike brought out the blood-stained coat from the exhibit cabinet and asked Boakes if it belonged to him. Boakes glanced, looked away and said it was not his.

When they started talking about Gwen's murder Boakes suddenly slammed his fist on the table and said, 'A man might have had a connection with her, but that is not to say I murdered her. There is another Charlie, besides me, who knows her well and does not get on with his wife.'

He went on to implicate someone who worked in a coal yard in Colombo Street, but police already knew of the two men to whom Boakes was trying to shift blame. Charlie Keyes worked in the coal yard, but also drove a taxi from time to time.

He fitted the description of the man who delivered Gwen to the Federal Hotel the evening she checked in. When interviewed, Keyes said he had last driven a taxi in January 1927, and he had not seen Gwen Scarff since March or April that year. He admitted owning a military coat but said he had given it back when he returned from the Great War. His story checked out.

The other man, Charlie Brown, was also a middle-aged taxi driver who had driven for White Diamond Taxis, and knew Boakes and Gwen Scarff. When interviewed, Brown seemed nervous so police spent a bit more time with him. He denied murdering Gwen Scarff but suggested police check a certain pharmacy.

Police had already heard from Derisley Wood about the package Gwen received and Jessie McClure confirmed Gwen hoped the contents would trigger an abortion. There were two bottles of liquid found at the murder scene, and these were thought to be poisonous. Tests showed one bottle contained Friar's Balsam and oil of pine, and the other a mouthwash. Toxicology tests had already confirmed that Gwen had not ingested poison at the time of death. The black market in illegal drugs, such as abortifacients, was widespread and lucrative. Following up on Brown's tip-off detectives began canvassing local pharmacies.

Almost three weeks had passed with no hint of an arrest. The Commissioner beefed up the team working on the case and announced a reward of £250 for information leading to the conviction of the killer. On the same day the reward was announced, Detective Laugeson went to the Scarff family home and produced a warrant to search Gwen's room and personal effects. He found a small piece of paper with 'MC Boakes, Nelson Street' written on it—Charlie Boakes' former address.

Despite visiting all hotels and boarding houses from Burwood to New Brighton, and hotels in Christchurch, detectives were no closer to knowing where Gwen had stayed on the night of 14 June.

On Monday 17 July, barely one month after the murder, Bickerdike had a breakthrough at Coltart's Pharmacy in central Christchurch. The assistant, Sidney King, was taken to the police station for questioning. King reportedly went white when Bickerdike asked if he had supplied pills to Boakes. He denied he had, but when it became clear to King the detective knew more than he was letting on, King knew he had to tell the truth.

He said he was introduced to Boakes by Charles Brown and Boakes immediately asked him for something to fix up a girl he had gotten into trouble. King agreed to help and told Boakes to come to the back of his pharmacy the following day when he knew he would be alone. He duly gave Boakes two small bottles of pills in cylindrical cardboard boxes wrapped in yellow paper, which matched Jessie's description of the parcel delivered to Gwen. Boakes paid King 3s.6d.

About ten days later, King met Boakes again and he was annoyed the pills had not worked. King said he could fix him up with something stronger the following day—Smith Ergot Apial pills—that he claimed would have an immediate effect. Boakes returned the very next day, pleading with King who gave him a small, unlabelled vial of liquid extract of Ergot with instructions to tell the girl to take all the contents at once, after a meal. Boakes paid King 3 or 4 shillings.

After the interview King seemed relieved to have got it off his chest, but returned the following day to amend his statement. This time he added that he had sold the Smith Ergot pills to Boakes three days prior to the liquid—not the day before. So, King had admitted supplying Boakes with abortifacients presented in packaging that matched Mr Wood's and Jessie's descriptions. It was probably sufficient to charge Boakes with supplying illegal abortifacients, but was it proof enough that he murdered her?

Gwen had told a number of people she was pregnant to her boyfriend, Charlie—most likely Charles Boakes who, she claimed, was responsible for her earlier pregnancy. On the other hand, Boakes said his marriage could not have been better and he knew that Gwen had had a number of sexual partners, including Les Arps. He did admit to having sex with Gwen's friend Winifred Capes at the beach the previous summer.

Police believed Boakes had strung Gwen along with promises to leave his wife—she was clearly naïve and believed every word he said. He was enjoying a sexual relationship with an attractive young girl who was willing to keep it secret. Finding she was pregnant, Boakes panicked and whether he was genuine in his intentions to leave his wife, it is difficult to say. Either way, in early July Gwen prepared to leave Christchurch.

Police had come to the conclusion Boakes made up his mind to kill her on the night of 8 June, but for some reason didn't and he delayed things for another week. This was all circumstantial—based on testimony from reliable witnesses. There was no direct evidence to prove that Boakes had murdered Gwen—there were no fingerprints on the murder weapon or the badly hemmed military coat that undoubtedly belonged to the murderer.

Despite the lack of evidence, on 27 July Boakes was arrested and charged with the murder of Ellen Gwendoline Isobel Scarff, and also with supplying a noxious drug to one Ellen Gwendoline Isobel Scarff on or about 15 June 1927, knowing that it would be used unlawfully to procure an abortion. Boakes was gobsmacked but went without fuss to be interviewed by Bickerdike once more.

As the interview was being conducted, Detective Walsh and a team searched Boakes' home. They found 13 large and 17 small military, brass buttons. Most military overcoats had five large and seven small buttons—there were enough buttons there for two coats, yet Boakes contended he had only ever owned one.

The overcoat found at Boakes' was traced to a returned serviceman named Haycock, whose name was still stitched into the collar. Haycock confirmed he had handed his coat to Defence authorities when he returned home from the Great War, as many thousands of other servicemen had—40–50,000 coats were sent to be cleaned at the Ordinance Department at Trentham before being distributed for sale in various second-hand clothing stores around the country. No records were kept after the coats arrived in Wellington so it was impossible to determine where or when Haycock's coat had been purchased.

Bickerdike read out Arps' and Jessie McClure's statements. Boakes said most of what was contained in the statements was true except the points that incriminated him. He said McClure was incorrect about the insurance policy—it only amounted to £30.

He admitted knowing Sidney King, but said King was lying about selling him abortifacients. King was summonsed and directed to read out his statement in front of Boakes. King broke into a sweat as he read out his statement and left quietly, carefully avoiding eye contact with the accused throughout the exercise.

Boakes was formally charged at Christchurch Magistrates Court before magistrate HP Lawry. News of the arrest caused a huge stir around Christchurch, although most people knew of Boakes before the formal announcement. The courtroom was packed with onlookers as Boakes kept his head down and attempted to shield his face from the cameras.

He was remanded until 4 August, and by 9am that day crowds of people had gathered outside court to see the accused. This time he was remanded in custody until 31 August. At the end of August, Boakes appeared again before a packed court and confidently pleaded not guilty to both charges. The magistrate concluded a prima facie case had been made for the charge of supplying a noxious drug, but in regards to the murder, it was only right and fair to give it consideration. After a two day hearing, with 60 witnesses, Mr Thomas, Boakes' lawyer, agreed a prima facie case on the minor charge but contended that no jury in the country would convict Boakes for murder on the evidence tendered. Nonetheless, Boakes was committed for trial on both charges. He was stunned but Thomas remained confident the police case was very weak.

Boakes stared desperately towards his loyal wife, who stood tensely in the public gallery, her ears reddening at any reference to her husband's alleged sexual dalliance with the murdered girl. Throughout the whole investigation, she had been largely unco-operative with police—even after learning about the beach trip where Boakes admitted having sex with another young woman.

The Criminal Sessions at Christchurch Supreme Court opened on 15 November 1927, Mr Justice Adams summed up for the jury as follows, 'The crux of the whole question is what evidence is there to connect Boakes with the actual murder?'

He went on to say he could see no hard evidence to prove Boakes had any association with Gwen around the time of the murder and, furthermore, there was nothing linking the spanner or military coat directly to Boakes. The second charge of supplying the noxious drug in relation to the capital charge was only relevant so far as to show motive.

Finally, he looked over to the jurors and paused before closing with, 'I must confess, Mr Foreman and gentlemen, that so far as I personally am concerned, I have the gravest doubt as to whether a true bill should be returned against the accused on the capital charge.'

The Crown Prosecutor and police present could not believe their ears, and Mr Thomas could not believe his luck. The jury had to determine whether, on the evidence heard, Boakes should be put on trial for Gwen's murder. Nonetheless, after just four hours deliberation, they brought in true bills against Boakes on both the capital charge and the minor count. His trial was due to start on 21 November.

However, just two weeks before the trial, King decided to change his testimony, although he was aware he could be prosecuted for perjury. This was a huge blow to the prosecution who had to now regard King as a hostile witness—they would simply have to wait and see what they could draw from him during cross-examination. Most likely, King was only out to save his own skin—by denying selling the drugs, he could keep his job.

Once again, there was a large crowd outside the Christchurch Supreme Court several hours before the doors opened on Monday 21 November. In anticipation of the crowd, Boakes was transported to court in the early hours while most people were still in bed.

Boakes pleaded not guilty to both charges. Donnelly, acting for the Crown, opened his address by outlining the facts of the case and said the case should be considered under three main headings:

- The life of the girl and her relationship with the accused.
- Gwen's movements between 8 June and 15 June, and her relations with the accused during that period.
- The movements of the accused after the murder.

After addressing the summary of facts, Donnelly mentioned King's change in statement and denied Bickerdike had bullied the witness, as he now claimed. King was cross-examined at length and it was obvious his testimony lacked credibility. The rest of the first day was taken up with testimonies from Gwen's family, Jessie McClure and Mr and Mrs Wood.

On the second day, the Court heard from most of the taxi drivers and it was proved none had been in the Cashmere or Burwood areas on the days in question. They all said they knew Boakes to be a fair man. Some admitted knowing there had been an association between Boakes and Gwen Scarff.

Police were interviewed and Bickerdike was given special attention by Thomas, who accused him of bullying King. However, he knew Thomas' techniques almost as well as Thomas himself and he remained cool and calm throughout the cross-examination.

At the end of the day, Donnelly announced he had finished the case for the Crown. Thomas was so confident he did not bother to cross-examine many of the witnesses. Justice Adams released the jurors with a warning that there was bound to be very lengthy addresses the following day.

On the morning of Wednesday 23 November, Thomas addressed the court saying the case was high profile, and his client was the subject of much speculation and rumour. He warned of the problems of circumstantial evidence. Although some of it could be very strong, it could never be as strong as direct evidence. With direct evidence a witness could make a mistake in what he or she saw, but with circumstantial evidence the witness could also make a mistake in deduction. With regard to this case, he argued:

- Much of the Crown case was based on the relationship between Gwen and Boakes, but there was nothing in the evidence to connect Boakes with Gwen beyond three or four days before the murder.
- There was no evidence as to who was responsible for Gwen's pregnancy.
- Boakes, Capes and Arps all admitted going to the beach and Arps admitted having sex with Gwen. If Boakes was really in a relationship with Gwen, would he have allowed Arps to have sex with her?
- McClure and King described the different packaging for the pills. Thomas conceded King's evidence could not be depended upon. Either way, there was no evidence that Boakes had procured abortifacients from King or anyone else.
- Boakes went to the Cashmere on 8 June to pick up an unidentified male passenger and it was probably him talking to Gwen, but this did not make him the murderer.
- Although it was White Diamond taxi number 22 that Mrs Watts saw beside the Avon, she did not see the driver. It may not have been Charles Boakes.
- Boakes had probably lied about being in Burwood and taking the tram. The reason he had lied was because he was frightened of being accused of being the murderer.
- There was no motive for Boakes to murder Gwen Scarff.
- Mugford saw the murderer and the description he offered did not fit Boakes.
- Mugford's story of a man in the area on the afternoon after the murder tallied with Neate's testimony.
- Gwen Scarff was known to be associating with other men. She was seen by Neate talking to a man at 2pm on 14 June—the day before she was murdered.
- There were no traces of blood on Boakes.

Mr Justice Adams began summing up at 3pm. In his opinion there may have been improprieties in Boakes' relationship with Gwen Scarff, but there was no evidence of that—the relationship may have been platonic. The accused and the girl may have had meetings between 8 and 11 June, but there was no sign of any argument between them. It could be as simple as an old family friend showing concern for her troubles. There was nothing to support a guilty verdict on the murder charge.

The only thing to connect Boakes with the murder was the fact he was seen returning from the Burwood shelter on the tram on the night of 10 June—the shelter was about 400 metres from the murder scene. There was nothing to show how he got to Burwood or why he was there.

Not for the first time, Justice Adams conveyed his personal thoughts to the jury, swaying them towards a not-guilty verdict, and questioning the strength of the police case. Police and the prosecution team did not object—they were resigned to losing.

The jury retired at 4.15pm on Wednesday and took just 45 minutes to return a not-guilty verdict to the charge of murder. On the minor charge of supplying abortifacients, he was remanded until 30 November on bail of £100.

The minor charge was primarily based on a conviction for the murder charge, so on 30 November the charge was withdrawn and Boakes was a free man. Police were disappointed but not surprised. They were most disappointed the judge had spoken in favour of the defence and they got stick from the media, who reported the case against Boakes as 'one of the weakest ever to be put in front of a jury in the annals of murder in this country'.

Thomas was generous and said police had done a good job under immense public and media pressure to bring about a quick result—hence the arrest of Boakes on circumstantial evidence. Even if police had taken longer, it was unlikely to have made a difference, given the complete lack of evidence.

If Boakes lied, it was only in not revealing the true extent of his personal relationship with Gwen Scarff, and being in Burwood. So, in court he was found not guilty, but most people thought he simply had luck on his side. Boakes knew things would never be the same for him again—he could not continue driving taxis in Christchurch. Despite being found innocent of murder, the public had a very long memory.

He made attempts to be reinstated in his job, but no company would have him. Soon after, there was a rumour that Boakes had been lured into an alley by a young woman and given the beating of his life. There are a number of different versions of this story, including one where the attackers were plain-clothed policemen. In another version, two observers—Walter Scarff and Jim Bickerdike—were seen walking quietly away after the beating. Was summary justice delivered?

Within weeks of his release Boakes and his family left Christchurch.

Walter Scarff wrote a letter to the commissioner thanking him and his detectives for the work they did to try and bring his daughter's killer to justice. He and his family attempted to put the tragic affair behind them and get on with their lives.

The police never reopened the Gwen Scarff murder case. They believed Boakes was responsible, but by sheer good luck or cold and careful planning there was nothing linking him to the murder or murders—after all, Gwen was four months pregnant.

One thing that was never considered was whether there was more than one person involved. Could Gwen have been murdered by somebody else?

It is clear Boakes and Gwen were carrying on a relationship, but they each had different ideas about the status of that relationship. When Gwen became pregnant and Charlie's attempts to procure an abortion failed he drew proceedings out for as long as possible, hoping a solution would present itself. Perhaps it did.

It was evident Gwen's relationship with Charlie Boakes was not exclusive, and she would do anything to please him. She had sex with Arps and Boakes suggested she also had sex with Syd Neate. It was also alleged that she may have had sex with other men at Boakes' bidding.

Neate was a close friend of Boakes and, as police were piecing together Gwen's movements, he seems to be involved at crucial stages before and after the murder. The description of the middle-aged taxi driver who dropped Gwen off at the Federal Hotel and delivered her bags the following day matched Neate. Was Neate the man they had been meeting in Burwood? Was he the driver who was supposed to drive them to Lyttelton on the night of 8 June and then 14 June?

Neate said he had seen Gwen talking to a tall, thin, man on the afternoon of the fourteenth. He also happened to be in Burwood on the afternoon the body was found, to witness a short, stocky man in short-sleeves race out of the bush several hundred metres from where the body was found. Coincidence? Neate was never able to identify either man, but one thing is certain—neither description was anything like Charles Boakes. Coincidence again?

Could Neate have been the killer? Could he have beaten Gwen in a jealous rage? He was not seriously considered to be a violent man, although he had committed a string of petty offences in his youth. Boakes had asked his friend to help him out of a bind —whether he was in on it or not, Boakes would say anything Neate asked because of the trouble he was already in.

However, like the Crown case, this is purely circumstantial and the tragic case of Gwen Scarff remains unsolved. It is partly remembered for the sexual scandal and sensationalism attributed by the media at the time, which almost superseded the bare facts of an innocent girl being brutally murdered.

Six years later, publican Don Fraser was murdered at the Riccarton Racecourse Hotel. Somebody wrote a letter to the *Christchurch Star* blaming the murder on Boakes. Bickerdike was asked to follow up the story. He found that Boakes and his wife had sailed to Sydney in May 1928 and were still living there. The Boakes children had been placed, under assumed names, in the care of Cholmondeley Home in Lyttelton. They joined their parents later. Reverend Revell from the City Mission said Boakes' mother-in-law had visited them in Sydney in 1931, and Boakes was driving taxis. Family members, who had visited the Boakes in Sydney in 1936, said they had no intention of returning to New Zealand.

5. The Death of Elsie Walker

In all my 34 years of work in the police department, I can say this case has received much more attention than any other case I have known in New Zealand.

Chief Detective Alfred Hammond addressing the
Commission of Inquiry on 27 February 1929

College Road in Auckland's Panmure is now a largely residential area but in October 1928, it was rough farmland completely covered with scrub. There were only a few farms scattered along the road. The main building there was Knox Home, a sanatorium housing 41 patients who all had incurable diseases. Opposite Knox Home was a large overgrown scoria paddock that contained a disused quarry.

Late on the afternoon of Friday 5 October 1928, James Thompson, who lived nearby, met up with his chum Dick Pye. The two 11-year-old boys raced off to have some adventures in the scoria paddock, unfazed by the 1.2 metre rock wall that surrounded it. They decided to go and check a rabbit warren they had come across the previous weekend. They couldn't see any sign of the rabbits and it was starting to get a bit dark so they headed for home at about 6pm.

As they walked along a little-used dirt track, hemmed with thick scrub, they noticed what appeared to be a pair of feet sticking out from under the scrub. They inched closer. There seemed to be a woman sleeping there. She was lying on her stomach and it looked as if she had crawled as far as she possibly could into the bush and fallen asleep.

Intrigued, the boys made their way home. They told James' uncle, Steve Carter, what they had seen. Steve and his brother Jim accompanied the boys back to where they'd seen the woman lying. By the time they got there, it was nearly dark. They could just about make out the prone figure and called out to ask if she was all right. There was no response.

Carter struck a match and edged his way closer. The woman was dead. There was a small white handkerchief smeared with blood lying close to her body.

Frightened, they raced across to Knox Home and called the police. The call was answered at Panmure police station by Constable Charles Collins. At 7.20pm, he met the foursome at the entrance to the paddock and they directed him over to where the body lay.

Collins carefully checked the body before heading back to the station and placing a call to Auckland police. Detective Sergeant Tom Kelly answered the call and instructed Collins to return to the scene to check if there were any suspicious circumstances.

From his initial scene inspection, Collins ascertained that the woman was of small build. She was dressed in a brown men's overcoat that was too big for her. He thought the coat would have fitted a boy aged about 12 or 14 years old. Under the coat she was wearing a mauve coloured frock with a white collar, over which there was a red apron. Her dress had not been ruffled and her underclothing appeared intact ruling out any initial thoughts of her being violated. A handkerchief appeared to have dropped from her right hand. It was smeared with blood and had the initial *F* stitched in the corner.

As he turned the body over, Collins noticed a small pool of blood that had formed by her head, it looked to have come from her nose. The girl looked to have been aged about 20 years, and was about 5 foot 2inches (1.5 metres) in height, with dark hair and brown eyes. Her black hair was matted with blood, which appeared to have come from a small wound above her right eye. She had a couple of superficial looking cuts on her jaw and her right arm.

Because her face appeared flushed and there was a trail of brown liquid running from her mouth down her chin, Collins thought she may have died after ingesting poison. He didn't think she'd been murdered as there were no obvious signs of an attack. It was difficult to tell how long she had been lying there. It looked like she had been dead for several days.

There was no broken bracken or foliage around where the body lay, so it did not appear as if she had been thrown under the bush. It looked as if she had carefully crawled in as far as she could and died.

At 9.30pm, Collins telephoned Detective Sergeant Kelly and reported his observations. Collins told the detective that he thought the girl had committed suicide by ingesting poison. He didn't think there were any suspicious circumstances. Kelly then instructed the immediate removal of the body to the morgue.

Collins, Carter and several bystanders helped pull the girl carefully from the bushes and she was taken to the Auckland mortuary by a local undertaker. The medical inspection of the body began at 11pm, conducted by doctors Noakes and Spencer, in the presence of Detective Waterson and Constable Bowman.

The doctors concurred the girl had been dead between three or four days.

When her clothing was removed, a tag bearing the name Godfrey Bayly was found in the coat she'd been wearing. Two letters addressed to Tom Bayly, c/o W. Allan B. Matthews, 27 Bond Street, Claudelands (Hamilton) were in the pocket of the coat along with a handkerchief bearing the initials *GNL*.

Her other clothing was clearly the clothing of a housemaid. It was unusual that the girl had broken convention by walking out in her working clothes—in 1928, people tended to wear their Sunday best to go out, only wearing work clothes while working.

There was nothing to identify the deceased. There was no sign of any attack and it appeared she died from natural causes or perhaps from poisoning.

Detective Waterson had been present at the examination of the body, but in the middle of the night he inexplicably sent an error-ridden report around all police stations in the North Island. The message reported an unidentified woman had been found dead, and that 'she met her death through violence, as her head is bashed about, her face badly bruised, and a lot of blood about the head, and one eye badly knocked about.' A further error was in the description of the deceased. She was described as being 'a woman with fair hair and blue eyes'.

The report was read by Constable Harris of Hamilton who immediately responded via telex that the body could be that of a girl who had been reported missing by her family in Papamoa in the Bay of Plenty. She had disappeared several days ago having taken the family automobile. Constable Harris recalled hearing a car had been found abandoned in Papatoetoe three days earlier, which was reasonably close to where the body had been found. A telephone call was made to the girl's family at 6.30am.

Detective Sergeant Kelly was roused from his bed by Chief Detective John Hollis at 7.45am and summoned to the Auckland Public Hospital to attend the girl's post mortem, which began at 8.30am. Dr Murray, the police surgeon, and Dr Gilmour, a pathologist conducted the procedure. Hollis instructed the doctors to test for pregnancy and any signs of violation.

The medics concluded that the girl was aged between 17 and 20 and she had been dead for about 72 hours. They explained the wounds on her face and arm as having been caused by rats or similar vermin.

There were no signs that the girl had been sexually violated and there were no signs of sexual activity in the 24 hours prior to death. The girl's internal organs were all healthy and there was no evidence of a brain injury. There was slight bruising on her scalp but for the injury that caused the bruise to be fatal the girl would have had to have been struck from directly above or she would have to have fallen directly on the top of her head as if she had been standing on her head, which seemed unlikely.

The girl had eaten about four hours before her death and there were no signs of any corrosive poison in her stomach.

Upon completion of the examination the doctor and the pathologist concluded that, 'there was no evidence as to the actual cause of death.'

Despite the post mortem not finding any poison in the girl's stomach and the fact that there was no sign of any poison bottles at the scene, Detective Sergeant Kelly remained convinced that the brown stain on the her chin was a trace of some kind of poison and that the girl had committed suicide.

A Hamilton constable called around to the address on the letter found in the girl's pocket. Annie Matthews confirmed that the letters were addressed to her 11-year-old brother Tom, who lived with her parents in the Bay of Plenty. He had spent the last school holidays with Annie and her family in Hamilton.

The officer described the deceased to Mrs Matthews and she said it sounded like her 17-year-old cousin Elsie Walker. Elsie had disappeared with the family car several nights earlier and her disappearance had mystified the family.

There was nothing remarkable about Elsie Walker's life. She was a shy girl who was born and raised on the East Cape, and in 1927 moved from her isolation to become a housemaid for Frank and Constance Bayly, a rich and very well-respected couple who lived at Papamoa in the Bay of Plenty. Yet her death saw her become a household name.

Elsie's parents, Charles D'Renzy Walker—also known as Whisky—and Mere Walker married on 18 April 1910 in Opotiki. The couple lived on Mere's ancestral land at Raukokore, a tiny coastal settlement a 99 kilometres away. Walker leased adjacent farmland from his in-laws and set up a large farm.

One month after their wedding, the couple was blessed with the birth of Ann. Her sister Elsie Grace Walker followed on 21 September 1911. They then went on to have five more children.

The Walkers were a close family who lived a simple life in the remote settlement. Whisky Walker ruled the roost. While he toiled away on his large farm, Mere busied herself with bringing up her brood as well as spending time with the kuia of Tu Kaihi marae.

When Ann Walker was a teenager, her father packed her off to Auckland to complete her education. Being close in age, Ann wrote regularly to Elsie, boasting about the lifestyle she was leading in Auckland. Her descriptive letters had a profound effect on Elsie, who dreamed of life in the big city. She begged her father to send her to Auckland but Whisky was loath to do this. Elsie was needed to help care for her siblings and she wasn't as academically capable as her sister so at the age of 14, she left school to work on her father's farm.

During 1925, Elsie went behind her father's back and wrote two letters to a relative Mrs Barters, whom she had never met, pleading for permission to live with her. When he found out, Whisky was highly embarrassed. He forbade Elsie to continue her correspondence and told her she was not going to Auckland. As a compromise, she went to work as a live-in housemaid for Mr Fairweather in Te Kaha.

Elsie was unhappy in Te Kaha and again begged her father to allow her to move to Auckland where she wanted to train to become a dressmaker. He would not allow this but did not relish the alternatives. Despite having married a Maori woman himself, Whisky didn't want his daughter to marry into the local iwi but the prospects for her marrying a European was limited. Besides, Elsie had no distinguishing qualities to attract a suitor. Employment prospects were also limited.

One day, Whisky walked in and caught Elsie masturbating. He believed the girl to be 'subnormal' and he feared the onset of madness. Her maternal uncle was in a lunatic asylum and Whisky began to worry madness was hereditary. He consulted his GP who suggested the girl was 'sensually inclined', and was not considered healthy. The doctor recommended she be placed in 'better surroundings'.

Whisky had another sister, Constance, who lived in Papamoa, close to the thriving port town of Tauranga. Constance was married to farmer Frank Bayly. Over the years, Bayly had been successful in his various business ventures and amassed a great deal of wealth as well as acquiring large blocks of farmland in the south Auckland area. His business acumen meant he and his family were able to live a comfortable life.

In June 1926, the Baylys had moved to a farm outside Papamoa. While Frank was gruff and taciturn, Constance valued her high social position and was ever present at balls and afternoon teas.

Whisky spoke to Constance about Elsie and she decided it was a good idea for her niece to come and live with them in Papamoa. Her role would be as 'a live-in housemaid and lady's companion' for the lowly sum of 12s.6d per week.

Sixteen-year-old Elsie moved into the seemingly palatial Bayly homestead in August 1927. Along with Constance and Frank Bayly, she shared the house with their sons, Bill (21), Trevor (17), Godfrey (15), Tom (9) and Charlie (3). The Baylys' eldest daughter, Anne, had married and moved away.

Despite the size of the Baylys' house, Elsie was not given a bedroom of her own. Instead she slept in an enclosed porch separated from the master bedroom by a curtain. She was only allowed to enter and exit from the outside verandah. In stark contrast to the comfortable rooms the Baylys occupied, Elsie had a small bed and a chest of drawers.

If Elsie had been looking forward to a life with more independence and access to shopping, fashion and theatre, she would have been disappointed. She worked tirelessly and little attention was paid to her. Her normal day consisted of rising early and seeing to three-year-old Charlie. She would then prepare breakfast for the rest of the household. After breakfast, she cleaned up before carrying out the day's chores.

Constance was very socially active, and spent most afternoons in the company of other well-to-do women from the district. Elsie often accompanied Constance on these afternoons but her role was to supervise Charlie. Constance did allow

Elsie to foster a friendship with the daughter of a neighbouring family. Elsie Walker and Lorraine Morten would talk while Lorraine's mother and Constance gossiped and drank tea. On Sunday afternoons, Elsie was allowed to visit the Mortens and the girls would play croquet, drink tea and listen to records.

Constance kept a watchful eye on her niece and discouraged any male attention. She was allowed to attend dances and socials but only if chaperoned by one of her cousins. The older Bayly boys were outgoing, popular and keen dancers. Elsie's cousins didn't seem to have a very close relationship with her and only agreed to chaperone her as a favour to their mother. Like their parents, the Bayly boys seemed to treat Elsie as a maid rather than a relation.

Elsie was shy and socially inept. She enjoyed dressing up and was excited to attend the dances with her dashing cousins, but she was usually dumped at the door and left to her own devices. She would then sit quietly in the corner and watch others enjoy themselves. The Bayly boys would ignore her all evening and collect her when it was time to leave. Elsie would shake her head when any young man politely asked her to dance. Not because she didn't want to but because she had never learned how to dance.

To make up for her social discomfort, Elsie would embellish stories and make things up to try and impress people. Lorraine Morten found Elsie to be shy, but like most 16-year-old girls the pair talked about their hopes and aspirations and, of course, romance. Elsie told Lorraine that she was only staying in Papamoa briefly because she was moving back to the East Cape to marry an Opotiki storekeeper. Another time, she said she was engaged to a man named King who ran a large sheep station near Opotiki. When Lorraine asked about the storekeeper, Elsie blushed and said she had so many suitors she couldn't make up her mind.

It wasn't just Lorraine that Elsie told fibs to. She told Constance Bayly's friend, Agnes Ryburn that she was marrying a boy on 31 September 1928. As September only has 30 days, she assumed Elsie was mixed up and meant 1 October.

Another one of Constance's friends, Minnie Jordan, befriended the girl feeling sorry for the way Constance treated her. Elsie once told Minnie she was engaged to a man who owned racehorses, but on future visits, Elsie never mentioned this man again.

Elsie was even prone to lying to people she was close to. Among her possessions was a letter from a relative in Taneatua, replying to a letter from Elsie. In it she said, 'So you been right to Auckland you lucky beggar, I wish I saw you go past why didn't you stay for a while you mean shet (sic), and to think you are engaged eh good luck to you but I don't quite believe you.'

The writer had reason not to believe Elsie as she was not engaged and she had never been to Auckland.

One of Trevor Bayly's friends, Reginald Lees, took a shine to Elsie. At socials he frequently asked her to dance and she would usually respond by giggling shyly and shaking her head. One day in early September 1928, Lees drove to the Bayly farmstead and asked Constance's permission to take Elsie to a dance. She agreed as long as Trevor was going to the dance as well. Elsie was excited and for a few weeks it was all she could talk about.

On the night of the social, Elsie, Trevor and Reg drove to the dance. Elsie was excited and talked animatedly. She told Reg she had heard a couple say he and her were engaged, which he thought rather odd. Elsie agreed to dance and did so awkwardly. Embarrassed, she realised her shortcomings and sat the rest of the evening out. Reg danced with another couple of girls but regularly spent time between dances sitting with Elsie.

In May 1928, Elsie returned home to Raukokore for a two week holiday, which was then extended to a month. The reason given was that the Motu River had flooded and she couldn't leave. The truth is she probably didn't want to go back.

Soon after she returned to Papamoa, Elsie learned her dream was to be realised. She was going to Auckland to accompany Constance on a three week holiday. Elsie could barely contain her excitement. All of a sudden her future seemed bright. She counted down the days.

On the morning of 1 August, Constance and Elsie packed and drove to Tauranga, where they were due to catch a train on the newly completed East Coast main trunk line through to Auckland. When they arrived in Tauranga the pair called to have morning tea with Minnie Jordan, a family friend of the Baylys.

Constance suddenly announced she was going to Auckland alone and Elsie would have to remain with Mrs Jordan. She gave no explanation for her change of heart and Minnie Jordan was embarrassed and upset for the poor girl. She knew Elsie had her heart set on going to Auckland. The girl was devastated, remaining quiet and withdrawn throughout most of her three week stay with the family.

Constance Bayly returned to Tauranga on 18 August and collected Elsie. Later, Constance was to say the girl was very quiet on the journey home but in reality

Constance probably did not pay too much attention to her niece as she had other things on her mind. Family problems were simmering and back home there were obvious tensions in the Bayly household.

Frank and Constance's eldest son, Bill had been living at home and working on the family farm. Handsome, cocky and arrogant, 22-year-old Bill had a way with women, and if there was any trouble involving young girls in the area, then the Bayly home was usually first port of call for Constable Jackson. Police regarded Bill as being 'sexually weak'.

This was particularly harrowing to poor Constance who worried her son's antics would affect her reputation and social standing. She dreaded the thought of people gossiping behind her back about one of her precious boys. She was forever protecting Bill and lambasting the 'loose morals' of the latest girl he was linked to.

In August 1928, Phyllis Palmer, the daughter of a neighbouring farmer, was pregnant with Bill Bayly's child. Within days of his mother's return from Auckland, Bill and Phyllis quietly moved to Auckland. Constance's 'shopping excursion' may have been a ploy for her to arrange a safe haven for her son with friends and relatives in Auckland. If this was true, then she also kept it secret from her husband and sons who later said they had no idea why Bill had suddenly left the district.

Bill returned home on 3 September and finished up his contract with his employer and tidied up his affairs before leaving again ten days later.

On 24 September, three days after her seventeenth birthday, Elsie wrote a letter to her father saying that she was looking forward to coming home at Christmas. She added that, 'Bill is going to get married to a nice girl,' and intimated she was happy for him.

On the afternoon of Saturday 29 September, Elsie was cleaning the billiard room. She was bending down scrubbing the floor, when she stood up suddenly hitting her head on the windowsill. It was a hard knock and was heard by Constance who was on the other side of the room. Elsie was momentarily dazed. Constance rushed over and helped her to a chair then went to fetch a cold cloth. Elsie laughed at the fuss and said she would be all right. She seemed happy to resume her chores after ten minutes rest.

Lorraine Morton came over to visit Elsie the next afternoon and the pair played croquet. Elsie excitedly mentioned that Reg Lees had asked her to an upcoming dance at Te Puke Hall. Elsie said she was keen on Reg but did not want to go by herself so asked Lorraine to accompany her. Lorraine said she couldn't go.

On Monday Audrey Bayly, a cousin from Auckland, was coming to stay for a week. Elsie and Constance spent most of the weekend cleaning in preparation for her visit. By early on the Monday afternoon, the work got too much for Constance and she went for a snooze. When she woke, she noticed Elsie sitting in a chair in the kitchen, in an apparent daze.

Constance asked her what she was doing. Elsie told her she was cleaning the china cupboard, but the cupboard had not been touched since the previous week.

When Constance told Elsie to go and bring the clothes in from the line, Elsie continued staring into space. There was a possibility the girl had been concussed when she bumped her head two days prior, but Constance figured her behaviour was more likely to have been because her period was due. According to Constance, Elsie was highly strung when she got her periods, which often caused dizziness and nosebleeds.

At 4.30pm, Audrey Bayly arrived at the farm and the Baylys rushed out to meet her. At home in Remuera, Audrey lived the kind of lifestyle Elsie could only dream of. She was introduced to Elsie who shyly said hello before resuming her duties.

Later, Audrey noticed Elsie quietly appear at the table for dinner. As the family excitedly chattered, Elsie kept quiet and only uttered a 'thank you' when the bread was passed to her. Audrey thought it highly unusual that this girl was family but was treated as an employee.

Over dinner, Audrey told the family that she had been present in September when Australian aviator, Charles Kingsford Smith had landed in Auckland. Elsie listened quietly, wide-eyed, as Audrey regaled tales of this historic event.

After dinner, Trevor left for a dance in Te Puke and Constance told Tom to help Elsie with the dishes. Eleven-year-old Tom later said Elsie had seemed angry as they cleaned up.

At around 8pm, Audrey went into the kitchen to fetch a glass of water. At that moment, Elsie came inside from the washhouse. Her face seemed flushed and she appeared surprised. Audrey asked her for a glass of water and Elsie walked over to the sink. She said, 'I have just come in from emptying the bucket.' But she was not carrying the bucket. Then Elsie began to giggle. Audrey thought this an unusual reaction but figured the girl was just shy or embarrassed.

Godfrey Bayly excused himself at 8.30pm, saying he was going to bed. The sixteen-year-old noticed the kitchen lights still on. He went into Elsie's room to ask why she had not turned out the lights but she wasn't there.

The rest of the family went to bed at about 9.30pm. Constance hadn't seen Elsie all evening but this wasn't unusual. Elsie often went to her annexe early, where she would quietly knit before turning in.

Between 1.30 and 2am, Reg Lees dropped Trevor Bayly off at the gate. Trevor was surprised to see the front gate onto the main road and the gates leading to the shed and the house still open. Elsie's last job of the day was to ensure all gates were closed. As he went through the last gate, about 350 metres from the house, he noticed that the family car—a blue Overland Whippet—was not in the shed. The absence of the car worried Trevor. He thought someone must have taken ill. His brother Godfrey was still awake so Trevor asked him who was sick. Godfrey said he didn't know and then told his brother that he had noticed the kitchen lights still on when he went to bed. Perplexed, Trevor went to bed.

At 7am the next morning, Trevor came out to the kitchen to find Godfrey already at the table with Constance grudgingly fixing breakfast. She complained that Elsie was still asleep and told Godfrey to call for her. When he received no response, he went to her room. Her bed looked as if it hadn't been slept in. Returning to the kitchen, he told his mother and brother that Elsie was not there. At this point, Trevor mentioned that the car wasn't in the shed.

All three went outside and followed the car's tracks out to the road. The marks on the verge indicated that the car had gone towards the east.

When they returned to the house, the other members of the family were in the kitchen. Adding to the mystery, there was £7.1s.½d missing from Audrey's handbag—the equivalent of about $600 today.

Constance Bayly could not understand where the silly girl had got to. The boys could not believe Elsie would steal the car as not only was it not in her nature, but she couldn't drive—at least none of the Baylys had ever seen her drive.

Constable Jackson at Te Puke was informed that the car and girl were missing on the morning of 2 October. As a matter of course, Jackson asked if the Baylys were all at home the night before. Constance told him the whole family had been at home, it was only Elsie that was missing.

In the meantime, the family went from room-to-room to see if anything else was missing. Frank Bayly was missing £3,15s from the pocket of his trousers. Godfrey reported that his silver Ingersoll watch was gone. Also missing was a coat belonging to Tom.

It was strange. There was no reason for Elsie to take the coat, the watch or the money. She'd left her purse, containing two shillings and threepence, in her room and she was due about £10 in back wages. Her own wristlet watch was on her dressing table although it had stopped working some weeks earlier. She also had her own perfectly good coat.

There were two keys to the Whippet. Missing was the main key, which was kept in a small red box on the dressing table in the Baylys' bedroom. No one outside the family knew where this key was kept so the assumption was made that Elsie must have taken it some time before the couple went to bed at 9pm. The other car key was found in a drawer.

At 7pm that evening, Constable Jackson phoned the Baylys to see if Elsie had returned home. She hadn't and there was no word from her father, who had been told of his daughter's disappearance by phone. Jackson spent the night telephoning police stations in Whakatane, Waihi, Tauranga, Opotoki, Katikati, Rotorua and Hamilton reporting the girl and car missing.

The message reached Auckland Central police station at 10pm and was read to all staff the next morning. Unbeknown to them, the car had already been located in Auckland the previous day. A woman named Christina Anderson had noticed a dust-covered blue car parked opposite her house on Station Road in Papatoetoe at 8.50am on 2 October. It was still there later that afternoon so she telephoned police who told her to call them the following day if the owner had not returned.

At 7.30 the next morning, Mrs Anderson called Papatoetoe police to tell them that the car had not moved and there was no sign of the driver.

Constable Maloney arrived at the scene at 9am and made a cursory check of the abandoned Whippet. It was covered in dust indicating it had travelled some distance on unsealed roads. In the back of the car, resting against the seat was a spare tyre, its rim and a jack. Somewhere along the journey, the driver must have stopped to change a tyre. Maloney had no idea the car had been reported missing so he climbed into the car and drove it to Butler's Garage in Papatoetoe. He issued a report around all police stations in the North Island saying he had located a 'blue Overland Whippet touring 5-seater car, registered 27.847'.

Within a few hours, a response came in from Hamilton police suggesting the car could be the one reported missing from Papamoa a few days earlier.

Up until this point, it was thought Elsie had had enough of her position and had become jealous hearing her cousin Audrey's tales of her exciting life in Auckland. Did Elsie steal the keys to make a trip to the city she was fascinated with?

There were two factors in this theory that were difficult to explain. The first of these is the abandonment of the car in Papatoetoe. Elsie Walker had never been to Auckland before and even if she had negotiated the hazardous roads herself during the night, why would she abandon the car in Station Road? She knew nobody in Auckland except her aunt in Epsom. If Elsie had been resourceful enough to drive all the way to the city, surely she would have completed her journey? Why would she have abandoned the car and walked 13 kilometres to the paddock where she was found?

The second was the fact Elsie could not drive. Even if she'd learnt the theoretical rudiments of driving by observing the driver's actions as a front-seat passenger, it would have been extremely difficult for her to back the car out of a narrow shed in the dark night and then drive for miles on unknown roads. How would she know what roads to take?

From Papamoa to Auckland, Elsie had three possible routes. It was approximately 300 kilometres from Papamoa to Auckland, via the conventional route through Rotorua, or about 250 kilometres over the difficult Kaimai Range road or 225 kilometres via Waihi. Each of these routes would have taken the most experienced of drivers at least eight hours.

The Whippet had a fuel capacity of 30 litres. The car was capable of doing just over 300 kilometres on a full tank. It could easily have made the trip from Papamoa to Auckland via any of the three possible routes. There was still a small amount of petrol left in the car when it was found.

Trevor Bayly had filled the car two days prior to its disappearance and said it had already travelled about 25 kilometres after being filled. Having been driven to Auckland, there would still have been enough fuel in the car for Elsie to get to Epsom where her aunt lived. Why had the car been abandoned here?

Then there was the question of the changed tyre. How could she have done this in the dark of night with no mechanical experience? Perhaps she'd stopped at a garage and been helped by a proprietor or mechanic.

Te Puke policeman, Constable Jackson telephoned Frank Bayly to tell him the car had been located in South Auckland. The policeman thought it strange that Bayly didn't enquire after the girl.

On 3 October, the day after the Whippet was found, a black cocker spaniel was found wandering in the vicinity of Knox Home. Robert Brown, who had been walking his dog, asked nearby council workers to distract the dog and tie it up. One of the council workers took it home and noticed that the dog had a Tauranga County Council collar that had been registered in 1926. A few days later the man was taking the dog for a walk, when it broke loose and ran off chasing a car. It was never seen again. Could this dog have been linked to Elsie's disappearance?

Three days later, Jackson went to the Bayly farm to tell them that Elsie had been found dead 14 kilometres away from where the car was found. Frank Bayly grunted when he heard the news and agreed to go to Auckland to identify the body.

Before catching the train he sent two telegrams: one to his sister saying he was going to need a place to stay and the other to his brother-in-law D'Renzy Walker informing him that Elsie was dead and saying that he would take care of the funeral arrangements.

With Frank Bayly gone, Jackson set about taking statements from the rest of the family. While interviewing Constance, Jackson casually asked about Bill. She told him that he was on holiday in Auckland and having his teeth repaired. Jackson was suspicious. The day before, Constance had told him nobody was missing from home. She did not tell him that Bill was away. The constable had had numerous dealings with Bill over the past two years and he suspect that the lad had something to do with his cousin's disappearance.

He asked Constance if there were any spare keys to the Whippet and she produced the set saying they were Bill's. Jackson uplifted them and took them back with him to Te Puke police station. There, he sent an immediate wire to Auckland police detective branch suggesting they get a statement from William Alfred Bayly. He added it was important to locate him before his father arrived in the city, describing the father was described as a 'shrewd man'.

Back in Auckland, Detective Sergeant Tom Kelly was feeling troubled. Constable Collins had convinced him that there were no suspicious circumstances in regards to Elsie's death. Yet something did not sit right in the detective's mind. The doctors had confirmed the girl was healthy and had ingested no poisons, so what could have killed her?

The explanation proffered suggested that she had driven the car perhaps bashing her head on the steering wheel or on the boot of the car as she changed the tyre. The blow had concussed her and she wandered some distance in a daze and crawled into a quiet spot beneath thick bushes and died. To Tom Kelly this didn't make sense. He was angry at himself for not ensuring the car had been secured as a possible crime scene. However in his defence, there was no evidence of any suspicious death when the car was located three days *before* the body was found.

Kelly went to Butler's Garage and located the car. It was still dusty and the punctured tyre was still in the back with the rim and jack. A forensic examination found no fingerprints on the tyre or any of the tools so it was impossible to determine who had done the job. Nor were there any fingerprints on the steering wheel or column, making it impossible to work out who'd been driving it. Despite its dusty state, there were no fingerprints on the exterior of the car.

There was enough fuel in the car for it to have been driven at least another eight to ten kilometres. The policeman couldn't understand why Elsie Walker would have left the car in South Auckland. He knew that Elsie's sister had lodged with an aunt, Ann Barters, in Epsom and that Elsie had written to her a few times. DS Kelly interviewed Ann Barters, who was Constance and Whisky's sister, but she denied having heard from Elsie since the letters from Raukokore several years earlier.

Kelly then sought out Bill Bayly, who was staying at the Glenalvon Hotel in Waterloo Quadrant, central Auckland. A private boarding house, the Glenalvon Hotel was run by Annie McCallum. When Kelly arrived on the afternoon of 6 October, Annie was highly suspicious and reluctant to answer questions about any of her guests. Annie did, however, confirm that Bill Bayly had been staying there but he had left several days earlier in order to start a job somewhere in Henderson.

Kelly asked to see view the hotel register to find out how long Bayly had stayed and in which room. Annie McCallum couldn't say how long he had been there and said that he had stayed in various rooms but had lately been in room one.

On further questioning, McCallum admitted that Bill was not a paying guest because he was her nephew. She told DS Kelly that her brother, Frank Bayly, would be arriving at any minute.

When asked about Bill's movements, Annie thought Bill had spent the evening of 30 September with the Barters before returning to the hotel at about 10pm. She was sure he had breakfast early the next morning but, as it was her day off, she had not seen him.

Kelly suggested that he might have to interview other guests at some stage which Annie was not happy about and she refused to answer any more questions. At that point, Kelly had no cause to be suspicious so he left.

Frank Bayly arrived in Auckland on the evening of 6 October and stayed the night at the Glenalvon. First thing the next morning, he caught a taxi to the Epsom address of his old friend and solicitor, Robert Lusk. The pair then travelled to the Auckland mortuary where they met Chief Detective Hammond. The three went in to make a formal identification of the body.

Having identified Elsie, Frank Bayly and Robert Lusk drove out to a farmhouse in Henderson where they found Bill Bayly and a frightened young pregnant woman. Bill had not expected their visit and was shocked when he learnt his cousin had stolen the car and had been found dead. Bill returned to the Glenalvon with his father that night. Over breakfast the next morning, Bill told his father that the police wanted to see him.

On Monday 8 October, Elsie Grace Walker was buried at Purewa Cemetery, in the presence of Frank Bayly, Robert Lusk and D'Renzy Walker, who arrived just in time to see his daughter buried. After the funeral Walker boarded the first train back to Tauranga and from there back to the East Cape. He was busy on the farm and he believed that the Lord had Elsie now and she was in His hands.

After the funeral, Frank Bayly and Robert Lusk returned to the Glenalvon and collected Bill. The trio drove to Auckland Central police station and asked for Detective Sergeant Kelly. Bill Bayly made a brief statement confirming his whereabouts over the previous days.

The next day, Bill Bayly and his father drove the Whippet back to Papamoa.

Police asked for the assistance of the media hoping readers who were out on the road on the night of 1 October might come forward with information on Elsie Walker's movements. Early reports dubbed the discovery the 'Tamaki Mystery' and reported possible suspicions around the cause of Elsie's death. This was partly fuelled by the fact that her body had been found in a paddock opposite Knox Home. The home was a sanatorium for people with incurable illnesses but it was reported in the media to be an insane asylum. There were rumours that a lunatic had escaped and strangled the poor young girl.

There were no unexplained absences from the home during the period in question and the home was so secure that it was virtually impossible for anyone to leave undetected. The reports of involvement by anyone from Knox Home were pure sensationalism.

Despite the sensational reports, several people came forward with sightings of Elsie. A newspaper vendor named Joseph Butler thought he saw the girl at 4.50am in Papatoetoe, walking in the direction of Otahuhu, but he could not give an accurate description of what she looked like or what she was wearing.

David Baldwin was able to offer more detail. On Tuesday 2 October, he was grading the road alongside Panmure Lagoon. At 8.15am he was turning his grader at the intersection of Panmure and Saint Heliers Bay roads when he spotted a girl walking in the direction of Panmure. What caught his attention was the fact she had no hat on, her hair was ruffled and she was wearing a coat that was miles too big for her. The girl appeared to be in a daze and walked straight towards the path of the grader. She did not seem too concerned but stopped in her tracks. Baldwin looked directly at her and she returned his stare. The driver said she looked as if she was not of sane mind. He noticed a distinct mark on her left cheekbone. Baldwin placed her about 2.5 kilometres away from where her body was found.

When police checked the details provided they found that he had described what Elsie was wearing exactly, before her full description and photograph had been published. When shown a photograph of Elsie, Baldwin was adamant it was the girl he had seen. Baldwin's sighting placed Elsie alive between where the car was abandoned and where her body was found. There was still no clear evidence of how she came to arrive in Auckland.

Detective Sergeant Kelly went to Te Puke on 16 October to continue enquiries already begun by Constable Jackson. The township was rife with rumours, none particularly favourable towards the Bayly family.

Arriving at Baylys', he received a frosty reception. Upon introducing himself, Frank Bayly laid a complaint against Constable Jackson because he felt that Jackson was spreading false rumours around town about his family. The local policeman was there with DS Kelly and the pair faced off. Jackson saying, 'Don't you talk to me, Mr Bayly, like you talk to your wife. You talk to her like a pig!'

Kelly managed to keep the pair apart and Bayly walked back to the house grumbling. Jackson told the Auckland detective that the overbearing patriarch was thwarting his enquiries. The hostility had started when he had visited the Bayly farm to re-interview Constance about the car. When Jackson had taken his original statements from Constance and the boys, Frank Bayly had been in Auckland. Now that he was back, Constance told the constable she wanted to withdraw what she had said about the car being stolen. Jackson told Kelly that Frank Bayly had interrupted his wife, saying, 'Don't tell him too much, mother. Leave it all to me. I have more brains than you.' On being asked not to interfere, Jackson said that the farmer had stared at him menacingly, saying, 'Leave it to me, mother. I'll fix it. I have some influential friends.'

Kelly talked at length with Frank Bayly who reluctantly conceded that Jackson had only been carrying out his duties and he agreed to co-operate fully with ongoing inquiries.

While at the farm, Kelly spoke to Constance at length about Elsie. The detective noted Constance as saying, 'Elsie Walker was not a bright or normal girl, but she was healthy. She was an obedient girl, clean and tidy. I know that she was untruthful. She was untruthful to me and from what I know that she told the neighbours, she was untruthful to them. I kept her strictly under discipline and it may be probable that she disliked me and wanted to get away, but she did not give me any indication of it.'

She also described her niece as being gentle and kind, but a bit simple. She said the thought the girl had the mental age of a child aged 10–12 years—a description that would later be unfairly accepted as an accurate assessment in court.

Constance also told the officer that Elsie had been acting strangely on the day she disappeared, which she put down to the girl's imminent period or her jealousy at the stories told by her cousin Audrey. She also told him that Elsie had received a bump on the head several days earlier.

DS Kelly asked whether Elsie had ever learned to drive. Constance said Elsie had expressed an interest in driving but was never allowed to. But then Mrs Bayly told the policeman that several weeks before her disappearance, Elsie had offered to change a tyre, but instead watched as Godfrey changed it. Four-year-old Charlie suddenly piped up saying, 'But her can drive the car'. They all looked at him in puzzlement and he added, 'Her backed the car out the shed to the water tank, walked all around it and drove it in again.'

There was no evidence to suggest a second person was involved but police couldn't rule out the possibility. If there had been an intruder there were three dogs which would have barked at any strangers on the property. One was tethered near the garage, and the other two at the rear of the house. Yet nobody in the house or nearby farms heard the dogs bark. If there was another person involved perhaps they were known to Elsie and the family?

Kelly was interested in Elsie's behaviour in the hours prior to her disappearance from the home. Audrey Bayly mentioned her encounter with the girl when she went to get a glass of water. When Audrey said that the girl had said she had taken the rubbish out, Constance Bayly was surprised as the previous day had been rubbish day, so the bucket would have been virtually empty.

The bucket was found in the shed where the car had been. It contained some potato peelings, a dishcloth and some brown paper. There was no reason for Elsie to take it outside but why didn't she return it to the washhouse when she came back inside?

There were no signs of a struggle in the shed. If there was a man involved, then it seemed likely it must have been someone Elsie knew. If she had disturbed a thief she would have immediately raised the alarm. If it was somebody she knew, she would have been willing to go on a night time drive. If she'd intended to be away long, or leave the district, surely she would have dressed in suitable attire.

Was the meeting spontaneous or pre-arranged? If it had been pre-arranged, that might account for her unusual behaviour the day she disappeared. Was Elsie carrying on an illicit affair and planning to elope? If so, who with?

Reg Lees was the only boy in the area to have registered any interest in Elsie. He had taken her to a dance and was supposed to be taking to another one the weekend after she disappeared. Reg hadn't invited her to the dance that he and Trevor Bayly went to the night she disappeared. Instead, they had taken the Morten sisters. Reg had been at the dance all evening and had dropped Trevor home at 2am. He was never considered a suspect.

Another young man who became a possible suspect was 22-year-old Algar Ferguson, who lived on his parents' farm in Papamoa. Despite being the same age, Algar Ferguson and Bill Bayly were not friends. They were, however, very much alike. Ferguson was a trouble-maker and fancied himself as a ladies man. Whenever there was a young lady in trouble in the area, Ferguson was usually the second person police visited after Bill Bayly.

Rumours were flying that Ferguson and Elsie had an immoral relationship and that they had been seen dancing in a risqué fashion at local socials. This was clearly untrue as Elsie could not and would not dance.

Initially it was thought the initial F found on the bloodstained handkerchief near her body stood for Ferguson. When interviewed, Algar Ferguson said that he had moved to Auckland in August 1928, staying at McBeath's Boarding House until November, when he moved back to Papamoa. He was living in Auckland on 1 October and was able to provide satisfactory alibis for the period 29 September to 2 October. He added that he knew Elsie Walker and where she lived but that she was not a personal acquaintance.

Police interviewed a number of men in Te Puke and Papamoa, including all known criminals, before deciding to cast the net wider to the East Cape.

The first person they spoke to there was Elsie's father. Whisky Walker was quick to reject the question of Elsie having a sweetheart. But Whisky spent most of his time toiling on the farm, did he really have any idea about his daughter's private life?

He was also adamant that his daughter could not drive and wouldn't have had the tenacity to drive a car through the night on difficult and unfamiliar roads. He was equally doubtful of her having the strength or knowledge to change a tyre. Whisky also thought it unlikely she would have left the property dressed in her maid's outfit as she had always prided herself on her appearance.

Elsie's father remained of the firm belief that she must have disturbed a stranger in the shed, catching him in the process of stealing the car. Then he had either suffocated or strangled her, and then bundled her into the car and dumped her at the spot she was found. He didn't think she would ever have gone willingly with a stranger.

Native Constable Pirina, based in Te Kaha, knew most people in the region and began discreetly asking questions. Mr King, the sheep farmer Elsie had said she was engaged to, was interviewed at length. He said he knew Elsie but he had not had any contact with her since she left for Papamoa. He also said he'd heard rumours of their engagement but said they were not true.

Another possible suitor was Bob Cricket, a cocky Englishman who had come to New Zealand a year earlier and was working his way down the country. His real name was Robert Shotton but he was known around the district as 'the Cricket'. Shotton was named in letters between Elsie and her 14-year-old sister Ivy.

In June 1928, when Elsie had returned to the Baylys after her prolonged stay at home, Shotton wrote to Constance asking if he could correspond with Elsie. Constance read the letter and immediately discarded it. She never mentioned his letter to Elsie so the girl never knew of his interest.

Could he have been the reason Elsie had prolonged her holiday during May 1928? One rumour circulating was that Whisky had caught Cricket and Elsie in 'a passionate embrace' and had sacked the young man. This was never verified.

In a letter to Elsie dated 26 June 1928, Ivy wrote, 'The Cricket got the sack.' Adding, 'He had a bad mouth, and had too much to say.' If there was a romantic relationship between Elsie and Shotton, she clearly never admitted it to her younger sister.

Police quickly tracked Bob Shotton to a farm near Opotiki. He was interviewed and denied any romance between him and Elsie. He said he had not seen Elsie since May 1928 when she returned to Papamoa. He also denied making any attempt to correspond with her.

The Baylys' neighbours were all interviewed and asked if they had seen or heard anything on the night Elsie disappeared. Robert McPike lived in a house on a section in front of Bayly's farm. He claimed he saw the lights of the Whippet leaving the property in the direction of Te Puke at about 8.30pm but he couldn't see who was in the car.

If Elsie had left around 8.30pm, as McPike alleged, then the route from Papamoa to Auckland via Rotorua was roughly 300 kilometres and she would have arrived in Papatoetoe between 3am and 4am providing there were no obstructions along the way. This would have coincided with the sightings of her by Butler and Baldwin. At some stage she must have stopped to change the tyre but police never found out where this was done.

Weighing up their inquiries to date, senior Auckland detectives believed Elsie had become dissatisfied with her position at the Baylys' and decided to steal the car and drive to Auckland. Confused, tired and scared, they thought that she then abandoned the vehicle. Overcome by exhaustion, they surmised, she then crawled under the bushes and died of fright or exposure.

This was all to change 17 days after Elsie's body was found when somebody finally thought to send her clothes for examination by Frederick Armitage, a bacteriologist at Auckland Hospital. After they had been removed during the post mortem, the clothes had been stored in a damp room. When they were retrieved, they were sodden and had to be left out to dry.

Armitage tested the stains on all of the garments, focusing particularly on stains found on Elsie's underwear. He quickly returned his findings:

There were stains of human semen present on the bloomers. The stains were not in only one part of the garment but distributed in several parts. The large stain containing blood and semen appeared to have been produced by blood and semen ejected together; the small spots of blood nearby and lower down all bore the appearance of being produced by the same man. There were also traces of semen on the handkerchief found near Elsie's body.

Mr Armitage was not able to determine the age of the stains but said that he didn't think they were made at the time of or after Elsie's death but they were 'quite recent' as they had been deposited after the clothing had last been washed. When interviewed, Constance Bayly said they had last been washed on 24 September.

Elsie had come into sexual contact with a male within one week of her death. This was shocking news. The pathology report deemed Elsie to have been a virgin when she died.

Armitage's report arrived in the hands of senior police on 1 November 1928—the same date that the police commissioner relieved Detective Sergeant Kelly of his lead in the investigation, appointing a more experienced detective, James Bickerdike of Christchurch.

Bickerdike was still smarting at media criticism over the ruthless techniques he had used during the Scarff murder investigation. When he arrived in the Bay of Plenty, he refused to co-operate with the media and deliberately drip fed journalists minimal details of developments.

Even though police restricted the information they shared with the media, the newspapers continued to print articles about the young girl who disappeared from her rural home and was found dead in an Auckland paddock. This fascination only grew when the media got hold of a third-hand account of the semen stains on Elsie's clothes. Of all the newspapers, *Truth* was the one that really ran with the story and their articles read like a sexually-charged crime fiction serial. Fact intertwined with fantasy. It was the perfect mystery. The *Truth* headline on Bickerdike's first day on the case read: *Brutally slain while defending her honour. Little Elsie Walker was done to death whilst fighting to retain her virtue.*

The story accompanying the headline was largely based on rumour, speculating that 'innocent little Elsie Walker' was either startled by an intruder who was burgling the Bayly house or she'd run away with a lover who had promised to marry her in Auckland.

Because police were withholding information, reporters could not be blamed for filling in the blanks. The case had captured the imagination of all New Zealanders with *Truth* and other newspapers competing for the attention of readers.

According to the Armitage report, Elsie Walker had sexual contact with a man between 24 September and 1 October. Family and friends said Elsie had no boyfriend, and she was rarely allowed out. Did the semen, therefore, belong to somebody within the Bayly household? There was no proof that this sexual activity had any correlation with her death but identifying this mystery man might help to solve the puzzle of what happened to Elsie.

With the Armitage report in hand, Detective Sergeant Bickerdike called around to the Bayly house and re-interviewed the Bayly men one by one. Bill Bayly was initially ruled out as he was known to have left Papamoa on 13 September. Frank Bayly and his sons, 18-year-old Trevor and 16-year-old Godfrey, were questioned by Bickerdike. All denied having any sexual connection with Elsie. The detective was particularly harsh on Godfrey, as his initial statement said that he'd gone to bed at about 8.30pm and when he noticed the lights were still burning, he said he went into Elsie's bedroom to ask why she had not turned them out. Bickerdike suggested that it would have been more normal for Godfrey to just turn the lights off and go back to his room. The boy had no explanation as to why he had decided to check in on Elsie but he emphatically denied Bickerdike's accusation.

Trevor Bayly had a strong alibi that night as he was seen by a number of people at the dance in Te Puke. Yet he seemed nervous and fidgety when asked intimate details about his relationship with his cousin. When asked about the dance, he caused suspicion when he could not recall what time he was picked up or where exactly he was picked up by Lees. He said he could not recall whether he sat in the front or the rear of Lees' car but he could recall Lees dropping him at home about 1.30am.

As he left, Bickerdike asked Constance about Bill's whereabouts on the night in question. Constance told him that Bill wasn't in Papamoa, adding that Bill thought of Elsie as nothing more than a child.

In his report, Bickerdike wrote that he did not believe any of them but he didn't have one definite suspect. In his report he merely concluded that the sperm 'was a result of Elsie skylarking with the Bayly boys'.

The investigation was taking its toll on the Bayly family. They felt that they were being harassed by police, media and curious locals on a daily basis. The scandal ruined Constance's cherished social standing. Frank Bayly had several altercations with pressmen before eventually realising that the best way to deal with them was to be polite but wary.

The Baylys probably had no idea that police already had their sights set on one member of their family. Constable Jackson had always suspected that Bill Bayly was involved in Elsie's disappearance, thinking that Bill had sneaked back to Papamoa and eloped with Elsie.

Detective Sergeant Kelly had interviewed Bill, primarily because he was the only member of the immediate family living in Auckland. He had no reason to suspect Bill of any involvement with Elsie's death, so his questions focused mainly on the car and whether Bill knew of Elsie's intention to travel to Auckland. At that interview, Bill was accompanied by his father and a solicitor.

Several weeks after taking over the case, Bickerdike decided to interview Bill Bayly, tracking him down at a farm in Ruawaro, near Huntly. Bayly was clearly annoyed by the visit but politely answered the officer's questions. He refused to make a statement, saying he had already made two. The detective believed Bayly had something to hide.

Around this time, Commissioner McIlveney issued a memorandum to senior Auckland detectives asking for the inquest to be hurried, adding, 'No effort must be spared to clear up the matter as soon as possible.'

Upon reading the memorandum, Bickerdike approached doctors Gilmour and Murray to see if they could aid in the progression of the case. He asked both doctors independently whether there had been any mistakes in their original report. Murray said he could not add anything further.

On 6 December, Dr Gilmour added a postscript, which was shown to Dr Murray, who duly signed it. 'In our opinion, death was neither due to natural causes nor to exhaustion. The probable cause of death was concussion following a blow to the head.'

This change hinted at police pressure being brought to bear on the doctors. Now that there was a cause of death attributed to the case, the inquest process could move more quickly. This remarkable turn of events took everyone by surprise. Why the sudden change in the doctors' opinion?

The post mortem makes mention of the bruise several times but it also stated that the injury was not likely to have caused Elsie's death. The content of the report was not amended so the postscript was contradictory to the rest of the report.

The day after the postscript was added, police instructed the crown prosecutor to appear at the impending inquest. Their explanation for the instruction was due to, 'the intense public interest and unusual circumstances of the girl's death'. The crown prosecutor, Vincent Meredith was given the police brief on the case. The brief said that Elsie had been upset with her position at the Bayly household so had voluntarily absconded, stealing the car and driving to Auckland. There she hit her head and wandered in a daze to the spot where she collapsed and died.

Meredith was far from happy with the brief. In his memoirs, he wrote that he refused to accept the assertion, 'that Elsie had taken umbrage and in a fit of pique had taken the car and driven to Auckland, with no money and no clothes, dressed in her kitchen array, to a place where she knew nobody on a dreadful road she didn't know and in her dark when she couldn't see.'

He declined to act, labelling the brief as absurd and refusing to be associated with it. Meredith believed that Elsie had been murdered and he suggested that further enquiries needed to be made, particularly in relation to the movements of Bill Bayly on the night in question. He said he had read the statements taken by residents of the Glenalvon Hotel and he directed police to re-interview them. Within weeks, an amended brief was offered and Meredith agreed to proceed with a very tenuous case against Bill Bayly. Police, under Bickerdike's command, scrutinised Bill Bayly's movements during the days leading up to the discovery of Elsie's body, speaking to anyone and everyone that might be able to provide them with the lead they so desperately needed.

William Alfred Bayly was born on 15 July 1906 and spent the first 19 years of his life in Auckland. In June 1925, when his father bought the farm in Papamoa, Bill moved there to manage the place. The rest of the family moved a year later. Handsome and cocky, with a magnetic personality, Bill had a way with women.

Part of the reason Frank Bayly bought the farm and sent his son to manage it may have been to provide a solution to a recent problem. Bill Bayly had seduced the 15-year-old daughter of his then employer and she became pregnant. He was arrested and charged with carnal knowledge, a charge to which he pleaded not guilty. The case was dismissed but, to the consternation of his mother, it was widely reported in the newspapers.

Bill Bayly didn't learn his lesson and after moving to Papamoa, Constable Jackson received numerous complaints about Bill's behaviour and Frank Bayly was regularly accosted by angry fathers. By the age of 19, Bill Bayly's police file already had him labelled as being 'sexually weak'.

Throughout 1928, Bill worked on his father's farm and was paid a wage of 30 shillings a week. If he ever needed extra money, his father would give it to him.

For most of 1928, Bill and his cousin Elsie both lived in the house at Papamoa but they had little to do with each other. Elsie regularly wrote letters home to her family telling them snippets of news. In this correspondence she never mentioned Bill except for in the very last letter she wrote. A week before she died, Elsie wrote to her father saying, 'Billy is getting married to a very nice girl in the district'. No one had told her that Bill was already married.

According to his mother, Bill had little to do with Elsie. Bill had once driven Constance, Charlie and Elsie to Rotorua for a day trip earlier in the year but that was the only time they had ever spent together away from the farm.

Bill's latest girlfriend, Phyllis Palmer, was the daughter of a neighbouring farmer. When Phyllis told Bill she was pregnant, he made secret plans for them both to leave the district—probably to avoid being arrested again. It seems that Constance knew the truth, which might have been the reason for her last minute decision to leave Elsie in Tauranga when she went to Auckland.

Within four days of Constance's return to Papamoa, Bill and Phyllis abruptly left for Auckland. Bill allegedly told his brothers he was going to Auckland to have his teeth fixed and would remain there for a short holiday. It was some weeks before they found out the real reason for his departure.

On the evening of 22 August, Bill and his heavily pregnant girlfriend were picked up from Papakura station by Stanley Wright, an old friend who farmed at Karaka.Wright drove Phyllis to her aunt and uncle's house in Newmarket, before taking Bill back to his place in Karaka. Bill stayed there for a week and would catch the early morning train to Newmarket to visit Phyllis every day.

On the cool winters' day of 29 August, Bill Bayly and Phyllis Palmer married at All Saints Church of England in Ponsonby. Even though they were married, Phyllis continued to stay with her aunt and uncle, while Bill moved into the Glenalvon Hotel, which was owned by his aunt.

He stayed at the Glenalvon until 3 September, when he caught the train home to Papamoa. When he got back to his parents' place, he didn't tell anybody about his marriage, continuing to work and live at home until he announced his intention to move to Auckland.

On 13 September, Constance and Godfrey Bayly dropped Bill at the train station, where he handed over his set of keys to the Whippet saying he had no use for them anymore.

In the days following, rumours began to circulate around Papamoa that Bayly and Phyllis Palmer had eloped. On 24 September, Frank Bayly travelled to Auckland and confronted Bill, demanding an explanation. Bill admitted that he was responsible for Phyllis' pregnancy. He also told his father that they had married.

Bewildered and disappointed, Frank handed his son £10 and said he was on his own from now. Then, as he left, he relented and offered his son the running of the family farm in Papamoa. Bill declined saying he and wanted to make a fresh start. Frank then suggested that he might be able to secure the farm at Karaka for him but that it would take time to arrange.

Soon Bill was back sharing a farmhouse with Stanley Wright in Karaka. Each morning, Wright would take Bayly from Karaka to Papatoetoe railway station. The direct route by car would have taken them down Station Road where the Baylys' Whippet was later found.

Before the Bayly family moved to Papamoa, they had lived in Kohimarama and Frank Bayly still owned land there. Bayly and Wright regularly travelled from Karaka to Kohimarama to check on that piece of land. They would have travelled directly along College Road, past Knox Home and the paddock where Elsie's body would be found.

Bayly was determined to find work. Since he left Papamoa, he had been living off savings but the money was quickly running out. With his wife ready to give birth any day, he needed to find a farming job that came with living quarters.

On 27 September, Bill Bayly moved out of Wright's house. As he was leaving, he asked Wright to care for his dog and some personal effects, saying that he would pick them up once he secured a job.

Later that afternoon Bill made his way out to Henderson to apply for a job on Avis Edwards' dairy farm. The job entailed hand-milking a herd of 18 cows as well as keeping the farmhouse tidy. Mrs Edwards told him she wasn't going to make a decision yet and said she was going away for a week and she would contact him a week later to advise him whether or not he was the successful applicant.

Three days later, on Sunday 30 September, Bayly spent most of the day at the Fowlers' with his wife. He then spent the evening with the Barters before leaving at 9pm to return to Glenalvon. As he left, he told his aunt that the next day he was either going to Henderson to see about the job or to Papakura to pick up his dog.

Elsie Walker disappeared on the evening of Monday 1 October. Bill Bayly's movements from this day onwards were scrutinised by police.

At 7am on Monday 1 October Glenalvon housemaid Haidee Swinton brought Bill a cup of tea in his room. She told police that when she collected his cup half an hour later, Bill Bayly was lying on his bed reading the paper.

After breakfast Bayly caught the 9.30am bus to Henderson. None of the drivers were questioned, so there was no proof that he had indeed been out to west Auckland. According to Bayly, no one was about on Avis Edwards' farm so he returned to town. Strangely, one of Avis Edwards' employees told police he was at the farm all morning and did not see Bayly.

When he returned to town, Bayly said he had lunch at Cooks Dining Rooms before meeting his wife at 3pm. Together they walked to the Electric Power Board Office on Wellesley Street where Phyllis paid a bill while Bayly waited outside. They then walked to Karangahape Road where, according to Bayly, they spent time browsing in George Court and Rendells before Phyllis went to Miss Nidd's Millinery, where she bought a hat. Again her husband waited outside. They then went to the Blue Bird Tea Rooms in Queen Street for a light meal. When interviewed, no one at Cooks or the Blue Bird remembered seeing Bayly but this was hardly surprising given how busy both of the establishments would have been. Interestingly, the only places where Phyllis had any interaction with staff, the power board and Nidd's, Bayly waited outside. Miss Nidd's could not produce dockets for the day in question. The shop assistant who had been working that day was not given an opportunity to identify Phyllis Bayly so there was no solid proof that they had been in the shop at all.

They returned to the Fowlers' house where Phyllis was still staying with her aunt and uncle. They were not home so the couple had the house to themselves for the evening. Bayly said he left there for the Glenalvon at 9.30pm.

Annie McCallum didn't work at the hotel on Monday nights. In her absence, a long-term resident of the Glenalvon, Leonard Wilson acted as unofficial manager. In Wilson's initial statement he said he had no recollection of seeing Bill Bayly at all during that week. When police returned in December to take detailed statements, Wilson could recall a great deal more about Bayly's movements.

He told police that Bayly had occupied room one in the hotel's annexe from 27

September to 3 October. On the night of 1 October, Wilson said he had attended the opening night of the opera *Lohengrin* at the Saint James Theatre, returning to the hotel at about 11.20pm. As he went around the building extinguishing all of the lights, he said he heard someone walk towards the annexe from the verandah. Suspicious, Wilson said that he went to check the annexe and knocked on the door of room one. According to Wilson, Bayly answered the door at about 11.40pm.

If these statements were all correct, then Bayly was in Auckland on the day Elsie Walker vanished. But were Phyllis Bayly and Leonard Wilson telling the truth? Even Bayly himself queried whether it was that night that Wilson had come and checked the annexe. He told police that it had happened another night. Despite this, Wilson's statement provided a key part of Bayly's alibi for his whereabouts that crucial day—an alibi that could otherwise only be backed up by Bayly's wife.

No train or motor car tickets to Tauranga or Papamoa had been issued in Bayly's name for that day so if he had caught a train from Auckland, it's possible he'd climbed onto a goods train and jumped off near the family farm as the train slowed to enter Te Puke.

According to several interviews with staff and residents of the Glenalvon, Bill Bayly was there on the day following Elsie's disappearance. The chef, John Guilding, said he saw him at 6.45am. The pantry maid, Hazel Check, said she saw him at 7.30am. Annie McCallum said she saw him at 10am and Don Ogilvie, a resident, said he saw him at 1.15pm, adding that Bayly was in a foul mood and his clothes were dusty, 'as if he had been on a farm'. An ex-tenant, Colin Coutts, also said he saw Bayly at the hotel that night at 9.30.

There was, however, one staff member at the Glenalvon who wasn't so certain of Bayly's presence on 2 October. Marie Lego, a maid, claimed that she had been on duty that morning and initially told police she couldn't recall whether or not Bayly had been there. Later she told the crown prosecutor, Vincent Meredith, that she had gone to make Bayly's bed that morning and it hadn't been slept in. She also said that there had been a cup of tea left over that morning but she couldn't be sure that it was meant for Bayly.

According to Bill Bayly, he had collected his wife from the Fowlers' just before midday. Mrs Fowler and her daughter were both at home that day and confirmed that Bayly had visited. From the Fowlers', the pair went to Newmarket train station where he signed a goods delivery note for three boxes and a tin trunk from Phyllis' father, Thomas Palmer at 12.15pm. Bayly then completed another consignment order for the luggage to be dispatched to Henderson station.

According to the couple, they then had lunch at Cooks Dining Rooms before doing some shopping and going to the movies. That afternoon, they ran into a friend called Mrs McDonald and she joined them for afternoon tea at Milne and Choyce. At some stage that day, Bill told Phyllis that he'd got the job in Henderson so when they got back to her aunt and uncle's place that afternoon, the pair set about packing Phyllis' belongings. Bill said he then caught the bus out to Avis Edwards' farm, where he saw Alf Dodds and told him he would be out the next day. Dodds was confused as he had just started work for Avis Edwards and she had not mentioned anybody else being employed.

On the morning of Wednesday 3 October, Bayly and Phyllis moved into the farmhouse. At midday, Avis Edwards returned from her week away and Dodds told her that a man had moved in to the workers' cottage and had started working.

Extremely surprised, Edwards went over to the cottage and found Bill Bayly there. She asked him what he was doing and he told her that he had already started work as arranged. According to Avis Edwards no such arrangement had been made. She was quite clear that she'd told Bayly she still had other applicants to interview and would make her decision on her return. In any case she had already decided before she left and had hired Dodds.

Phyllis Bayly began to cry. Her husband was indignant, saying that he had already begun work. Avis Edwards agreed to pay him to work until the end of the week and to let the couple stay in the house for one week after that.

On the following Sunday morning, Bayly was visited by his father, Frank, and his lawyer Robert Lusk. Bill said he was shocked to learn that his cousin had stolen the car and even more shocked to hear that she'd been found dead. That night he returned to the Glenalvon with his father. Frank Bayly attended Elsie's funeral the next day and then accompanied his son to Auckland Central police station, where he was interviewed by DS Kelly.

Bill told Kelly he'd been in Auckland all week. When asked about Elsie, he described her as a very quiet girl and he said she had no sweethearts that he could recall. He told police that he didn't know if she could drive, adding that if someone could reverse out of the narrow and awkward driveway at the farm, then they would have no problem driving.

The next day, Bill and his father picked up the Whippet from Papatoetoe police station and drove home to Papamoa. During the trip, Bill confided in his father the misunderstanding about the farm job. Frank offered his son a job running a farm in Ruawaro, west of Huntly.

Bill remained at home for three days before returning to Henderson. He still owed Avis Edwards several days work but she was not interested and demanded he leave at once. Despite promising to leave the house by 14 October, he stayed for nine days after that. During this time, Phyllis had given birth to their son and was convalescing with the Fowlers.

On 10 November, Bayly finally moved his new family and belongings south to Huntly. He stopped in to see Wright to thank him and to collect his dog and belongings he had stored there. When police interviewed Stanley Wright he told them Bayly had asked him if he remembered what day he had left his house to stay at the Glenalvon. Wright said he couldn't remember but Bayly asked him if he would sign his book saying he had left there on 27 September. Bayly allegedly told his friend that that was the date he had told police and he didn't want any more trouble. Wright agreed and signed the book. When interviewed by police, he was quite open with them that he didn't remember the exact date and had signed the document at Bayly's behest.

Bill Bayly and his young family's move to Ruawaro in November came with hopes of a fresh start. Despite the isolation, he couldn't escape the allegations being made against him and a visit from Detective Sergeant James Bickerdike was inevitable.

Bickerdike arrived at the Ruawaro farm on the afternoon of 27 November. According to the policeman's report, Bayly was suspicious and unforthcoming.

In Bayly's account of the meeting, the hard-nosed detective made casual small talk before launching an all-out offensive. According to Bayly, Bickerdike asked straight out whether Bayly had been having a sexual relationship with Elsie Walker. He claimed the policeman told him that, given Elsie was seventeen, having a sexual relationship with her didn't make him guilty of anything. Bayly said Bickerdike then went on to tell him that if he admitted to a casual sexual relationship, then the officer would keep it a secret—it would just serve to lift suspicion from the rest of his brothers and he wouldn't be incriminating himself if he admitted it.

Bayly, on the defensive, told the officer he was not going to admit to something he hadn't done. He went on to say that Bickerdike had downplayed the question saying that Elsie was an attractive girl and that he would be a fool if he hadn't tried to have sex with her. According to Bayly, he told the police officer that she wasn't the sort of girl he was attracted to and, besides, she was his cousin.

Whatever was said during this meeting, Bickerdike did not elicit the responses he wanted. One week later, the doctors added the addendum to the medical report and the inquest date was announced.

The inquest opened to a packed courtroom at Auckland Magistrates Court on Thursday 10 January 1929 before the coroner, senior magistrate Frederick M Hunt. Vincent Meredith, crown prosecutor, represented police. Erima Northcroft represented the Bayly family and Mr Mowbray watched proceedings on behalf of D'Renzy Walker.

The inquest was held to determine the cause of death not to apportion blame. Police had not made an arrest nor were they likely to by the time the inquest started. A modest 23 witnesses were to be called to give evidence and it was envisaged that the coroner's hearing would take around three days. It took much longer. When Bill Bayly took the stand, he must have felt he was on trial.

He spent a full day on the stand on Friday 11 January and when the hearing resumed the following Monday, the cross-examination continued for another half day. Bayly appeared cool and remained true to his account of his movements. There was no evidence produced to contradict him.

Trevor Bayly also took the stand to respond to reports that he had seen his brother in Papamoa the day Elsie disappeared. Rumour had it that Bill had threatened Trevor with a hiding if he told anyone he'd seen his brother. Trevor strenuously denied this to police and to the coroner.

When Dr Murray, the police surgeon, took the stand he appeared unconvincing. He said that he could not swear to the cause of Elsie Walker's death, adding that he thought the bruise on her head may have had something to do with it but he could not assert to the cause of the blow.

Murray also gave evidence that it was possible to suffer concussion from a blow that would produce very little bruising of the skin. In cases of concussion however, it was usual to find traces of haemorrhage of the brain but there was none in this case. It was a recognised medical fact death could follow a blow on the head which would cause concussion without injury to the brain. The surgeon said that cases like this were very rare but that it was possible this had happened in Elsie's case. However, such a blow would have caused her to lose consciousness as soon as she was struck. This would seem to rule out the possibility of Elsie hitting her head while changing the tyre or hitting her head on the steering wheel while driving across potholed roads.

It also ruled out the possibility that the injury had been caused several days before when she hit her head on the window sill at the farm. She could not have suffered the effects two days later and *after* allegedly having driven 230 kilometres. More importantly, the colour of the bruising was such it could not have occurred two or three days prior to death. It was likely the blow which caused the bruising occurred shortly before death. After receiving such a heavy blow, the victim would be unable to walk even short distance, much less the 13 kilometres between where the car was abandoned and where Elsie's body was found.

'The only evidence we had of the probable cause of death was the blow on the head, but we could not say definitely what had caused the death.'

The cause of the blow was also discussed at the inquest. Given that the injury was situated at the upper right side of Elsie's forehead, the blow would have had to have come from above. The skin was not broken, thereby eliminating a stone or sharp object as being the cause. It was thus decided that it was more likely to have come from a fist or a wooden object.

By the time the pathologist, Dr Gilmour, took the stand the hearing was heading into its second week. When the Baylys' lawyer began to question Gilmour closely about the change in the conclusion to his report he drew the ire of the coroner, who seemed to be running out of patience.

Hunt asked Northcroft what the object of the cross-examination was. To which Northcroft replied, 'I am asking the witness all these questions with the object of helping Your Worship to come to a finding in this case.'

The coroner was not pleased. 'Can you tell me where this is all leading to? All I am concerned about is the death of the girl and not this scientific talk. I have the doctors' report on the girl here before me in black and white.'

Northcroft responded with an equally unimpressed, 'If Your Worship's mind is not capable of being enlightened by the cross examination, I will desist.'

The line of questioning ended there and the real reason behind the amendment to the post-mortem report was left unexplained.

While DS Kelly was giving evidence, he attempted to raise the question of the cocker spaniel with the Tauranga tags that had been picked up near where Elsie's body was found. The dog had been registered in the year that the Baylys moved to the Bay of Plenty and there was a possibility that it was linked with the case.

The coroner was completely uninterested in what might have been a key piece of evidence. His response being, 'We don't want all that! If you tell us of all the inquiries you followed up without result, we will be here a month.'

When Constable Jackson took the stand, the coroner's mood had not improved.

Northcroft believed Jackson had written his suspicions as to who had killed Elsie in a memorandum to his superiors. He then challenged the constable to produce the document. Jackson looked over to some senior officers who were in attendance, then replied that he could not produce the document.

Hunt told the court that he had no power to direct that confidential police documents should be made available to counsel.

Northcroft responded, 'We started off to inquire into the death of Elsie Walker but since then we have gone further. We have gone from that to see if any charge of murder can be got out of the case and now the proceedings have become a police inquiry.'

The coroner had had enough. 'We are here to see into the death of Elsie Walker, how, when and where, and what has been done to discover who was in it! There is a poor girl lying in her grave. I am inquiring into her death. I have her father before me in the front seat. I want to satisfy him and show him that the country is doing all it can and that the police have made inquiries I am quite prepared to leave it to the public to judge for themselves!'

When Northcroft began his closing address on Tuesday 22 January, he told the court that the hearing had been more than an inquest to determine the girl's death, adding that it felt like the trial of one family who had been victimised by police.

As to the cause of death, Northcroft agreed it was improbable that Elsie Walker had driven to Auckland by herself but it was not impossible. He inferred she could have surreptitiously crept out at night and practiced driving while everyone else was in bed.

He said that it also seemed unlikely she had been abducted or taken to the paddock and dumped, as there was no evidence of this. Northcroft said he believed that it was clear from the position of the body that death had occurred following a long tiring journey, occupying a day and night of panic.

In his conclusion he asked why Bill Bayly had been targeted when his movements had been accounted for. Northcroft then asked why Bayly would elope with then kill the girl when he had been married for one month.

The coroner made his address on Friday 25 January 1929, 14 days after the hearing had opened. 'I am of the opinion that either the girl discovered the thief in the yard and he struck her unconscious and took her away with him in the car or he induced her, which I think the more probable, to accompany him for a short run in the car, then attempted to assault her during which attempt she received the injury to her head.

'The man drove on through the night, hoping against hope that she might recover. When she did not, he feared to stop until he decided on a place to conceal the body. He drove to the quarry and hid the body. The position of the body with the coat pulled up at the back of the head proves to me, then, that he pulled the body under the shrubs. Then he drove the car as far away as time or light would allow, eight miles to Papatoetoe, and either walked or caught an early bus or train to Auckland. Who that man was there is not sufficient evidence for me to say!

'I very much regret that I find it my duty to draw attention to the way the police handled this case in its early stages. The superintendent of police for the Auckland district was present throughout the inquiry. He must have seen as I did the mistakes that were made and the inefficient way the inquiries were carried out. I feel sure that he will see the necessity for holding an inquiry at once into the whole matter.

'The public are entitled to a better service from the police than they received in this case. It is possible that suspicion may rest against a perfectly innocent man for the rest of his life. This might have been avoided had prompt and intelligent inquiries been made.

'My finding is that the deceased Elsie Walker died about the first day of October 1928 somewhere between Papamoa and Auckland, and that the cause of her death was concussion following a blow on the head, but whether that blow was accidental or homicidal there is no evidence for me to determine.'

With that result, the Bayly family emerged from court feeling vindicated. They were anxious to return to their lives, hoping to put this misfortune behind them.

The police, however, remained in the firing line. The coroner was deeply critical of police handling of the case and insisted on an immediate commission of inquiry. He believed there were several grounds for the inquiry. The first of which was the fact that Elsie's body had been removed from the scene without properly identifying the cause of death. He was also concerned that Elsie's clothes had been removed at the morgue but not sent for analysis for some time. Hunt believed that the police had been too slow to start their inquiry and that they had not tested Bill Bayly's alibi sufficiently as no statements had been taken from others at Glenalvon immediately after Elsie's death. The coroner also believed that Constable Jackson had acted on his suspicions without proof.

The Minister of Justice, Thomas Wilford asked the Governor General to appoint senior magistrate Edward Page to preside over the commission in Wellington. His brief was to, 'inquire into and report upon the conduct of all or any members of the police force in relation to the inquiries made and the steps taken by them concerning or consequent upon the death of Elsie Walker.'

The Commission of Inquiry opened on Friday 22 February 1929 at the Auckland Magistrates Court before Mr E Page SM. Evidence was led by Mr A E Currie of the Crown Law Office, Wellington. The police officers involved in the case were represented by some of the best legal minds in the country.

Public interest in the inquiry was high due to heavy media coverage so the gallery was filled to capacity.

In his opening address, Mr Currie stated that this was not an inquiry into the death of Elsie Walker, nor was it an inquiry into the manner in which the information obtained by the police was presented at the inquest. Neither was it an inquiry into the general administration and control of the police force. It was a question whether, in the event of the finding of anything remiss on the part of any individual, the commissioner should indicate that officer should be the subject of criticism.

The commissioner and Superintendent Wohlmann were both questioned over the length of the investigation and the tactics used. When the questions got too challenging, both officers deferred blame to the doctors. The commissioner going as far as to say, 'We were of the opinion the medical men did not go far enough and we decided to ask Dr Murray to discuss it with us at our conference. The doctors' verbal report made to me by Inspector Hollis was that the girl had not died from any unlawful violence.'

Police had clearly been shaken over the addendum to the report, suggesting that Elsie died from a blow with a degree of violence attributed. The commissioner told the inquiry that the police were surprised at the sudden change of opinion of the doctors, 'We were left in the air. We thought we could not rely on the medical evidence and we did not know whether we were going to get another supplementary report.'

The lack of testing of Bill Bayly's alibis was also addressed. Page asked Inspector Hollis, 'Was there any evidence briefed or to be tendered by William Bayly?'

Hollis said he was confident that there wasn't. 'We did not think he could give anything of value. Very early in the inquiry the detectives satisfied themselves Bayly was in Auckland over the critical period. A most searching investigation carried on for months since that time has shown that belief was justified. At least nothing has arisen to shake it.'

Hollis added that Bayly had been interviewed by Kelly and had nothing of substance to assist the inquiry. When asked why police had continued with inquiries if they believed no crime had been committed, Hollis answered that a case such as this when sudden or unexplained death occurs, officers would spare no relaxation of efforts to obtain information.

Hollis told the inquiry that he firmly believed Elsie had died of natural causes and that there was nothing at all suspicious about the case until the bacteriologist's report came through on 28 October. He also defended Kelly's authorisation to remove Elsie's body before determining the true cause of death. In accordance with regulations, Kelly had instructed Constable Collins to check for any obvious signs but none were found. Collins believed the girl died of natural causes or poison and was therefore justified in his decision to authorise removal of the body.

Addressing the issue of Elsie's body being stripped of her clothes before the coroner or pathologist had seen her, Hollis said the lack of obvious injuries justified removing the clothes to check for any signs of violence on the body.

No explanation was given for the lengthy delay in sending the clothes to a bacteriologist. This was acknowledged as having been unacceptable.

Doctors Gilmour and Murray were originally not required to appear, but it seemed police were deferring much of the criticism from themselves onto the medical team so Page called them to give evidence. Both men were extremely upset and angry at having to defend their actions and shifted blame back on police.

Dr Murray, the police surgeon, testified that when he first examined Elsie Walker's body, he believed there was no obvious cause of death but he saw a small injury below the eye he couldn't explain.

The thought vexed him and at night he telephoned Chief Detective Hammond, thinking afterwards the girl could have been hit hard on the head or sandbagged.

Hammond had dismissed the idea saying it was likely she died of exhaustion. Murray disagreed because she had eaten a meal four hours before death and appeared to be very healthy.

He told the inquiry that it was a recognised medical fact death could follow a blow on the head which would cause concussion without injury to the brain and without showing any obvious outward sign. He said he believed that this was such a case. 'We cannot say whether she died of concussion or not. But it was probable the bruise on the skull had something to do with the cause of death.'

Inspector McIlveney asked Dr Murray whether, supposing a crime had been committed, a man arrested and a charge of murder made, there would be sufficient evidence to convict. Murray's answer was no.

Under cross examination, Murray said it was possible for the girl to have died from shock following a rat bite at night as had been originally suggested by police. Murray eliminated shock because of the blow on the head. 'You can eliminate all those possibilities but it all comes back to the blow.'

When Page asked why the doctors had waited two months before altering the report, Murray explained that they had been waiting for the results from poison tests on Elsie's stomach contents and forensic tests on her clothing. These results did not come through until 21 November.

Dr Gilmour, the pathologist, testified that he had seen the mark on Elsie's head and found congestion of the brain. The doctors had been unable to account for the cause of the congestion, which was usually attributed to disease. Assuming Elsie received a blow on the head, which caused concussion, Gilmour admitted that it was possible for the girl to have the head injury and the brain congestion and still live. However, he did say that he thought Elsie would have lost consciousness immediately that the injury was sustained. Gilmour explained to the inquiry that while they knew the injury and congestion had some significance, it was insufficient evidence to form a definite opinion until all angles had been discussed.

The pathologist was then asked if he thought the coroner would have been justified in coming to the conclusion that Elsie's death was due to concussion, had he and Murray stuck to the findings in their original report.

Gilmour replied, 'No. In fact I do not think he was justified in finding that verdict on the second report.' He then conceded that the doctors were no closer to learning the cause of death than when they carried out the post mortem. 'The only evidence we had of the probable cause of death was the blow on the head, but we could not say definitely what had caused the death.'

The laboratory was under Gilmour's control but he said he never saw any of Elsie's clothes. Had he seen them at the post mortem, the presence of blood and other stains would have been detected and he could have determined the likelihood of sexual contact within 24–48 hours. He also said that they might have been able to prove more conclusively whether the blood on the clothing had come from a source other than Elsie. Gilmour stated he assumed police were testing the clothing and did not ask. It was not in his jurisdiction to inquire.

With regard to the police theory that Elsie had died from fear, Gilmour said that he had never performed an autopsy in a determinable case of fright, which was essentially a 'sudden death'.

The Commission of Inquiry concluded on Tuesday 6 March 1929. Fourteen days later, Page submitted his report, finding no fault with police methods and that existing rules and regulations were adequate. He concluded the correct steps were taken during the investigation into Elsie Walker's death. Despite the fact that police failed to establish the manner of the girl's journey from Papamoa to Panmure or the actual cause of death, police had been prompt, thorough and exhaustive. They had interviewed over 1000 people, taken 155 written statements and made 343 written reports. The police were exonerated. But the case refused to go away.

At the conclusion of the inquest in January, Bill Bayly, his wife and baby son returned to their farm near Huntly. Bayly had been cleared of any involvement in his cousin's death but the stigma of association would remain and people found it hard to forget. Newspaper reporters would not let the case be forgotten and regularly beat a trail to his door. As the months progressed, any snippet of news, however trivial, continued to make front page headlines.

D'Renzy Walker accepted his daughter's tragic misfortune and continued to believe she had been abducted by a stranger and murdered. He would never elaborate except he believed it was God's will that Elsie was taken.

The Bayly family in Papamoa took some time to shake off the stigma that the case had caused. The continued media attention saw reporters continually arriving on their doorstep expecting a quote on recent developments. Frank Bayly would answer the door and politely decline interviews. Constance Bayly's status in local society never returned to what it had been before Elsie's death. At one time this would have bothered her, but she had other things on her mind.

A week after the inquest, Constance received a letter from an old friend named Margaret Thomason. As a former neighbour of the Baylys, Margaret had followed the case with interest. Now she felt she was carrying a burden she could no longer bear. From her home in Wanganui, Margaret wrote to Constance to tell her that on the afternoon of Elsie's disappearance, she and her sister had caught the train from Tauranga to Papamoa. On the train, her sister saw Bill Bayly.

Once the sisters realised the significance of this sighting, they agreed not to discuss it with anyone. With the inquest over, and Bill Bayly cleared, Margaret was no longer certain they'd made the right decision.

At the time of Elsie's death, Margaret Thomason and her husband Arthur lived on a block of land directly in front of the Baylys. The Thomason property was near the Baylys' house and the shed where the Whippet had been parked. The car would have left the shed and travelled along a driveway beside the boundary between the two properties, which was about 30 metres from the Thomasons' house.

Margaret Thomason was interviewed by Constable Jackson on 22 October 1928. In that interview she told the officer that she had caught the train some weeks earlier with her sister but could not recall the exact date and adding that she had noticed nothing unusual during the trip.

Margaret also knew Elsie Walker. She recalled Elsie boasting about having several boyfriends on the coast. She told Jackson she had only seen the girl once since May.

In her statement to Constable Jackson, Margaret said she had been at home with her husband on the night of 1 October. They retired to bed around midnight and heard nothing whatsoever after that. She also said she had seen the Baylys everyday thereafter, and believed that Elsie had driven off on her own volition. When asked about Bill, Margaret said she had last seen him at the farm about ten days before Elsie disappeared.

Within a week of reading the verdict, Margaret had a sudden change of heart. A flurry of correspondence between Margaret and Constance ensued. Constance told Margaret that she was going to see Bill to ask him whether he had been on the train. Margaret's response, dated 28 February 1929, makes her view on the matter very clear. 'My dear, if he told you the truth there would be no need of a letter from me. I told you both Mrs Langdon and I were on that particular train, and if Bill won't tell you the truth then I will, as I think you ought to know. He was on that train. I should have told you before I left Papamoa but I did not think that things would have turned out as they have done. Mr and Mrs Bayly, we mourn for both of you and the cross you have to bear, but can you imagine how I feel knowing what I know but not doing my duty as I ought to? I feel a certain degree that I am commit (sic) a crime myself by keeping this knowledge.'

Over the next few months, the exchange of letters increased, with Constance Bayly pleading with Margaret Thomason to resolve the issue privately. Constance viewed the letters as inducements for hush money but she stopped short of actually making that accusation. A telegram received by Constance on 17 June forced her hand. It read, '*Truth* coming to see me next week. Wire immediately if you can come and will remain in town to see you.'

Constance Bayly replied immediately saying she was on her way to Wanganui. She also informed her solicitor, Robert Lusk, who immediately passed the telegram and letters to the police.

The two women arranged to meet at Fosters Hotel at 1.30pm on 22 June. Margaret was late and Constance was about to leave when she finally walked in. The pair walked towards the elevator but Constance grabbed Margaret's arm and said she preferred to take the stairs. Margaret was confused by this but agreed to walk upstairs to Constance's room.

Mrs Bayly was loath to take the lift because at that very moment it was carrying a policeman, Detective Revell, to the second floor. Another officer, Detective Sneddon, was already hiding in the room next to Constance's. Once inside, Constance directed Margaret to sit at a small table. Constance then sat on the other side of the table. She told Margaret that her hearing was deteriorating and to speak up. Sneddon had his ear to the wall next door and made shorthand notes of the hour-long conversation.

According to Sneddon's notes, Thomason told Bayly that she thought that the reporters from *Truth* were only guessing about what she knew. But she was also sure of who she had seen, 'I was on the train and saw Bill. I was not in the same carriage. I am sure it was Bill. He spoke to me and lifted his hat. Mrs Langdon knows Bill. Mrs Langdon drew my attention. I worried. I wish I had not been on that train. . . If he had not lifted his hat, spoken, may not have known him. Not actually spoke, raised hat. What was he doing there?'

For the next hour Constance kept asking Margaret what it was that she wanted the Baylys to do. Margaret constantly evaded the question insisting that she'd just come to talk and that it should be the Baylys to suggest 'what to do'.

At one point Sneddon heard someone check the bedroom door and the wardrobe door. It seemed that Margaret had her suspicions that the conversation was being listened to. She refused to buy into Constance's clumsy attempts to induce a bribe. Money may have been on Margaret's mind but it seems she was waiting for Constance to suggest a figure. Suspicious or not, she continued her conversation with Constance, telling her that she wasn't only afraid of the reporters from *Truth*.

To which Mrs Bayly responded, 'The police are the right ones to ask questions. It would kill him [D'Renzy Walker] if his girl's name is dragged over again. Do not let *Truth* worry you. Why do you not go to the police? Police are best friends better than *Truth*.'

Mrs Thomason replied by reiterating that she'd seen Bill on the train. At this point, Constance decided that the conversation was near its end and asked Margaret again what she wanted, 'Tell me what to do and I will do it'

Thomason's response a suitably cagey, 'You will have to let me think.'

The pair left the room and talked for a few minutes in the lobby, passing Detective Revell as they went. They walked together for ten minutes before Constance returned to the hotel. There she told police that Margaret had suggested returning to her home. Constance declined and once again asked her what she wanted.

According to Constance Bayly, Margaret asked her how much she valued her boy's life. Constance responded that it was a difficult question as she had many sons but, if forced, she would value his life at £10,000. Having named the amount, Constance said she then asked if that was the amount Margaret wanted.

Margaret's alleged response, 'Yes and in cash.'

There was a further condition, according to Constance, and that was that Margaret Thomason refused to sign anything to guarantee that she wouldn't demand more money later. Constance told Margaret that she would need to consult with her husband before releasing that amount of money then bade her former neighbour goodbye.

The next day, Detective Sneddon visited Margaret Thomason at her home. She agreed to give him a statement. In it she admitted that she had seen Bill Bayly on the train from Tauranga to Papamoa on the day of Elsie's disappearance.

She said her sister, Kathleen Langdon, had pointed him out saying, 'There is Billy Bayly.' Margaret said that he appeared to have heard them, because he looked towards them, raised his hat and bowed.

When the train stopped at Papamoa, Margaret and her sister got off and waited for Bayly as they thought they could walk home together. He did not get off the train and they figured he might have alighted earlier at Otaimatua, about five kilometres from Papamoa.

Margaret admitted not mentioning any of this in her first statement saying that she did not want to bring additional problems to the Baylys. She told Detective Sneddon she had wanted to discuss the matter with Constance Bayly and had lied about a representative of *Truth* coming to get Constance to come to Wanganui. She denied being motivated by money.

Of the discussion that had taken place outside the hotel the previous day, Margaret's version of events was very different. She said that Constance had offered her £10,000 and she had been horrified. She said she had not met Mrs Bayly expecting a pay-off.

At the end of the interview, Sneddon told Thomason that he was going to interview her sister. As soon as he left, she packed her suitcase and headed for Te Puke. There she booked an appointment with her solicitor and attempted to contact her sister.

Police had already traced Kathleen Langdon to a boarding house in Auckland. She had not been in contact with her sister since the Thomasons had moved to Wanganui in November 1928 and therefore had not had a chance to collude with them on the latest developments.

Kathleen Langdon was somewhat taken aback when approached by the intimidating figure of Detective Sergeant Bickerdike. He asked her whether she had seen Bill Bayly on the train. She was quite clear in her response, 'I did not see any of the Baylys on the train that day. My sister made no mention of seeing any of the Baylys on the train. I am positive I did not see any of the Baylys on Monday 1 October 1928, certainly not Bill Bayly, and no person has ever told me that they saw Bill Bayly that day.'

And with that Kathleen Langdon promptly disappeared.

In the meantime, Margaret Thomason decided to sell her story to *Truth*, and yet again the case of Elsie Walker dominated the headlines. Upon hearing of the contradictions to her story, Margaret and another sister, Mrs Richardson, travelled to Auckland to try to locate Kathleen Langdon but she could not be found.

Kathleen Langdon suddenly resurfaced on 28 June, having spent several weeks on Great Barrier Island, seemingly unaware of all the fuss. She was shepherded to Te Puke by her sisters where she made an amendment to her statements in front of Mr Cooney, and in the presence of the disbelieving detectives Bickerdike and Sneddon.

'On Monday 1 October 1928, I saw Bill Bayly standing in passageway as the guard came through. I had a good view of Bill Bayly. I drew my sister's attention to Bill Bayly. She nodded to him. I spoke to him.'

When asked why it had taken her until now to come forward, Kathleen said that she had made a pact with her sister never to say anything.

Truth broke the story of the sighting of Bill Bayly with a front page headline along with excerpts from the conversation that had taken place between Margaret Thomason and Constance Bayly in Wanganui.

As a result, the whole case, the coroner's findings and the subsequent commission of inquiry were once again called into question. The coroner, Mr Hunt, publicly recommended the inquest be reopened or a prosecution be instituted for perjury.

Truth led with the question which was on everybody's minds: 'It seems imminently logical to say that the new evidence now available warrants a Supreme Court order for a fresh inquiry into the Elsie Walker tragedy.'

The question was put to the Minister of Justice, Thomas Wilford, in parliament. He told the house that there was no statutory provision for the reopening of an inquest, unless some illegality had taken place during the conduct of the first inquest. He also said that if there was any new evidence in a case it should be put before a Supreme Court judge who would then decide on the merits of the evidence before him.

Wilford was not prepared to grant a new inquiry despite the new evidence from Margaret Thomason and Kathleen Langdon. He had good grounds not to accept their evidence: their statements were made eight months after they had originally spoken to police; there was no record of Bayly booking a ticket to Papamoa that day; and to have been on the 4pm train from Tauranga, Bayly would have needed to have been on the train from Auckland the night before and there were witnesses placing him in Auckland that evening. Despite the weight of evidence against the sisters' claims, a public outcry ensued and the minister was accused of ignoring vital new evidence in the case.

In October 1929, hundreds of people braved a cold wet night to pack into the Auckland Town Hall. There they heard various speakers who called for the government to take some action on the Elsie Walker case. Mrs Soljak, the secretary for the Auckland women's branch of the Labour Party, had organised the meeting. She urged the Minister of Justice to change the necessary laws so that the Elsie Walker case could be reopened, adding, 'It would not benefit Elsie Walker but it was for the sake of any other Elsie Walkers.'

Mrs Soljak then asked the gathering, 'Do men and women acquiesce and thus agree to connive at the unfortunate Elsie Walker case being hushed up finally and for all time?'

The response was a loud and animated, 'NO'.

A petition with over 15,000 signatures was presented to parliament. But the minister was not one to be pressured into making a decision.

Eventually Wilford agreed that a bill to change the law should be passed but not until the following year and he made it clear that he would not order the reopening of the inquest. While the public believed he was hiding behind the law, Wilford did actually spend some time considering the case and examining the new statements provided by Thomason and Langdon. He concluded that it was unnecessary to re-open the inquest into Elsie Walker's death because no fresh evidence had come forward that would establish the cause of death and he believed that the current laws were adequate to deal with any new evidence. He also felt that the women's statements were contradictory and of little evidential value, and he said that he believed Thomason had attempted to blackmail Constance Bayly.

At the completion of his investigations, Wilford concluded that there was not the slightest justification shown for reopening the inquest, nor any evidence discovered to throw any light on the cause of Elsie Walker's death. 'I refuse absolutely to assist in what must only be a farce and cannot help in the slightest degree to elucidate the cause of her death.'

The public were not appeased and by the end of the year, Wilford had been seconded to London to become New Zealand high commissioner. The new Minister of Justice, Sir Thomas Sidey, announced an amendment to the Coroners Act giving power to reopen an inquest or to hold a fresh inquest. The amendment did not allow for retrospective cases to be considered so the case of Elsie Walker was never reopened.

The case remained in the memories of many who had been involved in it for years to come. In his 1966 memoir, *A Long Brief*, crown prosecutor, Vincent Meredith gave an account of what he believed had happened to Elsie Walker. 'My own personal view was that the actual death of Elsie Walker was an accident. In the attempt at seduction in the dark garage at the back of Bayly's house it was quite possible that, while struggling, Elsie Walker hit, when falling, some object such as the handle of the car, which made the small bruise on the skull from which she died. It was certainly not an intentional blow, as the injuries to the skull would have been very much greater. Whoever it was, finding he had what he thought to be a dead girl on his hands, took the car and the body with him in fear.'

Whether Meredith's version of events—or anyone else's for that matter—is the true one will never be known. Through all the controversy, court hearings and debate, people seemed to lose sight of the fact a 17-year old girl had died. It's hard to imagine what Elsie, a timid girl from the backblocks of New Zealand would have made of all the fuss.

6. Serial Killer?

I understand that some years ago, the accused was linked with the death of a young woman. At no time was it proven, or indeed seriously suggested that the accused who now stands in the dock, charged with multiple murder, was in any way connected with that matter. You must dismiss from your minds anything you have heard or read about this affair. The accused is entitled to a fair trial on the serious charges he faces and the facts attendant to those charges are all you are to weigh and consider in his trial.

Sir Justice Herdman in his opening address to the jury
in Rex v Bayly, 21 May 1934

Situated 14 kilometres north-west of Huntly, Ruawaro was sufficiently isolated for Bill Bayly to hide away from the scandal of being accused of killing his cousin, Elsie Walker. Having moved to Ruawaro in November 1928, Bayly made little effort to become part of the tight-knit local community.

Once a confident and cocky young man, the death of Elsie Walker and subsequent events hardened him. Family members said the ordeal of the investigation, inquest and commission of inquiry had made Bill defensive, bitter and suspicious of most people. While fiercely loyal to, and protective of, his wife and family, Bayly would overreact to trivial things.

Although he chose not to integrate into the social aspects of the small community, Bayly would go out of his way to help other farmers. An unwitting comment, an innocent innuendo or some other action not meant to cause offence would often cause Bayly to end his friendships with local farmers. At any supposed slight, he would cut himself off from any future communication and only in rare cases would he ever forgive.

A local couple who would feel the full force of Bayly's wrath was Samuel and Christobel Lakey. Samuel had worked for Frank Bayly as a carpenter before he went to fight in the First World War. Upon his return, Lakey was one of 10,000 returned servicemen who were given loans to buy or lease farms through the Discharged Soldiers Settlement Act. He purchased land from his former boss in 1919.

In 1933, Sam Lakey was 47 years old, and Christobel, or Pet as she was affectionately known, was 54. They were described as a quiet and well-respected couple who were very popular with their neighbours. While her husband was busy on the farm, Pet Lakey looked after an array of domestic animals, including ducks, geese and turkeys. While she might have had a way with the animals, Pet was also known for having a colourful turn of phrase and a quick temper.

For the first few years after Bill Bayly and his family moved to Ruawaro, the Lakeys and the Baylys enjoyed a cordial working relationship. While the two couples didn't socialise, Bill Bayly and Sam Lakey worked alongside each other when necessary. Lakey helped Bayly build and alter farm dwellings. Bayly would return the favour by assisting on Lakey's farm when he was needed. Together they built a milk stand and shelter by Lakey's gate, which housed both of their cream cans until they were collected and taken to the local dairy factory.

The pair also enjoyed a working arrangement whereby Lakey allowed Bayly's sheep to graze on his land, and once ready, Lakey would slaughter them and they would share the mutton.

This cordial relationship soured one day in August 1932 when Bayly did not receive his fair measure of meat. He found out that Lakey had given away two hoggets without his knowledge. Bayly was furious believing that Lakey had ripped him off.

A few days later, Lakey went into the paddock where the sheep had been grazing and was shocked to see they had all vanished. Together with a neighbouring farmer, Lakey went searching for the sheep. They soon found tracks that led onto Bayly's property. Rumour had it that Bayly had mustered his sheep into a neighbouring yard, before trucking them to Franklin for sale.

Samuel Lakey was furious. When he found Bill Bayly at the sale yards, his neighbour didn't deny what he had done. Lakey threatened to tell police: he had fattened the sheep therefore he was entitled to a half-share of the profits. Bayly offered to pay him but he refused saying he would not accept dishonest money. He would not be bought and made sure that everyone else around the district knew of Bayly's dishonesty.

Around the same time, a thief had been stealing pieces of machinery, particularly separator parts, from cowsheds during the night. This wasn't one or two isolated incidents and most of the local farmers had been hit. When Lakey's farm was hit, he happily spread the word that he suspected Bill Bayly.

Lakey did nothing about his suspicion but another local farmer, Arnold Wright, contacted Huntly police and suggested Bayly as a suspect. Constable Robertson visited all farmers in the area. Bill Bayly told the officer that there was nothing missing from his shed, adding that a thief would have a hard time because his property was not easily accessible by road. Bayly blamed Lakey for what he saw as an outright accusation from the police.

The animosity turned to open hostility with harsh words continually exchanged between the two men, with Pet Lakey also chipping in with her harsh tongue.

The police investigation didn't assuage the Lakeys' belief that Bayly was responsible for the rash of thefts. They continued to tell other locals of their suspicions, saying that Bayly was the only farmer in the district who had not had anything stolen and adding that his equipment always seemed to be in a pristine condition and did not suffer the same problems faced by other farmers.

Bayly scoffed at the insinuation that he kept his machinery in good order by stealing from other people. It was no secret that his father was very wealthy and provided him with the most modern equipment available.

To counter the Lakeys' stories, Bayly began spreading rumours that his neighbour was in a dire financial position and was close to having to walk off his farm. For a farmer in that era, this was the cruellest insult. While he was regaling local farmers of the Lakeys' problems, Bayly was also allegedly heard to say that if Lakey ever set foot on his land, he would shoot him.

In October 1932, Bayly decided he did not want to keep using the gate through the Lakeys' property near their house to reach the road. He wanted to cut a gate through their property further down the boundary fence. He asked Len Stent to accompany him to put the proposal to Lakey. Stent worked for Bayly as a farm labourer but had previously worked for the Lakeys and knew them well.

The pair rode up to the Lakey house and called out for Sam Lakey. According to Stent, the Lakeys were not pleased to see them but Bayly came straight to the point and asked to be allowed to cut a gate further down the property closer to Bains Road. Lakey refused point blank, saying, 'You won't cut no fence.'

In Stent's account of the meeting, he said Lakey then looked towards him and said, 'Keep out of it, Stent. This game is more serious than what you think.'

The conversation between Bayly and the Lakeys lasted about ten minutes with both sides becoming increasingly abusive. As Bayly rode away, Stent said he remarked that the couple would not see the next season out.

It's not known whether Pet Lakey heard the comment but she called out after Bayly, 'Your guilty conscious is pricking you! You murdered Elsie Walker and we expect the same!'

According to Stent, Bayly was so furious he rode down to Bains Road and removed the roof of the cream stand and carried it over to his own gate, saying, 'I'm not going to let those miserable bastards have it!'

Over the next few months, Lakey regularly complained to neighbours that his milk cans had been tampered with or the contents tipped over. In the tough economic times, the Lakeys—like many other farmers around the country—were struggling financially. Their feud with Bill Bayly was costing them money they could not afford yet neither side relented.

Some friends of the Lakeys from Auckland came and stayed at the farm for their Christmas holidays in 1932. One morning the visitors walked outside and witnessed Lakey and Bayly arguing over the fence. The argument was said to have been over one of Bayly's bulls, which had broken through the boundary fence and was found grazing on the Lakey's property. Pet Lakey had set her dog onto the bull, which made it very difficult for Bayly to calm the creature and lead it back to his land.

Bayly stormed up to the house to confront Pet Lakey. Her husband came out of the house and ordered Bayly to leave the property at once, adding that if Bayly ever set foot on his land again, he would beat him.

Bayly made a similar threat back causing Pet Lakey to threaten him. 'You bastard! I'll tell your father about you. You can't leave us alone! You won't leave us alone!'

The New Year brought no respite to the feud but each man toiled away on their farms struggling to keep up with the economic situation.

On Thursday 12 October 1933, the Baylys went into Huntly to shop for their weekly supplies. There Bill Bayly bought a new single shot .22 Spandau pea rifle and 200 cartridges from Farmers Trading Company.

At about 11.30 am the following Sunday, 15 October, Raymond Brader, the 11-year-old stepson of Arnold Wright, rode over to the Lakeys' for lunch. He arrived in time to help Pet feed the animals and prepare lunch. Sam Lakey came in at about 12.30pm and the three enjoyed their lunch together, talking about what Raymond had been up to and indulging in a bit of local gossip.

While Pet did the dishes, Sam played cards with Raymond before going back to work on the farm. The lad stayed at Lakeys' until about 2.30pm when Pet kissed him goodbye and he headed home.

At about 4.30pm that afternoon, one of the Lakeys' neighbours, Gwen Stevens looked across to the Lakeys' paddocks and saw Pet Lakey walking towards the cowshed carrying a cream tin. Sam Lakey was following close behind his wife bringing the cows in for milking. Gwen and Pet didn't get on and had recently had a row over Pet Lakey's use of foul language in front of the Stevens children.

At around 6.15 that night Gwen's husband, Bertram, was just finishing milking when he noticed a man turning the cows out of the milking shed onto pasture on the Lakey's property. It was getting dark and Stevens was surprised Lakey was only now turning out his cows. Lakey usually finished milking well before anyone else but Stevens decided that Lakey must have been behind schedule that day.

At five o'clock the following morning, Gwen and Bertram Stevens went to do their morning milking. Gwen Stevens was surprised to see the Lakeys' cows still in the paddock where they had been turned out the evening before. Lakey was usually just as diligent with his morning milking as he was at night. Bertram wondered to his wife if Sam Lakey might be ill.

At 7.30am, Stevens took his cream cans down to Bains Road for collection. The truck driver was there talking to Arnold Wright. He told the two farmers that when he collected the Lakeys' cream cans, they had been lighter than usual and in a different place. The driver said that Lakey was always methodical about how he placed his cans but that morning the cans looked as if they'd been left by someone in a rush. Adding to the mystery, an empty can from the Saturday pick-up was still on the road.

Stevens told the driver and Wright that the Lakeys' cattle had not been milked and wondered why Sam would have put his cream cans out before the morning milking. The two farmers decided to investigate and walked up to the Lakey house.

When they reached the house, they found the door open. They called out to the Lakeys but received no response so they headed to the cowshed to see if the couple were there. The milking apparatus and separator shed looked clean as if Lakey or his wife cleaned the shed after last evening's milking but there was no sign of the couple.

Wright and Stevens were worried and decided to head back to the house to investigate further. There they found the table set for a meal. The meat and potatoes had been cooked but had cooled some hours earlier. There was also a rice pudding waiting to be served. In the sink were two empty cups. It appeared the Lakeys had had afternoon tea but had not eaten dinner.

The men decided the best course of action was to call the police. Wright headed over to see Charles Sanson, another neighbour, and called the Huntly police from Sanson's house. He spoke to Constable Robertson and told him that the Lakeys were missing.

Before going out to the farm, Robertson telephoned everyone in Ruawaro to find out if anyone had seen the Lakeys. When he telephoned Bill Bayly, he mistakenly asked Bayly if he had seen Sanson. Bayly asked him to clarify whether he meant the man with three children. In response, Robertson corrected himself and said he meant Lakey. Bayly did not respond.

Charles Sanson and Arnold Wright joined Bertram Stevens in the cowshed. With nothing else to do, the three milked the Lakeys' 35 cows while they waited for the police to arrive. Just as they were turning the cows out, another neighbour, John Slater, arrived offering his assistance.

The farmers returned to the house just as constables Robertson and Elms arrived. They walked around the house and noticed that the beds had not been slept in. A double-barrelled shotgun and a single-barrelled shotgun stood against a wall in the passageway. Neither looked as if they'd been fired for a long time.

The officers then headed to the cow shed. While they were there, John Slater walked over to Pet Lakey's duck pond, which was between the house and the shed. Slater lightly kicked at a pile of manure sacks by the pond before lifting one of the sacks.

The men in the cowshed heard him cry out.

'Here's Pet!'

Constable Elms carefully lifted the sacks off one by one. There were 11 in total. Beneath the pile was the body of Christobel Lakey. She was face down in the duck pond. Carefully turning her over, Elms noticed a small abrasion to her chin. Some of her teeth looked to have been knocked out and there was blood and froth oozing from her nostrils. She was dressed in the clothes she normally would wear in the cowshed.

As the men scoured the farm for Sam Lakey, Constable Robertson telephoned for a doctor. He then carefully placed Pet's body on an old door frame and brought it into the kitchen. Robertson then phoned senior police in Auckland. A message was then relayed to Inspector Hollis of the Auckland detective branch. Hollis had been involved in the Elsie Walker investigation and later said that when he heard about the discovery in Ruawaro, he wondered whether Bill Bayly was involved.

Around midday, Constable Elms began visiting Ruawaro residents, starting with the Baylys. As Elms approached the house, Bill Bayly sauntered out. The police officer told him about finding Mrs Lakey's body. He said that in response, Bayly stared at him for a few seconds and said, 'I suppose you already know we were not on friendly terms?'

Elms said he was not interested in any petty squabbling, his only interest was in finding Samuel Lakey. Bayly said nothing and returned to the house.

An hour later, Constable Robertson was returning to Huntly when he passed Bayly's property and noticed Bayly riding quickly towards him trying to get his attention. Robertson stopped and Bayly pulled up asking if anything was being done about Lakey's cattle. Robertson said it was all taken care of. He told Bayly he was organising a search for Sam Lakey and asked him if he would join. Bayly turned and rode off without replying.

Detectives Thomas Allsopp and Thomas Sneddon along with constables McEachern, McCurragh and Watts travelled directly to Ruawaro from Auckland.

The Auckland police team arrived at Lakey's farm at around 4pm. They spent Monday evening encamped at the Lakey house, carrying out a detailed search. Among the pile of correspondence found in a bedroom drawer was an unsealed envelope which had been addressed but not sent. The letter read:

Ruawaro,
Huntly, 9/1/33

Dear Mr Bayly,
I am writing to ask you if you could make it convenient to come and see us. I am so sorry to trouble you, but Bill is on the warpath again with his spiteful annoyances.

We won't want to send for the police until we have given you a chance to settle with him. He will have to be made to keep the peace. We are sick of his dirty spite.

Please come, and we will tell you all. We have waited for the Christmas holidays to go before writing, and I hope the New Year will be a happier one for yourself and Mrs Bayly and family. Believe me,
Yours sincerely,
Christobel Lakey

With the author dead and her husband missing, the police could not know what had driven Pet Lakey to write this letter or why she had not sent it. At this stage of the investigation, there was nothing suspicious to suggest Bill Bayly's involvement.

Early on Tuesday 17 October, a number of volunteers left their farming duties to search for Samuel Lakey. Constable Robertson was in charge of the search.

Despite police assurances that no foul play was suspected, the searchers didn't think they'd find Lakey alive. Rumours abounded in Ruawaro that Pet Lakey had drowned and her husband had killed himself. If he had gone away to commit suicide, he might be found hanging in one of the ti trees or lying dead from a shotgun wound. The likeliest area would be the long grass and scrub in the marshes surrounding nearby Lake Whangape.

Among the searchers was Bill Bayly. Before the search briefing, he was seen to quietly detach himself from the main group and wander over to peer in the manure shed and down a rubbish hole where Lakey was known to discard old paint tins and similar material.

As the morning wore on it began to rain and Bayly decided to return to his farm. Constable McEachern asked if he could accompany him and Bayly consented, inviting the officer to stay for lunch.

Over lunch, Bayly told the officer he didn't believe that Lakey would have killed himself. He said that he thought his neighbour had found his wife's body and wandered off. Bayly said he thought Sam Lakey would be found sitting in the scrub on the other side of the lake.

Mid-morning on Monday, Dr MacFarlane of Huntly and Dr Waddell of Hamilton performed the post mortem examination on Christobel Lakey's body. Police briefed the doctors to pay special attention to the possibility that Lakey had been poisoned on account of the froth around her mouth. No traces of poison were found.

They found bruising on and around her jaw and two scratches on her right cheek. These were consistent with her having received two heavy blows to the face or having suffered a heavy fall. There was also bruising on her right elbow and on one of her knees.

The post mortem found that she had probably been unconscious but still alive when she was put face first in the pond. Her death was likely to have been as a result of being unable to raise her head to breathe. However there was no water found in her lungs to suggest she had drowned.

The doctors were unable to give an exact cause of death but when pressed later, Dr MacFarlane stated, 'I have suggested suffocation. That would be smothering. Strangulation would show visible signs. Smothering is one of the causes of asphyxia which leaves no traces behind. A face immersed in water would not cause smothering unless water was drawn into the nasal passages or unless the patient died immediately on reaching the water.'

Dr Waddell believed Lakey had been rendered unconscious following a blow to the face and that she died with her face under the water. He believed her death was probably due to asphyxia caused by 'occlusion of air by water', which was, in effect, drowning.

Detectives Allsopp and Sneddon had noticed Bayly loitering around the Lakey property on the first day of the search. Later that afternoon, Sneddon called at his house to take a statement.

Bayly said that on Sunday between 4.00pm and 4.30pm, he was returning from Charlie Calvert's place and had seen Samuel Lakey rounding up his cattle. After having tea with his wife and children, Bayly said he'd brought his cows in for milking which finished around 7.30pm. After that he said he'd returned home to eat his dinner before going to bed some time between 9pm and 10pm.

As Detective Sneddon left the Bayly property, he met Constable McEachern. The constable said he had walked the boundary fence between the Bayly property and the Lakey farm. In the damp grass on Bayly's side he said he'd noticed what looked like sledge marks in a semi-circle leading from Bayly's private road, over to the fence and back again.

Underneath a wattle tree about 40 metres from the tracks was an old cart. The officers went to have a look at the cart and found that the grass beneath it was fresh indicating that the cart had been put there recently. The cart was covered in chicken droppings, which was unusual as there was no evidence of fowls roosting in that particular tree.

Police traced the wheel marks from the wattle tree across to a point at the boundary fence. Almost directly across on Bayly's property were the sledge tracks, which appeared to have come up to this point from Bayly's private road. Between the cart tracks on the Lakeys' property and the sled marks on the Baylys' property were a fence and a space of about three metres. Cart tracks were also found in the direction of the Lakeys' cowshed. On further investigation, police found that the cart had stood in the Lakeys' backyard near their hen house for the last 10 years.

On the morning of Wednesday 18 October, the detectives asked Bayly if they could examine his sledge. He obliged but objected to them removing the front board as it would leave him being unable to use it.

The detectives told Bayly about the tracks between his farm and the Lakeys' place. Bayly seemed surprised but told them he had taken the sledge up to the fence as he had noticed a telegraph pole that he thought was broken. He said that when he got up there he realised the pole was secure and came home.

Allsopp noticed Bayly carrying a knife in his belt and asked if he could inspect it. It was razor sharp and seemed to have several small turns at the edge of blade. Allsopp commented that it was so sharp it would have been useful for shaving.

The detective also noticed that Bayly had several small cuts on his hand. He explained that he had got them while helping a neighbour, George Furniss, erect a windmill.

The following morning, while loading Lakeys' cart onto a truck for transportation to Auckland, Detective Allsopp noticed some bloodstains on the cart's cross bar. There were also numerous small blood specks visible underneath the cart.

This immediately threw suspicion on Bayly's sledge. A re-examination of it showed minute blood specks. In several places, though, the underside of the cart had been carved or whittled away as if someone was trying to remove something—possibly bloodstains.

Meanwhile, during a search of the Lakeys' implement shed, Constable Flynn found a fence batten covered with blood specks. Allsopp directed officers to make an immediate close examination of the shed. As they proceeded, they found further traces of blood on some benzene drums, boxes and on loose stone chips and wood shavings on the floor. Some of the battens at the rear of the shed also looked as if they had been carved out as if to remove something.

Officers also searched the manure shed that they'd noticed Bayly peering into on the morning of the initial search. More bloodstains were found on the shed wall and specks of blood were found on fence palings stored at the back of the shed. It was too early to confirm whether these were human blood stains, but Allsopp was suspicious. He believed they were no longer looking for a missing man but rather they were looking for a murder victim.

From the locality of the various bloodstains, Allsopp surmised that Lakey had probably been shot as he walked back onto his property after milking. If this was true, he would not have seen his wife as she lay dying—or dead—in the duck pond.

That afternoon an Auckland pathologist, Dr Gilmour, arrived to examine Christobel Lakey's body. Gilmour had been asked to undertake the examination as doctors MacFarlane and Waddell had been unable to confirm a cause of death.

Gilmour was only too familiar with the Bayly family as he had been the pathologist who first examined Elsie Walker five years earlier and he had also been the author of the controversial addendum to Elsie's post mortem stating that she had died from the blow to her head.

Given that the body had already been examined, putrefaction had set in. Gilmour was therefore at a disadvantage and had to rely on notes taken at the initial post mortem. He largely agreed with the initial post mortem but elaborated, 'The findings point to death by asphyxia. There is no evidence that the air was cut off by strangling or foreign body in the throat or other method of depriving the body of air. The findings are not consistent with a comato-asphyxial death. They are entirely consistent with death due to immersion of the face in water while she was not making a serious struggle for breath.'

He concluded that Christobel Lakey had died of asphyxia due to drowning.

Gilmour was then asked to test the blood on the wheels and frame of the cart. He was able to confirm that the blood found was indeed human blood. The blood type corresponded with specks found on Bayly's sledge.

On the afternoon of Saturday 21 October, detectives Allsopp, Sneddon, Findlay and Chief Detective Sweeney went to see Bill Bayly. Allsopp asked him for his sheath knife and he handed it over. The knife was now extremely blunt.

Bayly was then asked to provide a further statement outlining his movements on the morning of Monday 16 October.

Bayly said he got up between 6am and 7am and went straight to milk his cows, finishing between 8.30am and 9am. He said he then cleaned up the shed and carried his two cream cans down to Bains Road. He said that as he returned to his house, he noticed that the telegraph pole near the boundary fence looked to have been damaged so he rode there to check it out. When he got to the fence he realised that the pole was in order. He shook the pole several times to be sure before returning the empty cream cans to the cowshed and going home for breakfast.

Bayly said he didn't know why he hadn't told the police about inspecting the telegraph pole in his first statement but that he didn't think it seemed important at the time. He denied riding his horse near the boundary fence an hour earlier and returning with a sledge. He added that anybody who claimed to have seen him was a liar.

Sneddon served Bayly with a search warrant and in response Bayly invited the detectives to search his property. Sweeney asked Bayly to fetch the clothes he had been wearing the previous Sunday. He came back with a pair of denim trousers. As he handed them over, a .22 calibre shell fell out of the pocket. Bayly explained it away by saying he had shot some pukeko that Saturday.

Detectives also found a shirt with faint blood stains on it. Bayly said he couldn't remember if he'd worn that particular shirt on Sunday. He explained the blood stains by saying that he'd been wearing it while one of his cows had calved.

Bayly then led police to his cowshed where he handed over his shotgun, explaining that the traces of blood on the gun's barrel were from shooting a hare and then hitting it over the head.

When asked about ammunition, Bayly said he had purchased 200 rounds the previous week. However when he reached for the box where he kept it, there was no ammunition. Bayly could not explain its whereabouts, inferring that it must have been stolen. When asked who would have stolen it, Bayly replied, 'I do not know. I would not suggest the police would.'

Detectives also interviewed Charlie Calvert and George Furniss, a couple of local farmers who were on friendly terms with Bill Bayly.

Charles Calvert said that Bayly had visited him between 3pm and 4pm on Sunday 15 October. Bayly told him that he was going to Auckland for a couple of days on the following Tuesday and asked Calvert to milk his cows. Calvert told police that he had just returned from Auckland when Bayly visited him and the pair discussed the condition of Churchill Road, a back road on the way to Auckland. Calvert said he'd told Bill that conditions were rough but by taking this route he would be able shave at least 45 minutes off the trip. When Bayly was leaving he mentioned that he was going to call in and see George Furniss on his way home.

When they interviewed George Furniss, the farmer told police that he hadn't seen Bayly that afternoon. He said it was strange as Bayly usually came over on a Sunday afternoon to play tennis and have a few beers. Furniss was one of the few farmers in the area who home killed beasts so Bayly invariably left his place with his meat for the week before heading home to do the evening milking. George Furniss was also one of the few people in the district who Bill Bayly truly counted as a friend.

While he told police it was unusual that Bayly hadn't called in that Sunday, Furniss said he put it down to the fact that Bayly had said something about planning one of his regular trips to Auckland to visit family and friends. He said Bayly had also mentioned going to a play at the Saint James Theatre while he was there, which had made Furniss laugh as Bayly didn't seem like the type to go to the theatre. According to Furniss, Bayly had taken the jibe well and had replied saying that he was really quite cultured.

Furniss said he couldn't recall when Bayly had said he was going to Auckland but because he hadn't turned up for his regular Sunday session, he thought it might have been that weekend.

When asked whether Bayly had cut his hand while helping him to put up a windmill, Furniss said he didn't know anything about the cuts or the supposed windmill.

Furniss and his wife claimed to have seen Bayly on Monday afternoon at 1.30pm when he collected his meat and they discussed the disappearance of Lakey. Mrs Furniss had noticed Bayly's eyes had been extremely bloodshot, as if he had been exposed to thick smoke. Constable McEachern also noticed Bayly's bloodshot eyes when he had lunch with Bayly earlier that day.

Another neighbour, named Herbert, told police that his cowshed had a clear view across the lake to Bayly's cowshed. He said that on the Sunday evening as he finished milking, he noticed thick smoke rising from Bayly's cowshed. When Herbert was getting ready for bed a few hours later, he noticed that the smoke seemed to have got thicker.

The number of police camped out at the Lakey property had swelled to 18 and the painstaking search for Samuel Lakey continued. Bayly did not take part in the search but was often seen sitting on his horse observing events from a safe distance. Bayly never initiated contact with police but when they tried to engage with him, he responded politely with an air of sarcasm. Several times he asked police if they believed he was hiding Lakey or if they thought he had something to do with his disappearance. Often he would turn and ride away refusing to listen to their responses.

On the night of Wednesday 25 October, detectives were seated around the Lakey kitchen table, planning the next day's search, when Bayly suddenly appeared at the door. He displayed no emotion but told the officers that at about 7.30pm he had finished milking and cleaning up, and had returned to his top shed. His dog had started barking at another dog, which Bayly quickly cornered. He told police he believed the dog belonged to Arnold Wright, with whom he did not get along. He said he then saw a man running across the ridge but he wasn't sure if it was Wright. He then told police that he thought someone was planting things on his property that could land him in trouble. The officers listened to Bayly's story and told him they would investigate.

One of the Auckland constables who was billeted with the Wrights confirmed that Wright had not left the house after he had returned from milking that evening.

Allsopp and Sneddon found Bayly in his yard the next day and took a statement. The detectives noticed a short-handled shovel that had been leaning against the wall of the cowshed and asked if they could examine it. Bayly told them it was his only shovel and he needed it. The detectives scraped a sample off the tip of the shovel and sent it for testing.

Police and volunteers continued searching the swamps surrounding the lake. Late on the afternoon of 30 October, a constable unearthed the double barrel of a shotgun from swampy land on Bayly's property. A few minutes later the fore end of a double barrel shotgun and the stock of a pea rifle were unearthed. All of the gun parts had been forced down into the swamp.

Detective Allsopp told Bayly what he had found. Bayly seemed surprised and told the officer that he didn't know how the guns came to be there. He then left saying he wanted a cup of tea. A few minutes later, Bayly returned and demanded to know who else's swamps had been searched that day. The officers explained that they had searched a number of other properties, assuring him that they were not just concentrating on his. Bayly seemed satisfied with the response and left.

Allsopp followed Bayly back to his cowshed. In a statement, Bayly denied being responsible for putting the guns in the swamp.

At 6pm, while Allsopp was still at the cowshed, Constable Taylor found another rifle barrel in the swamp. It was getting dark so Allsopp ordered two constables to guard the swamp until morning. In order to not draw attention to themselves, the two men lay flat in a silage pit. At about 8.45pm, the constables heard the rattle of cream cans coming from the direction of Bayly's cowshed. About ten minutes later, they saw Bayly walking down the hill towards them. It was dark but from their vantage point, there was sufficient moonlight to see him approaching the swamp. Bayly walked across to the sticks that marked where the gun parts had been found. He looked as if he was about to touch them, when the constables ordered him to stop. Bayly recoiled in surprise but then told the policemen that he knew they were there all along.

Early the next morning, more police joined the search of the swamp. The talk that morning was of Bayly's bizarre behaviour and his growing hostility towards police. However there was no firm evidence he had any involvement in Pet Lakey's death.

On 1 November, Commissioner Wohlmann visited the Lakey farm, and announced a reward of £100 for any person who could succeed in locating Samuel Lakey. Numerous false sightings of Lakey were reported and these were followed up but discounted. Initially newspapers reported the murder-suicide theory but this quickly gave rise to the story of a killer husband on the run. These theories were concocted by reporters listening to local gossip. The police were giving little information away.

When Bill Bayly's name was thrown into the mix, the nation's fascination was revived. Five years earlier, the Elsie Walker case had stirred public sentiment and Bill Bayly's presence in Ruawaro saw his dead cousin's name back in the headlines.

On 2 November, police employed the services of a De Havilland Moth aeroplane to fly around the area to take scene photographs of the farms. Police had never used aerial photography as a means to solve a crime before, which proved their dedication to finding Sam Lakey.

On 16 November, the results of the examination of the scrapings from Bayly's shovel were released. The ash residue contained wood charcoal, burnt bone and molten lead globules. Detectives Allsopp and Sneddon visited the Bayly farm and asked to check his cowshed. Sneddon swept the floor and removed further samples.

Outside the shed was a 12 gallon copper sitting on top of half of a benzene drum. In the bottom of the drum was ash from a fire, in which was found some burnt nails and staples from a boot. Bayly explained that he used the copper and drum to dress pigs, boiling the water in the copper over a fire in the drum. The boiling water would be used to strip the hair and bristle from the pig before it was butchered, which was a common farming practice.

Within days, examinations confirmed that the residue in the bottom of the drum contained wood charcoal and burnt bones.

Dr Brown, an Auckland gun expert, tested Lakey's pea rifle. All pea rifles make distinctive marking on cartridges when they're fired. The test cartridges fired from Lakey's pea rifle left distinctive ring markings identical to the markings found on the cartridge that had fallen out of Bayly's pocket.

On 29 November, the detectives returned to the Bayly farm armed with a search warrant. Bayly was clearly annoyed but allowed them to proceed. Bayly gave another statement offering much the same information as earlier.

As they left the property, Detective Allsopp showed Bayly some unburnt animal bones they'd found strewn along the fence line. Bayly told him that he often smashed up animal bones and threw them away or buried them in his garden. Samples of these bones were taken by police.

Two days later, on 1 December, the district was alive with rumours that Bayly had disappeared. Allsopp called over to the house where he found a distraught Phyllis Bayly. She handed him a brief letter written by her husband that seemed to be a suicide note. Given the large police presence in the area, nobody knew how or when Bayly had managed to slip away unnoticed.

Police immediately moved to carry out a more extensive search of Bayly's garden and sheds. Within minutes of digging over the garden, police found pieces of burnt wood and charcoal in the garden. They carefully examined pieces of what looked like burnt bone fragments. In and around the garden they found the metal runner from a pair of men's braces; pieces of burnt fabric and various pieces of boot leather.

The bones were carefully gathered and sent away for forensic testing. Some of the bones were large enough to quickly be verified as human. There were several pieces of rib, a piece of fibula, part of a backbone and pieces of a skull.

On the evening of 4 December, Bill Bayly was located at the Greenlane home of his family solicitor, Robert Lusk.

The search of the garden continued and police unearthed two false teeth, more bones and a sack believed to be from Lakey's implement shed. The sack was thought to have been used to wrap Sam Lakey's blood-soaked head as he was transported across to Bayly's cowshed.

Bayly's sheep dip was emptied and further discoveries made: a piece of skull bone which fitted precisely with other pieces of skull bone found in the garden; several shotgun cartridges, and a piece of a cigarette lighter with a homemade wick which was verified as belonging to Lakey.

Bones and leather were found scattered throughout the orchard. The metal rim of a watch was found under a tree and some other pieces from this watch were found in the car shed. A damaged watch case was found under the tool shed.

Bayly was charged with the murder of Christobel Lakey on 5 December 1933, and remanded in custody. On 10 January 1934, he was charged with the murder of Samuel Lakey.

The police believed that at some time on the Sunday evening, Bayly had gone over to the Lakeys' and had encountered Christobel Lakey as she returned home from milking. He was then believed to have struck her several times causing her to lose consciousness, before dragging her body over to the pond and covering her with sacks. Police believe Bayly then shot Sam Lakey, before attempting to cover his tracks by placing the Lakey's cream cans on the road and removing Lakey's body to his own cowshed. There, police thought that Bayly had placed the body into the 40 gallon drum and incinerated it along with Lakey's clothes and boots. This would have taken Bayly all night. Once the fire was extinguished, police believe that Bayly strew the remnants of Lakey's body around his garden and orchard as well as in his sheep dip. He is then thought to have disposed of the guns in the swamp and swept out his shed with his shovel.

Bill Bayly's trial opened on 21 May 1934, at the Auckland Supreme Court before Sir Alexander Herdman. The crown prosecutor was Vincent Meredith, who had acted for the Crown at the inquest into the death of Elsie Walker five years earlier. Erima Northcroft represented Bayly, as he had at the Walker inquest. The Crown had to prove:

- That Mrs Lakey died through her head being submerged in the duck pond after she had been knocked unconscious by heavy blows on her face.
- That of the large number of pieces of bone discovered on Baylys farm at Ruawaro, 61 pieces could be definitely identified as of human origin, and of these 55 were from a human skull. All had been burned recently.
- That many of the stains found on slats of wood on the old wheels and frame, and on battens found on the Lakey property, were human bloodstains.

The trial took 29 days and was the longest recorded trial in the country at that time. Northcroft's final address took three and a half days. Northcroft's defence that Bayly could not be the killer rested on the following points:

- The evidence against Bayly was circumstantial. There were serious questions as to the nature of Christobel Lakey's death that the scientists failed to answer and there was no substantial proof of Samuel Lakey's death.
- Nobody had any evidence there was a feud between Bayly and the Lakeys, therefore there was no motive.
- There was no absolute evidence proving the identification of the cartridge.
- Bayly's sledge had stopped short of the boundary fence by three metres. This was consistent with Bayly going to observe the telegraph pole. If he was responsible for removing the body, there would have been obvious marks right up to the fence and through the other side.
- Bayly did not have the strength to carry a body across the fence.
- Why would Bayly plant the guns on his own property?
- Bayly openly assisted police, allowing them to search his property and answering questions.
- There was no proof Bayly's knife made the cuts in the wood, and significantly, no blood was found on the knife.
- No blood was found on Bayly's oilskins or any of his clothes.

- There was no proof all the bones found belonged to the same skeleton. They could conceivably have come from a Maori burial ground or they could have been discarded by a medical student.

On Saturday 23 June 1934, the jury retired and an hour later returned with a verdict of guilty on both counts of murder. Bayly displayed no emotion as he was sentenced to hang.

Bayly was remanded at Mt Eden Prison awaiting his execution date scheduled for 20 July 1934. Meanwhile petitions were filed by his family and his defence team. They failed. Bayly was hanged.

The 5 August 1934 edition of *Truth* ran the headline: DID BAYLY COMMIT FIVE MURDERS IN ALL? The story suggested Bayly was also responsible for the deaths of Elsie Walker, Arthur Blomfield and James Blair. He had been hanged several weeks earlier and therefore could not be questioned and held accountable if he was guilty. Was he New Zealand's first multiple murderer?

Bill Bayly will be forever linked to the death of Elsie Walker. Whether he killed his cousin will never be known because even though police proved Bayly had lied about his movements, they could not prove Bayly killed Elsie.

The death of Arthur Blomfield sent shockwaves through Auckland much as Elsie Walker's had. Blomfield was a 75-year-old chemist who managed Mackay's Dispensary in Wellesley Street, near the corner of Queen Street. On the evening of 30 October 1931, he had been in the store by himself when he was attacked by an unknown assailant. A pharmacy assistant returning to work found Blomfield lying on the floor out the back of the shop, semi-conscious and bleeding profusely from his face and head. He uttered the words, 'Go away George, don't do it!' before passing out. He died in hospital that night without regaining consciousness.

Whoever killed Blomfield must have known he was alone in the pharmacy at the time and police believed that the attack was part of a robbery. The till had been emptied before Blomfield was attacked as there were no blood stains on it so police surmised that the old man had heard the till being opened and gone to investigate. The assailant had then pushed the old man through the door into the back room. Police believed the murder weapon to have been a heavy spanner or hammer.

No controlled substances had been taken which seemed to rule out the possibility that the killing was drug related.

There were several witnesses who described a young man who had been seen near the shop at the time of the attack on Blomfield. They all said that the man was between 20 and 23 years old, about 1.8 metres tall with dark eyes and short, wavy, dark hair. He was wearing a navy-blue coat, dark vest and brown trousers. Unfortunately the description was so broad it fitted most of the young men in Auckland.

Three weeks after Blomfield's death, a young man carrying a parcel wrapped in newspaper calmly walked into the Remuera branch of the Bank of New Zealand and set upon the sole teller, Fred Youngs, with a hearth brush he'd concealed in the parcel. As Youngs tried to steady himself, the attacker threw sand into his eyes, temporarily blinding him.

Youngs quickly grabbed his revolver and fired point blank. The attacker managed to stagger clumsily out the door and along Remuera Road before collapsing and dying outside Maxwell's Bakery, to the horror of lunch time shoppers.

The attempted robbery quickly relegated Blomfield's murder from the headlines and within two days police identified the robber as Oswald Laurence Coulton, aged 24. Australian-born Coulton was described as a polite and affable gentleman who regularly flashed large amounts of money, but had no job to speak of. A search of his room led police to suspect him being responsible for a number of recent burglaries.

Police found a jack hammer in Coulton's room they suspected to be the weapon used to kill Blomfield. Two witnesses who had seen Blomfield's killer failed to identify Coulton as being the same man. One witness was shown a grainy photograph of Coulton and said the man bore some resemblance to the killer but she wasn't sure. Tests failed to indicate whether the jack hammer was the murder weapon. The police were unable to link Coulton to the attack with any certainty.

The inquest into the murder of Arthur Blomfield was heard at the Auckland Magistrates Court on 20 March 1932, in front of Mr W.R McKean. The magistrate heard evidence and returned a verdict that Blomfield had died of injuries wilfully inflicted by blows to the head by blunt instrument by a person or persons unknown.

Three years after Blomfield's death, *Truth* tried to link Bill Bayly with the case. However, the description of the old man's killer did not resemble Bayly at all.

Bayly's movements on 30 October 1931 are not known but it is unlikely he had any connection to Blomfield.

Truth also suggested that Bayly had killed Auckland taxi driver James Blair in the early hours of Sunday morning on 15 October 1933—the same day that Christobel Lakey went missing.

Blair had been found badly beaten in his taxi at 5.30 that morning by a local milk man. He was suffering from severe head wounds and died on arrival at Auckland Hospital.

The taxi was covered in blood and it was evident Blair had been severely beaten with a blunt instrument while he was still sitting in the drivers' seat. The blows had been so hard his false teeth had been knocked out. The engine was switched off but the meter was still ticking over. By the time this was realised, the meter had registered 18 shillings.

Amongst Blair's personal items was £2.9s.9d so robbery was ruled out as a motive for the attack but the possibility remained that the driver had been killed by someone who was unable to pay their fare. Blair's last passenger was described as being about 30 years of age, 1.7 metres tall and of a slim build, inclined to be dark, and dressed in a dark suit with a brownish overcoat and felt hat.

By the time the inquest opened in March 1934, police had interviewed 1500 people, and checked at least 300 boarding houses, 80 hotels and taken 100 statements. The coroner concluded that Blair had died as a result of injuries inflicted by a person or persons unknown.

The accusation in *Truth* that Bayly had been responsible for Blair's death had little basis. Again the description of the supposed killer bore no resemblance to Bill Bayly. The question of financial motive for the killing made no sense as Bayly was never short of cash due to the financial backing provided by his father. It also seems extremely unlikely that Bayly would have driven up to Auckland for the evening, then caught a taxi to Mt Roskill, where he knew no one, before killing the taxi driver and driving back to Ruawaro in time for the next morning's milking.

Bill Bayly definitely killed two people—Samuel and Christobel Lakey. It remains possible, even probable, that he killed Elsie Walker. However, any more purported victims of Bayly seem to have been made up by a media who were desperate to keep the infamous legacy of Elsie Walker going, and establish Bayly as some kind of outlaw. Perhaps conspiracy theorists were also keen to attribute the crimes to someone who could no longer fight back.

7. The Small Town with Big Secrets

On the evening of Tuesday 20 September 1921, Arthur Kennedy addressed a packed Auckland Town Hall. Recently returned to New Zealand, he told the enthralled audience about his 20 years working in the tea plantations of India and Ceylon. He concluded his talk with a warning to the government that if they were to allow the free immigration for Indians—Parsee, Hindu, Mohammedan, it did not make any difference to him —they would arrive in hordes, get about in loin cloths, and set up squalid shanty huts in Auckland. And there would inevitably be mixed marriages and a huge increase in the prevalence of venereal disease. He also suggested censoring letters written to and received by Hindus already in New Zealand to and from their loved ones in India.

It is unthinkable now that an opinion that extreme could be voiced publicly without causing national outrage, yet extracts of Kennedy's speech were published in newspapers nationwide as a lesson in culture—at that time, such comments were considered acceptable, even informative.

Indians began migrating to New Zealand in the late nineteenth century and were subject to racial discrimination from the moment they arrived. In the 1890s, there was an outcry in parliament over the 'menace of itinerate Hindoo Hawkers'. Indian traders travelled the country attempting to sell often worthless wares and their persistence was seen by many as rudeness. The hawkers often had doors slammed in their faces in anger.

Times were tough—the country was in a major recession. Tolerance was low—in a letter to the editor of a major newspaper the door-to-door hawkers were likened to 'annoying insects'. As a result, the Undesirable Hawkers Prevention Bill (1896) was passed to restrict their movement in and around the country, but it did not prevent immigration. Three years later, the Immigration Restriction Act (1899) made it possible to exclude Indians from entering the country, by imposing English competency tests on new migrants, but loopholes were there to be exploited and the act was difficult to enforce.

Things settled and, in general, Indians were accepted and integrated into communities and reported cases of racial abuse and prejudice were few until after the Great War, when disgruntled Pukekohe farmers formed the 'White New Zealand league' to protest against a seemingly large number of Indian families buying land in the region to establish market gardens. This was the first organised opposition and the League quickly found sympathy in many parts of New Zealand.

With rising unemployment and growing economic unrest, public meetings throughout the country were demanding the government impose restrictions on immigration. Returned servicemen believed they had a right to secure land for farming through the Land Settlement scheme, but there was not enough land available. Whatever the reason, Indians were blamed for buying land and taking over. In response, the Immigration Restriction Amendment Act (1920) was passed unanimously, setting a limit on the number of adult male Indians who could enter New Zealand each year.

Nana Chhiba, a Hindu born on 19 January 1900, in Surat, Bombay arrived in New Zealand in 1917. He was the youngest of four brothers. He married at the age of 13 and worked in his father's business for several years. He and his brothers all had business aspirations and decided they could make their collective and, later, respective fortunes in Australia or New Zealand. In 1917, the Chhiba brothers—Bhana, Bhika, Govind and Nana—sailed to New Zealand and settled in Wanganui.

They quickly established the fruiterers, B David and Co. Thanks to their collective hard work and business acumen, the venture was highly successful and their business expanded opening shops throughout Taranaki and the central North Island. However, another Hindu from the same caste as the Chhibas had already opened a fruit shop in Wanganui. This led to bitter rivalry that worsened when

B David and Co. began to offer cheaper prices and more choice. In 1924, Bhika was badly beaten in the street by members of the rival family. On another occasion, Govind complained of being beaten and threatened with a knife.

In 1926, the brothers decided to split their partnership and divide their capital. As his share of the sale, Nana received £6000, but he thought he should receive £12,000. Believing he had been swindled by his brothers, he broke off all personal ties with them. Reluctantly, he continued a business relationship of sorts, limited to them occasionally assisting in his new store as required—his brothers felt there was a code of honour requiring them to help each other. But now, they had amassed great individual fortunes and each had their own interests. They continued to buy and sell land together and individually throughout Wanganui.

In 1927, Nana returned to India. While he was away he received word his brothers had made a great deal of money selling a piece of land they had purchased together, without him. He was extremely jealous and this created more of a division between them.

The first thing Nana did upon returning to his village of Mataud, near Bombay, was to call a meeting of the village elders. In accordance with their custom, he requested a divorce from his wife whom he had not seen since abandoning her when he left for New Zealand. He then spent several months in India tying up his affairs. He even married another young girl, but returned to New Zealand without her.

In 1926, Nana and Bhana had established a small fruit store in the Taranaki township of Hawera and had installed a relative to manage the store. On his return to New Zealand in May 1928, Nana bought out Bhana's interests in the Hawera store and secured a valuable, freehold shop at the intersection of High Street and Union Street. He planned to operate the business himself. Six months later, he purchased larger premises further along High Street. The new location was ideal—it had a large shop front, a living area and kitchen behind the shop, and a loft upstairs, which he converted into sleeping quarters.

Nana Chhiba quickly became a highly respected member of the local community. He even received nominations for the local council. He was openly supportive of his community, providing employment for local lads and donating fruit to the poor.

He had numerous friends—Pakeha and Maori alike. The locals called him 'David', adopting the name of his shop. It seemed the only fly in the ointment was Chhiba Gopal Panchia, who had managed David's in Wanganui but moved to Hawera in March 1926 to branch out on his own. His shop, Patel Brothers Fruiterers, was virtually opposite Nana's new premises in High Street. The small township was not big enough to sustain two Hindu fruiterers and they became bitter rivals. Panchia was more aggressive and said he was determined to 'run Nana out of Dodge'. Nana, however, was more cunning than the uneducated youngster and dropped his prices, knowing Panchia would struggle with the competition. Nana also donated speckled fruit to widows, local pig farmers and swagmen passing through town. He was always willingly to help and contributed to local causes.

When he took over the business in Hawera, he resolved to make a completely fresh start. He estranged himself from other Indians, refusing to employ his countrymen. Instead, he employed local lads fresh out of school, who used his shop as a stepping stone to other jobs. The boys thought Nana was 'a good sort'—he was funny, easy-going and not at all strict with them. Plus, Nana was a poor record-keeper and it was easy to pinch money from the till or from any number of places around the house where he had poorly hidden stashes of notes. Whether or not he knew, Nana never reprimanded any of them.

Nana got along well with everyone and enjoyed pranks. He happily supplied the lads with alcohol and as much fruit as they desired. As a result, the store was a popular place for the lads to hang out and Nana was never short of employees. Whenever one boy left, he would have a friend lining up to replace him.

Meanwhile, Nana never forgave his brothers for swindling him. Only Bhana and Bhika remained in Wanganui and Govind had moved to nearby Stratford to open another branch of David's. In April 1930, Nana caught up with Bhana and received £9000 for the sale of some land he had invested in. Nana was furious as he had been excluded from the decision to sell and, once again, he had expected more money than he was given. Nana used £2500 of the money to take out an insurance policy with AMP and gave Bhana power of attorney over his affairs.

It was common knowledge in Hawera that Nana was a reasonably wealthy man, despite his bitter complaints to customers about how his brothers had swindled him. Nobody knew where Nana invested the rest of the £9000 of his savings, although he also owned the Rotorua branch of B David and Co. He received the profits from that business in cash.

Several boys spoke of Nana planning a trip overseas in 1935 and said they had seen him exchange cash for Bank of England notes—his preferred currency when travelling abroad—which was also still legal tender in New Zealand, although was more customarily traded on the black market. It was popularly rumoured he kept large wads of cash in a safe in his sleeping quarters upstairs.

Nana enjoyed running a successful business during tough economic times. He also enjoyed closing his store on Saturday nights with the anticipation of Sundays off. Every Sunday Nana would pack a picnic lunch into the basket on his bicycle and pedal four kilometres to Waihi Beach. He would spend the day looking out over the Tasman and walking along the beach before returning home around 3pm.

He was sociable during the week and often invited locals and travelling merchants to drink stout and share a meal. Gordon McCutcheon worked for Garton and Co, Fruit Merchants in Hastings and was a regular supplier of fruit and vegetables to Nana and his brothers. On Thursday 29 January 1931, McCutcheon visited Nana and enjoyed several bottles of stout while they discussed business. Over dinner, Nana suggested McCutcheon sleep in his spare room—it was late and they were both affected by the liquor. McCutcheon declined, having already booked into the Royal Hotel. Nana complained again that night about not receiving his fair share from land and business dealings with his brothers. He also said Patel was pestering him to sell-out.

The next day, Friday 30 January, some of Patel's workers were creating a din outside David's and Nana told them to take their argument elsewhere. He believed this was deliberately staged to annoy him. When the young men refused to move on, a scuffle ensued. Rogers*, one of Nana's boys, called Constable Healey who arrested the men for disorderly behaviour.

On Saturday 31 January 1931, Rogers commented to Nana that he had expected to be rushed off his feet with people heading to the beach, the Egmont Races and the Druids' Picnic. Instead, it was an unusually slow day for business. Rogers hadn't been at David's long—he had just replaced one of his chums who had got a full-time job in New Plymouth. Rogers thought Nana was not his usual affable self—he seemed distant that day and he couldn't understand why business was slow. Also, the confrontation with the Patel boys the day before had shaken him, and he may have been expecting more trouble.

It was sweltering that afternoon. Rogers wedged the back door open, using the tomahawk from the kitchen, and he used a meat cleaver to prop open the door between the living room and the shop. He stopped for tea at 5.30pm. When he returned, Nana cleared the shop till and took the cash upstairs to count, ready for the evening trade. When he returned he confirmed the takings were down.

The evening trade was steady with late shoppers and people purchasing fruit before and after the pictures. At 8.00pm, Nana and Rogers were joined by 16-year-old Gordon*—another of Nana's long-term employees who had recently moved on. He did, however, pop in on Saturdays to help with the evening trade and to close-up.

At 10.30pm, Constable Donovan was on his beat and saw Nana and the boys outside carrying the display crates inside and stacking them against the window. Donovan stopped for a few minutes to talk about the day. He thought Nana seemed cheerful—he said he was looking forward to his day off. Donovan asked if he had any more trouble from Chhiba Panchia, but Nana screwed up his face and said he had not seen him for a few days.

Nana usually closed up at 11pm on Saturdays. When Rogers washed up to leave he noticed the back door was still wedged open with the tomahawk. At around 11.05pm, a young man named Evans—another former employee who had moved to New Plymouth—called at the store. He needed some change and was pleased to see the shop was still open. He and Nana chatted for a few minutes and he left shortly after, noticing the shop was empty as he left. At 11.15pm, Gordon was out the back washing up when he heard voices out in front of the store. When he left, the back door was closed and the tomahawk was propped against a wall in the living room. As Gordon walked out Nana was sweeping the footpath and he asked Nana if he could borrow his bicycle the next day. Nana said he was riding his bike to the beach, so they bade each other good night and Gordon went home.

At 11.45pm, the Hawera night watchman cycled along High Street and noticed David's was shut, but the window blind was raised. Although it was dark inside the shop, he could see the light on in the living room. Howells was about to call out, but he noticed the door was locked so changed his mind. At 12.05am, Constable Donovan passed the shop and also saw the living-room light was on. He tried the door, but it was locked.

Genevieve Pickett lived in Victoria Street—her back fence overlooked the backyard Nana shared with the drycleaning business next door. Mrs Pickett's mother had owned the store and after she sold it to Nana she had been exasperated

* not real name

by the messy garden he kept. She chastised him, but Nana would laugh and say he would get around to it some time.

On Sunday 1 February, Mrs Pickett spent the day at the beach with her daughter. At 6pm, she was preparing dinner and realised she needed tomatoes. She climbed over the back fence and called out to David. As she neared the back door she noticed his bicycle propped up underneath the awning, which had come unfastened and almost completely covered the back door area. There was a wash basin outside the back door and she immediately noticed a tomahawk and hammer sitting in clear water. Mrs Pickett called out several times before pushing the back door open. She could hear something sizzling inside and assumed David was cooking dinner. She looked inside and was about to call out again when her eyes fixed on something. Suddenly, the door slammed shut.

Mrs Pickett went home in a daze and, at the dinner table, her concerned family asked her what was wrong. She stammered out something that seemed impossible—she thought she had seen a blood-splattered body on the floor at David's. Her family said it was probably a pig or some other animal and it was probably something to do with a Hindu ritual. Mrs Pickett calmed slightly but could not erase the image of a blood-soaked human hand. She decided to call her solicitor who said he would pass the information to the local police.

Constable Healey was on duty at Hawera Police Station when he received a call that someone might be seriously hurt at David's shop. He had walked past David's several times earlier in the day and had not noticed anything unusual. He went straight around to check the rear of the premises and tried the door Mrs Pickett claimed had been ajar earlier. It was now locked. He knocked at the door but there was no response so he returned to the station.

When Constable Donovan came on duty at 9pm, Healey told him about the call so the two of them went to check at 9.15pm. By now it was dark and the light in the living room was on. The constables knocked on the back door then went around to the front, knocking and calling for David to open up. Once again, there was no response and they returned to the station.

As the evening wore on, Donovan became uneasy. He returned to David's at 11pm. The shop was still locked and the living-room light was still on. Donovan called out again and there was no response. He tried the back door and this time it was unlocked. He opened the door and immediately saw a body lying face upwards in a large pool of blood on the floor in the middle of Nana's living room. There was a mat covering the head and chest and blood splattered across all four walls.

Donovan carefully lifted the mat and identified the victim as Nana Chhiba. His face and head were covered in blood and there were a number of deep head wounds. The right arm was flung back at right angles to the body with the fingers half closed. The left arm was at his side. The head and right arm were lying in deep pools of blood. Donovan raced back to the police station and called for Sergeant Henry and Dr Sinclair, who came at once.

An initial examination of the scene found loose, black hairs on Nana's forearms that matched the hair on his head. There were five visible head wounds.

There was a threepenny piece lying on the mat under his elbow. He had a knife, a gold chain with sovereign pendant, a nail file and a front-door key in his pockets. The right-side pocket of his coat was open and there were traces of blood on the inside of the left pocket. There were thick bloodstains on the outside of the right trouser pocket and more inside, as if a bloodied hand had reached into the pocket to remove something.

The splashes of blood on all four walls reached a height of 1.2 metres. There were large pools of blood on the floor to the right of the body and the newspaper in front of and under the body was splattered with blood. There were two empty cups on the table, suggesting the killer may have had a drink with Nana. There were 17 empty stout bottles under the table and another 16 were found in the bathroom.

The empty till was on a chair in the kitchen with a towel underneath it. It had been carefully removed. There was a blood-stained meat cleaver in corner of the living room. In the hand basin, half-filled with clean water, outside the back door, there was a hammer, tomahawk and a key ring with three keys on it.

After securing the scene, Sergeant Henry called New Plymouth and was instructed to wait for a detective to arrive. At 2am, Detective Arnold Mieklejohn arrived and approved the removal of Nana's body to the morgue for a post mortem that was performed by Dr Sinclair and Dr Thomson.

They found four deep fractures in the skull and 11 serious scalp wounds—six of the wounds were almost certainly caused by blows with a hammer and five with a tomahawk.

The blows were so vicious they had to be made by a homicidal maniac or someone in a fit of passion. The depth and angles of the wounds suggested an attack from three different directions, but they appeared to have been delivered by one person.

Detective Mieklejohn checked the rear of the property. The weeds and tall grass in the neglected backyard clearly showed two trampled tracks leading to the back fence. One track went to the Pickett's and had been made by Mrs Pickett. The other track went from the back door to the back fence where there was a private alley on the other side that led to High Street.

An examination of the basin and weapons found traces of hair on the head of the tomahawk that also matched the hair from Nana's head. The water was strained and more hairs were found.

On the afternoon of 3 February, Senior Detective Thomas Quirke arrived from New Plymouth. His departure had been delayed by news of a devastating earthquake in Hawke's Bay. A telegram had been sent to all police stations in the North Island requesting assistance and Quirke helped organise several uniformed police to travel to Napier. When Quirke finally arrived at David's store, Mieklejohn and Constable Lemm were in the living room taking measurements of the blood splatters on the walls.

Together the detectives set to work. They quickly established that Nana was last seen by Gordon at around 11.15pm when he was closing the store. The night-watchman passed the store half an hour later and the shop was closed, although the living-room light was on. Constable Donovan found the same thing when he passed at 12.05am. Neither Donovan nor the night-watchman could tell who was in the living room, but both had assumed Nana was still awake.

The doctors estimated the time of death as approximately 12 hours before the body was discovered. This placed the time of death at around 11am, but it was conceded that it was more likely to have occurred in the early hours of Sunday morning.

There were no signs of forced entry or of a struggle. This suggested Nana knew his assailant—the cups and empty bottles suggested that they had shared a drink. The attack had been fast and ferocious. It was likely Nana had quickly lost consciousness—the position of the body indicated he had no time to defend himself.

Oddly, it appeared the assailant had remained in the store for much of the next day or, at least, returned some time in the afternoon to clean up and remove evidence. The alleged murder weapons had been cleaned and left in a basin of water when Mrs Pickett called at 6pm. The empty cups had been wiped clean—there were no fingerprints to be found. The assailant may have been preparing to dispose of Nana's body when Mrs Pickett popped in. He may have then closed the door, locking it. He may have still been inside an hour later when Constable Healey found the back door was locked.

The assailant must have left some time between 9.15pm and 11pm—leaving over the back fence, down the alley and along High Street under cover of darkness. When Constables Healey and Donovan called at 9.15pm, the door was still locked. When Donovan returned at 11pm, the door was unlocked. It is difficult to imagine the killer being brazen enough to remain in the shop during the day at risk of being caught by one of Nana's boys.

The empty till suggested robbery as the primary motive and it, too, had been wiped clean.

Rogers estimated they had cleared £5 over the course of Saturday, but Nana had taken the balance up at 6pm, leaving a float of £2.10s in change. He said there would have been between £7 and £10 in the till when they closed up that night. He also said a man had come in on Saturday afternoon with a handful of Bank of England notes that Nana had bought. Rogers and Gordon confirmed it was common knowledge that Nana was well off and it was rumoured he had a substantial amount of cash hidden upstairs. He was a prime target for a robbery.

The detectives finished the scene examination downstairs on 3 February and climbed the ladder to the loft. They found a small room, cluttered with boxes, loose papers and clothing strewn across the floor. In the middle was an unmade bed. At first glance, the sleeping quarters appeared to have been hastily rifled through, but it was evident that this was the way Nana lived. A search found about £23 in notes in various places, and a cheque for £2 and another for £1.12s.6d were found between the mattresses. £26 in notes and another cheque for £1.5s were found in the drawer of a writing desk and there were stashes of loose change dotted around the room. In all, £85 were found, and none of it was well hidden. This contradicted the idea that robbery was the prime motive.

Detectives Quirke and Mieklejohn checked into rooms at the Royal Hotel, across the street from David's. As word spread of the murder, the footpath outside David's quickly filled with onlookers. Local gossip was rife. They thought Nana, or David as he was commonly known, was harmless—he was well respected.

Six days before the murder, Nana's three brothers had left for India, sailing to Sydney on the SS *Marama*. As a result, his body lay unclaimed in the morgue for several days. They had not spoken to Nana for a while, so were not very helpful when questioned. However, when Bhana had last spoken to Nana, in April 1930, he had mentioned the ongoing feud with Chhiba Gopal Panchia.

Police were not surprised—they knew Panchia was prone to violent outbursts. They had also heard rumours that Panchia was pressuring Nana to sell out and that Nana was on the verge of being closed down by market agents. Panchia played down the feud, but alluded to one possible reason why someone would want to kill Nana. He admitted he had recently made a polite offer to buy Nana out, which was rejected. He knew Nana was not as well off as many believed. In fact, he owed the Association of Providence Merchants, a predominantly Indian group, a great deal of money. Panchia said he was ashamed of Nana because his failure to make his payments disgraced their caste.

Detective Wright, from Auckland, went to Pukekohe to meet leaders within the Association of Providence Merchants, who confirmed Nana had owed the association £400. He had been meeting his payments until 12 months before, when payments stopped without any explanation. The amount owing was now £240. This was a large amount of money, but not enough to consider closing a business or murdering someone over.

The association's policy was to summon a debtor before the board to seek an explanation and arrange a payment plan. If this failed, sanctions would be imposed and, as a last resort, the debtor would be forced out of business. Nana had made irregular payments, but no action had yet been taken to summon him. They believed Nana would eventually pay up. Board members admitted they were disappointed with Nana, and not only over the debt. Years earlier, Nana had sacked all his Hindu workers and was unsupportive of his own caste—this breached their code that required them to support each other.

Police were satisfied the association had no reason to murder Nana. Besides, it was not in their nature to seek violent retribution. One association member did, however, suggest they check out Nana's cousin Vallabh from Rotorua. When Nana opened the Rotorua branch of B David and Co, Vallabh got the manager's job. The store struggled through the Depression under his poor management. Nana lent Vallabh a considerable sum of money to help, but this was allegedly lost on bad investments and gambling. Nana was furious with Vallabh. Vallabh also owed a substantial sum of money to the merchants' association and he had refused to arrange payments.

Vallabh attended Nana's funeral on 2 February, but acted strangely and avoided people, leaving straight after the service. In fact, he disappeared and did not return to Rotorua, which was highly irregular.

Jim Baldwin, a local, claimed he saw a small Indian with a bushy moustache driving a slate-coloured car at high speed out of Hawera towards Wanganui at 9.45am on the morning after the murder. Someone else reported seeing the same man and vehicle parked outside Mokoia Dairy Factory later that morning. The description of the man matched that of Vallabh.

It was possible Vallabh had been in the area—he was absent from Rotorua on the day of the murder. He was considered a suspect, but had no criminal record. Police struggled to come up with a motive other than Vallabh requesting more money from Nana and turning violent when his request was refused.

Police spent two days carrying out door-to-door enquiries in the vicinity of Mokoia Dairy Factory. None of the residents or patrons of the nearby Manutahi Hotel remembered noticing a strange Indian in the last few days. A full description of Vallabh was wired out to all stations and he was quickly traced to a house in Ngongotaha, on the outskirts of Rotorua. When police interviewed him, it was obvious Vallabh was scared witless—he thought Nana had been murdered by his own countrymen because of the unpaid fees to the association and he was worried that he might be the next victim.

He denied having financial problems—he said he felt ripped off by the merchants' association and had cut all ties with them. He had started purchasing his produce at the City Market in central Auckland. He denied murdering Nana and produced a season Rotorua-to-Auckland rail pass stamped to verify that he had travelled to Auckland on 31 January. He was ruled out as a suspect.

So, had Jim Baldwin actually seen an Indian? If so, who was it? During the first weeks of the investigation a number of people reported sightings of strange Indians in the district. Walter Lay had seen a Hindu swagman walking towards Hawera when he was driving between Eltham and Hawera at 6.20am on the morning of 31 January. Mr Lay knew most of the Indians in Hawera and was sure he had never seen this fellow before.

William Craigie had a store at 228 High Street and he reported an unusual encounter with a well-dressed Indian in his shop at 1.30pm on 31 January. The stranger said he was from Rangoon and asked Craigie if he knew the Patel Brothers and, also, how to get to David's. Craigie noticed that when he left the store the fellow walked away from David's store. He was aged between 30 and 35, and was 1.65 metres tall. He was stocky, with a very dark complexion, he was clean-shaven, and spoke good English. He flashed about some Bank of England notes. Customs checked their records for immigrants from Rangoon. Intriguingly, there was no record of any Rangoon Indian immigrating to New Zealand.

Craigie's Indian was carrying a wad of Bank of England notes and Rogers had seen Nana purchase some Bank of England notes from a Pakeha on Saturday morning. Because the customer and the stranger were seen with the notes before Nana was murdered, and Bank of England notes were still commonly used throughout the country, this was not considered as significant to the investigation.

Walter Whitten, publican of the Central Hotel in Hawera, served a small, thin extremely well-dressed Indian, wearing a dark suit, felt hat and gold chain on 2 February. This description matched Craigie's Indian. When the conversation turned to the murder, the man abruptly left the bar. Was he the murderer?

Police checked the records of all Indians who had committed criminal offences over the past two years. Remarkably, there were only fourteen and they all lived in Auckland or Wellington. None of the men matched the description of Craigie's Indian and all had alibis for the period in question.

Who was this stranger? He sounded too well-dressed to be a fruit hawker. Recently a representative from the merchants' association had closed down a fruiterer in New Plymouth. Rumours in the Indian community suggested the well-dressed stranger was an enforcer from the merchants' association, but the association assured Detective Wright they had not sent a representative to Taranaki that week.

As publicity of the stranger circulated, Mrs Sales came forward. She had seen a well-dressed Indian man sitting with another Indian man near the lake at the local park at 4.30pm on Sunday 1 February. They appeared to be deep in conversation and one handed a package to the other before they left. Was there any connection?

Well-dressed Indian travellers were a rarity in the area. He would have to lodge somewhere, so police checked all hotels and boarding houses in the area to no avail. Train bookings were checked, and railway staff and local taxi drivers were interviewed, but nobody else had seen this stranger.

Milne, who ran the drycleaning business next door to David's, said he overheard Nana at 8pm on the evening of 31 January say, 'Here is the soap,' to someone who replied in a foreign accent. The exact response was muffled because of the sound of running water, but Milne was adamant it was a foreigner. That's the same time Gordon started work. Neither he nor Rogers saw any foreign gentleman with Nana, but conceded they were busy working in the store at that time and Nana was out the back. It was possible someone came in through the back door and went straight upstairs without being seen by the boys, but he would have had to remain quiet and out of sight until they both left after 11pm.

Despite the large sum of money found upstairs, robbery was still considered the most likely motive, yet there were no obvious signs of forced entry anywhere downstairs. One option was the foreign man heard by Milne at 8pm. He may have headed upstairs straight after washing his hands—this would tie in with Craigie's Indian.

Another possibility was that Nana had met his assailant while closing the shop and invited him in for a few drinks. Unfortunately, the only fingerprints identified on the 33 empty stout bottles were Nana's own.

When police checked upstairs they found sets of fingerprints on the window sill. The same fingerprints were found on the window ledge in Nana's sleeping quarters, on the upstairs safe and on the ladder which was used to get up into the sleeping loft from the living room. Close inspection revealed tiny marks on the window latch and corresponding part of the sill—it was obvious someone had recently broken in and attempted to rob the safe. The same fingerprints were all over the place, suggesting the same person had broken in more than once.

All the witnesses interviewed so far had willingly been fingerprinted, so Mieklejohn was confident they would be quickly find a match. However, he was extremely surprised when he learned the identity of the would-be robber—the fingerprints had been left by Gordon, the lad who came in to help Nana on Saturday nights. The discovery also opened up a new sordid motive for the murder and a host of possible suspects.

On the evening of 1 March, Detective Mieklejohn went to Gordon's home and interviewed the lad in front of his father. When Gordon left to work in an office in New Plymouth, Nana was sorry to lose him and gave him a good reference. He asked Gordon to help out on Saturday nights and Gordon gladly accepted.

The detective wanted to know why Gordon's fingerprints had been found in Nana's living quarters and on the bathroom window sill. Gordon hung his head in shame.

Eventually, he admitted breaking into Nana's store on Sundays whenever he knew for certain Nana would be at the beach. He said it was easy to break in through the window and he had been taught the technique by the boy he replaced when he started working there. Most of the boys who had worked there did it—not all the time, just when they needed extra cash. They knew Nana left money lying all over the place upstairs and if he ever noticed some missing, he never said anything to any of them.

Gordon said he had not broken in for at least two weeks before Nana's murder and he repeated that he had left Nana's around 11.15pm. Mr Gordon confirmed the boy had returned home at about 11.20pm and lazed around home most of the next day.

This presented police with a problem. If it was common for the boys to break in to steal money from Nana when they were employed, why would they stop after they finished working there? They had to track down all the boys who had worked at David's to eliminate them from the inquiry. They could not rule out the possibility that one or more of them had continued to break in for some easy money.

Constable Lemm compiled a list of 12 boys—14 including Rogers and Gordon—and checked for any criminal activity. Meanwhile, Mieklejohn was still bothered by Gordon's reaction when interviewed—he felt Gordon was not telling the full story. Had he broken in on Sunday and caught the assailant cleaning up? Had he been coerced into shutting up?

After the scene examination, Nana's relations opened for business as usual, so Mieklejohn went to have a talk to Rogers. He found him unloading produce. Rogers said they all knew about the stash of money upstairs, but he had never been upstairs and he never had *any* intention of going there. Mieklejohn was puzzled at the last remark and asked what he meant. Rogers replied that, although he was a good friend and employer, Nana often said and did things that made him feel uncomfortable. Then he told his story.

One night, not long after Rogers started working there, Nana offered him a bottle of stout after work. As they had a quiet drink, Nana asked him if he knew many girls. Rogers said he did, and Nana suggested he bring one over so he could give her the 'jig-jig'. A few days later, Nana peeled a banana and asked Rogers if he had his 'skin on or off', meaning was Rogers circumcised? When Rogers did not reply, Nana sidled up to him and said he would give him £5 if he would show him his erection and let him photograph it. Some days when there was nobody else around, Nana would try and grab Roger's privates. Rogers would merely push him away and Nana would walk off laughing hysterically.

Rogers said he knew other boys had shown Nana their penises and Nana had given them money or fruit to take home. Once he arrived at work early and caught Gordon climbing down from Nana's loft with a box containing a new pair of expensive sports shoes. Gordon seemed embarrassed and refused to talk about it. Rogers believed Gordon was having a sexual relationship with Nana in exchange for money and expensive clothing and he thought Gordon had a spare key so he could visit whenever he felt like it.

Mieklejohn interviewed Gordon again—without his father present. He strenuously denied having a sexual relationship with Nana, but admitted to willingly exposing himself to him once or twice in return for money or clothing. He said Nana took gleeful delight in making a grab for his privates, but it never went any further than that. He also admitted frequently being out the back of the shop with a bunch of other boys when Nana laughingly exposed his erection to them. He would ask for a 'fuck', but they always ignored him and told him to bugger off. Nana never pushed further with this game. He denied having a key, adding that it would have been handy—he could have avoided having to break in through the upstairs window to steal money.

Mieklejohn asked about Nana's mood on the night he died. Gordon said he and Rogers were out the back and Rogers was lying on the couch. Nana came out, jumped on Rogers and attempted to 'dry-hump' him. Rogers pushed him off and Nana returned to the shop.

When interviewed, all the other boys had similar tales. One said Nana referred to them as his 'dirty bastards' even though he was the one making the sexual approaches. They all said Nana had asked them to show him their 'corks' for money, and they had all been regularly groped. Nine boys said Nana openly asked them for sex, but they all denied having a sexual relationship with him. Mieklejohn was suspicious—some boys probably had consented in exchange for money and goods, but were too ashamed to tell the truth.

In Hawera, Nana Chhiba had been a respected businessman. None of the boys appeared to have confided in anyone outside their own circle. To some, it was embarrassing. To others, it was no big deal—that's just how Nana was. This new disclosure, a month after the murder, offered an entirely different motive for the killing—revenge, if not by one of the boys then, possibly, by one of their fathers.

At the interview with Gordon on 1 March, Mr Gordon said he did not trust Nana and there was something about him he did not like. At the time, Mieklejohn thought Mr Gordon was racist, but now he suspected he may have heard something about what his boy had endured at the shop. None of the boys had complained to police. In fact, many of them spoke highly of Nana and were visibly upset at his death. It seemed, to most of them, Nana's lewd behaviour was tolerable—it was a small price to pay for the benefits of working at David's. They were paid well and did not have to work very hard. He gave them alcohol and there was always loose money lying around that he didn't seem to miss. In the Depression, fruit was a luxury and the boys were allowed to help themselves whenever they liked. Besides, he never really forced himself on them—all they needed to do was tell him to 'bugger off' and he would.

During interviews with the boys, Mieklejohn and Quirke heard another story about Nana's secretive and immoral life that opened up yet another possible motive and suspect. Tom and Ada Mitchell* used to manage the laundry and drycleaning business next door to David's. They lived in a flat behind the laundry, adjacent to Nana's living area. Ada Mitchell did Nana's laundry in exchange for the wood from his fruit crates. Four years earlier, Ada Mitchell became pregnant with her first child. The excitement of a newborn baby gave way to horror when she gave birth to a dark-skinned daughter. Tom Mitchell's shock turned to rage when his wife tearfully admitted having an ongoing sexual relationship with the Hindu next door. He stormed out, confronted Nana and gave him a beating. Nana was just as shocked but did not press charges. Instead, he became reclusive.

The Mitchells moved and opened a laundromat in Regent Street before going their separate ways. Tom stayed in Hawera running the laundromat, but became an alcoholic. Under the influence, he would occasionally threaten Nana. Ada moved to Patea, where she lived and worked with her sister at the Central Hotel.

Police learned that Tom and Ada Mitchell had met up in on the night of 31 January to discuss a possible reconciliation. They were seen walking together in High Street, before Ada was picked up by her brother-in-law at the Hawera

* not real names

Post Office at 11.00pm. Tom Mitchell loitered around town for half an hour before returning to his lodgings.

Mieklejohn was surprised such a scandal was not common knowledge around town. If it were true, they should have been investigating from this angle from the start. Mitchell was interviewed and denied murdering Nana. He admitted meeting his estranged wife and waiting with her for her brother-in-law until 11pm. He then walked home and slept until late the next morning. His story was corroborated by his landlady.

Ada Mitchell denied Nana was the father of the baby she had given up for adoption long ago. She said Nana had been a close friend and she was upset over his murder, but it could not have been her estranged husband who killed him.

Nevertheless, Tom Mitchell became a suspect. He had a motive and he was in the area at the time of the murder. Nana may have invited him for a drink in an attempt to make amends and Mitchell may have played along, but turned on Nana in a fit of sudden rage and killed him with the weapons to hand. He may have stolen the money from the till to make it look like the motive was robbery. However, none of Mitchell's fingerprints were found in the shop and he had a strong alibi, which is not to say he wasn't guilty. He quickly replaced Craigie's mysterious Indian as the prime suspect.

On 6 March 1931, police announced a reward of £250 for information leading to the arrest of the Hindu's killer.

Truth covered the case mentioning that the killer had stayed at the scene and 'coolly cooked a meal' alongside his victim's battered body. This was an exaggerated elaboration of Mrs Pickett's discovery, but it kept up public interest in the case. Even so, a battered Hindu did not generate as much sympathy as the mysterious deaths of young women like Elsie Walker and Gwen Scarff.

In Hawera, the announcement of a reward generated renewed interest in the case and prompted a few memories. Vince Pivac, who owned the local fish and chip eatery, reported he had heard rumours of four Maori going into David's just before closing time. He had done some prying and found out it was four young men who worked on a shearing gang in Okaiawa, 13 kilometres from Hawera.

When this discovery was reported in the *Hawera Star*, Dave Skipper read the newspaper and started to sweat. Skipper worked in a shearing gang in Okaiawa with the Katene brothers—Pi, Tonga and Dick. Every Saturday night the four of them would head into Hawera, have a decent feed and head straight for the pub—

often getting into a scrap or two. Soon after New Year, they were enjoying one too many drinks in the Central Hotel, when a local took exception to young Tonga showing an interest in his girlfriend. The local lad drummed up support from his equally liquored-up mates and it was all on. The publican turfed them all out and a fight ensued. Skipper and the Katenes were locked up for the night. Trouble usually followed the group and it got to the stage where they were seriously considering avoiding Hawera, but they fell back on the idea that it is better the devil you know and, besides, Hawera was the closest town.

Skipper remembered that Saturday 31 January was different. For once, they had avoided trouble, but he knew the police would come looking for them and probably try to put them in the frame. He took Pi Katene aside to talk with him, but Pi simply suggested they keep their mouths shut—it just might go away. The police took Pivac's story seriously, but Mieklejohn said he doubted four Maori shearers were capable of the cunning demonstrated in this case.

Besides, four killers would have made more of a mess at the scene, which looked as if there was only one assailant involved. It was unlikely Nana would invite a shearing gang into his living quarters late at night when he was alone. If more people had been involved it was more likely that information would have leaked out about what had actually happened. He didn't hold out much hope of locating the shearing gang.

Mieklejohn was surprised when Constable Donovan quickly identified the quartet as the troublemakers he had locked up. On 9 March, Mieklejohn and Quirke drove to Okaiawa. The four men, hats in hands and heads bowed low, told their story.

Late that Saturday afternoon, they travelled into Hawera as usual. They had tea at Pivac's before heading to the movies, and on to Snip Allen's Billiard Saloon to play a few frames. Around 11pm, they left and headed home. It was a rare Saturday night—they did not get into any trouble.

They reckoned it was about 11.20pm when they walked past David's and noticed it was still open. They went inside and Skipper purchased some grapes and Tonga Katene bought some grapes and bananas. Nana served them and seemed cheerful enough. There was another customer in the shop—a tall Pakeha man who was eating a peach and silently watching the four lads. There was a bag of peaches on the counter, which they assumed he had already purchased. They were only in the store for about five minutes and the stranger was still there when they left.

Skipper gave a pretty good description of the man—he was wearing a blue serge suit. In fact, Skipper said he had seen him twice since that night—once a week later eating alone at Pivac's and then just a few days earlier at the railway station. This reminded Constable Healey of an encounter he had in High Street at about 8.15pm on the evening of Sunday 1 February, just a few hours before Nana's body was found by Constable Donovan.

Healey was on the beat when he was approached by a stranger who said he was the baker from Cleaver's Bakery and was up from Masterton for the Hawera races. A few nights later, Healey noticed the same man walking in the middle of the road on High Street at about 3.30am—he said he preferred to walk on the road in darkness. The man was identified as Walter John Tinsley and he was staying in room nine at the Royal Hotel, just along from detectives Quirke and Mieklejohn. The detectives had seen Tinsley in the restaurant at the hotel but he did not stand out to them.

On 10 March, Mieklejohn approached Tinsley as he was walking back to the hotel after work. Mieklejohn said he wanted to talk to him about being seen in the Indian's shop on the night of the murder. Tinsley admitted calling into David's store some time after 11pm on 31 January, to purchase some oranges to take to the Druids' Picnic the next day. While there, he had taken a banana, which he was eating at the counter when the Maori lads came in. He said he had left the shop and returned to the hotel soon after—between 11.15 and 11.20pm. At breakfast the next morning, Mrs Gibson told him of the murder.

Mieklejohn remembered that a week after the murder, Tinsley approached him on the afternoon of 7 February complaining someone had moved his car and parked it around the corner while he was at the Hawera races. Mieklejohn had asked what the problem was—it had not actually been stolen or damaged and it was probably a prank pulled off by a local larrikin. Next morning, at breakfast, Tinsley complained his hat and some money had been taken from his room. Mieklejohn took a brief statement but the complaint was not followed up. On 25 February, Tinsley again complained to Quirke. This time it was about the noise and illegal drinking going on at Panchia's fruit store. Quirke immediately went to the fruit shop, but Panchia had a few customers he was serving alone and things seemed fairly quiet.

Detectives Mieklejohn and Quirke had heard good reports about Tinsley. Although he had only been in Hawera for a few weeks, he had quickly made friends. Nonetheless, his suspicions aroused, Quirke ordered a background check on Tinsley that showed up some interesting and disturbing facts. Walter John Tinsley was born in Masterton on 15 December 1904, the youngest of three boys. The children were doted upon by their mother, but she died when Tinsley was three, and their father walked out. The boys were raised by their grandmother who could not control them—they ran wild. Tinsley became aggressive and was remembered as a school yard bully.

As an adolescent, Tinsley was regularly in trouble with the law for minor crimes. In 1922, he was charged with the theft of a girl's bicycle, which led to his first conviction. He amassed three more convictions for theft during 1923. Disturbingly, his crimes became more selective—they had an anti-Asian motive.

On the nights of 27 and 29 September 1922, Yee Chong, who owned a green grocers in Masterton, heard someone moving around in the shop beneath his living quarters. When he went to investigate there was no sign of anybody, but he found a substantial amount of money missing from the till. Several nights later, on 3 October, he set a trap and caught Tinsley pilfering from the till. Yee pressed charges, and Tinsley was arrested, convicted, and placed on probation for two years.

Tinsley left school to take up an apprenticeship with McKays' Bakery in Masterton. At age 19, he moved to Eketahuna where he managed a billiard hall for a year before switching back to baking. He had a reputation for annoying Chinese and Indian shop owners in Eketahuna.

In 1928, he moved to Johnsonville to work at a local bakery. He married Julia, his childhood sweetheart, and for two years was happy and relatively settled. Tinsley enjoyed his job in Johnsonville and was regarded as a hard worker. However, the marriage was tumultuous and Julia left him in 1930 and returned to Masterton. At that time, members of the Chinese community in Johnsonville complained about being harassed by 'Wally the Baker', but authorities did nothing.

In December 1930, for the sake of his marriage, Walter returned to Masterton and briefly reconciled with Julia. He could not find steady employment there so, in January 1931, he took up the position at Cleaver's in Hawera. On 17 January 1931, he travelled to Hawera and checked in at the Royal Hotel. He began work on 19 January and was soon promoted to manager for two weeks while Cleaver went on holiday. At the beginning of February, Tinsley told Cleaver he wanted to return to Masterton and was actively applying for jobs there. Cleaver was impressed with Tinsley's work ethic and was reluctant to lose such an experienced baker. He thought highly of the young man and hoped he would change his mind.

After the check, the detectives decided they needed to interview Tinsley further. On 14 March, Quirke and Mieklejohn approached Tinsley in the foyer of the Royal Hotel and suggested they go to his room to discuss his movements on the night Nana was murdered. Once in the room Mieklejohn looked out the window and noticed Tinsley had a view overlooking David's store. Leaning out, he saw a narrow balcony leading to the fire escape—a ladder down to the street. The front door of the hotel was locked at 10pm and tenants coming back late had to use the fire escape to get to their rooms.

Tinsley told the detectives on the night of 31 January, he had fish and chips in Pivac's restaurant, leaving there before 11pm. Walking past David's, he noticed the store was still open, so went in and bought some oranges. While he was in the shop, an old man, later identified as an eccentric named William Grindley, and four young Maori men came and went. Tinsley admitted the only 'wrong' thing he did in the store was take a banana without paying for it. Afterwards he walked back to the hotel and re-entered via the fire escape. He did not know the murdered man, David, and he thought he had only ever been in the shop twice before that night. He said he had worked in the bakery from 4am until 11am that Saturday. On Sunday, he headed to the Druids' Picnic, but his car broke down near the racing track. It was the first race of the season and, more importantly, the cup race, so he decided to go to the races instead. Afterwards, he managed to start his car and drove very slowly back to Hawera. He decided to go to the bakery and help Mr Cleaver set the dough for the next day—that was between 4.30pm and 4.45pm. Then he went back to the hotel for dinner and an early night.

Tinsley was asked to provide accounts for the money he'd earned at Cleaver's. He was paid £5.10s per week. He sent his wife £1 per week, paid £1.15s board and the rest of his money was spent on food, beer and repairs to his car. When prompted he admitted betting £1 at the races that Sunday.

After Tinsley signed his statement, Mieklejohn produced a warrant to search the room. In the wardrobe, they found a bottle partly filled with benzene, with a rag forced inside the top where a cork should be. Quirke asked why the bottle was not kept in his car and Tinsley said he used the contents to clean his clothes. That seemed strange.

Mieklejohn checked the clothing and found a fawn gabardine coat with a blood smear and numerous blood specks on the right-hand side. The detective waited for Tinsley to offer an explanation. Tinsley paused before saying he must have got the blood when he called in to see about a job at the Masterton Freezing Works a few days before he came to Hawera. One of his mates, who was slaughtering lambs at the time, wrapped a piece of lamb's liver in newspaper and gave it to Tinsley. Tinsley remembered placing it in his coat pocket. Mieklejohn checked Tinsley's blue and grey suits and found minute specks of blood on the cuffs of the grey trousers. They took the coat and trousers for testing and went to search Tinsley's car. There was nothing of interest in the car so they headed over to the bakery. They asked Cleaver for permission to search the upstairs flour room and shed. Nothing warranting suspicion was found.

William Grindley was interviewed and admitted being in the store on the night of the murder. He remembered seeing the Maori men and the baker from Cleaver's. However he left while both parties were still in the store and headed directly home. He believed Tinsley and Nana to be on good terms.

The next day, Tinsley's wife arrived at the Royal Hotel, and Tinsley told Quirke he had decided to move back to Masterton. Quirke told him he would need to be present at the coroner's inquiry as he was the last known person in the store the night of the murder. Then he asked Tinsley what clothes he had been wearing on 31 January. Tinsley thought he had been wearing the grey suit.

Tinsley remained in Hawera while the clothes were sent to Dr Lynch at Wellington Hospital for forensic testing. Detective Mieklejohn believed Tinsley targeted Nana for robbery because he was a Hindu then, possibly, killed him when he was caught in the act. Police did not know exactly how much money was missing. Rogers had estimated there should have been between £7 and £10 in the till at closing time, but it was empty. Bank of England notes were found in various places upstairs, but there was no evidence of the 'bundle' Rogers had seen Nana put in his trouser pocket that Saturday afternoon. Masterton detectives checked the local banks and found Bank of England notes had only been cashed by legitimate businesses since the murder.

The detectives decided to have a closer look at Tinsley's financial position. During the interview on 14 March, Tinsley provided proof of his income and had satisfactorily accounted for his outgoings. Julia Tinsley was independently interviewed by Masterton police. She worked as a housekeeper at a store at Kuripuni, near Masterton, and confirmed she had received £1 per week from her estranged husband since he had been in Hawera, except on 7 and 14 February when she received £2.10s.

Two days after the murder, Tinsley took his car to a local garage. It needed a new piston, and the re-boring of four cylinders, which he was told would cost £20. Tinsley baulked at the cost and negotiated the mechanic down to £6, because of the age of the car, and ordered a new side screen for £3. When he picked up the car a week later, he had changed his mind about the side screen, but ordered a new hood instead and paid cash for the lot. If Tinsley had agreed to the £20 repair job, police would have cause to be suspicious. However, he haggled down the price to something he could afford from his earnings at Cleaver's.

A number of tenants at the Royal Hotel were interviewed and they were extremely reluctant to speak against the man they had come to know as a mate and a good bloke. Several said Tinsley told them he was going to the races on Sunday 1 February. They could not recall him mentioning he was going to the Druids' Picnic or that his car had broken down.

Cleaver and his 16-year-old assistant, Moody, were interviewed about Saturday and both confirmed Tinsley had worked until 11am. Moody mentioned he might go to the Druids' Picnic the next day, and Tinsley replied he would probably go, too, and would drive there. Moody said he did not see Tinsley at the picnic.

On Monday, when Moody asked Tinsley about his Sunday, Tinsley said he'd spent about £12 at the races. Still, Moody said he got on well with Tinsley, but did not quite know what to make of Tinsley's anti-Indian comments because Tinsley regularly popped next door to drink with Chhiba Panchia.

Panchia confirmed that he regularly entertained Cleaver and Tinsley and he couldn't recall any instances of Tinsley making racist comments. He did say Tinsley had asked him what he thought of the murder, and whether he was worried he might be next on the list.

After the interviews there was still no evidence to link Tinsley to Nana Chhiba's, murder, but there were obviously contradictory recollections of his movements the day after the murder. Nobody saw him at the Druids' Picnic on 1 February, and nobody actually saw him at the races either.

A report on Tinsley's coat and trousers came from Dr Lynch, the pathologist at Wellington Hospital. It was clear the trousers had been vigorously scrubbed, but there were still obvious red smears on them. However, tests for blood proved negative. As for the coat, the reddish stains on the lapel also tested negative for blood. However, the front and back of the skirt had more than 30 minute specks of something, there were several larger splashes on each sleeve and a thick 7.5-centimetre smear on the right-hand side of the hem, as if coat had brushed up against a wet object. These all proved to be human blood. Dr Lynch was unsure of the age of the stains, but he believed them to be 'not very old'—and it appeared to be the same age as the blood on Nana's clothing. He was unable to determine the blood types.

There was some conjecture about how the blood specks could have got on the back of Tinsley's coat. Dr Lynch thought it possible specks of blood could have been flicked onto the back of the coat from a bloody tomahawk or hammer held head high and behind the shoulder, as would happen in a frenzied attack. The cluster of bloodstains just above the main smear resembled an arterial spray—spurts from even a small artery go a very long way.

Sketches of the pattern of the spray on the coat matched the pattern of the sprays on the walls, although the sprays on the walls ran in different directions—some ran vertically down, some ran up and some ran horizontally.

Dr Lynch established three distinct features matching the stains on the coat to the stains on Nana's living-room walls:

- Smudging
- Arterial-spray patterns
- Wide distribution, as if flicked from a swinging object.

Since 14 March, Tinsley had been the most likely suspect. At last, the medical experts had provided some evidence to support this. On 12 May, Mieklejohn and Quirke travelled to Masterton and charged Tinsley with the murder of Nana Chhiba. He protested, accusing them of setting him up. He said he was the scapegoat simply because he had been the last customer in the store.

Quirke placed Tinsley in handcuffs and told him about the bloodstains on his coat. Tinsley paused, thought hard, and then repeated the story about being given a piece of lamb's liver at the Masterton Freezing Works two days before he headed to Hawera. Tinsley was taken back to Hawera. The following day he was picked in a line-up by three of the four Maori shearers. The fourth member of the shearing gang thought the man they had seen in the shop was of larger build.

The detectives picked up Tinsley's blue serge suit to send to Dr Lynch for testing because the Maori boys said the man they saw was wearing a dark-coloured suit. Tinsley said he was wearing the grey suit on 31 January. Perhaps this was a ruse? Tests for blood on the blue suit were negative.

Tinsley was remanded in custody and instructed Mr Patrick O'Dea of New Plymouth lawyers, O'Dea and Bayley, to represent him. He was adamant he was not the killer and insisted he could prove it. O'Dea immediately worked hard to bring a defence, confident the police case was weak, as it was largely dependent on circumstantial evidence. O'Dea made a formal request for disclosure, but this was slow in coming. Also, a number of locals suddenly became reluctant to answer any more questions.

On 21 May, O'Dea sent a strongly worded letter to the Commissioner, claiming Mieklejohn and Quirke were 'intimidating witnesses' and refusing to co-operate. He demanded to know why there were delays in providing exhibits and pathologists' reports to the defence.

Meanwhile, police worked to bolster their case against Tinsley. The current evidence warranted arrest, but it was not enough to gain a conviction. Dr Arthur Pearson of Christchurch travelled to Hawera and examined the bloodstains on the living-room walls and coat. He found a marked similarity to the angles, indicating the deceased was probably attacked by one person, with the blood thrown from the hammer and tomahawk during the attack. This concurred with the findings of doctors Lynch and Sinclair.

With the hearing approaching, O'Dea worked doggedly to come up with what he believed would be a robust and compelling defence, which included the following points:

- On 31 January an Indian man from Rangoon—a stranger to Hawera—asked Craigie about David [Nana], indicating he was going to see him on the day he was murdered.
- Was this the same Indian seen by Whitten two days later, who abruptly left the hotel when conversation turned to the murder? This man had not been identified but he may have been the killer.
- Three men from Masterton Freezing Works would testify that Tinsley visited them at work on 15 January, and one would say he gave Tinsley a lamb's liver wrapped in newspaper that Tinsley put in his coat pocket.
- Dr Lynch could not type the human blood on Tinsley's coat and Nana's clothes. They were probably not from the same source.

- A young jockey named Edwards would testify that at Christmas 1930 he had been involved in a fight in Johnsonville, and he had been knocked out. Tinsley had placed him on his coat in the recovery position. This would account for the blood found on the back of the coat. Later, when Tinsley drove him home, he struggled with Tinsley who hit him in the nose to subdue him. He was still clutching Tinsley's coat and the blood from his nose splashed the coat.
- A thief named Bregman was known to have committed a number of burglaries in the Hawera area during the last week of January 1931. He had been dressed in clothes similar to Tinsley's. He was arrested in early February and told a constable in Levin he had 'done something terrible to an Asian'. The constable was summonsed to appear, but Bregman could not be found.
- There was no proof to suggest robbery as the motive—large sums of money were located untouched upstairs. The thick blood found in Nana's trouser pocket was assumed to be from the murderer removing money, but there was no proof of this.
- It was heard that Nana had recently received a letter containing sensitive information, but this letter was not found in any of the searches. It is possible the assailant was after the letter and Nana was killed as a result.

In terms of the mystery letter, O'Dea had heard the rumours about the Mitchells' baby. He heard that Ada Mitchell had recently written to Nana confirming he was the father of her child. Was she blackmailing him? Did Tom Mitchell hear of this and visit Nana to demand the letter, killing Nana when he would not release it?

This is speculation largely based on local gossip. Ada Mitchell flatly denied writing Nana any such letter. However, the point O'Dea was making was that this theory for a motive was just as feasible as the unproven theory of robbery.

O'Dea had complained he felt Mieklejohn and Quirke were being unco-operative and withholding information from the defence. The Commissioner disregarded O'Dea's letter, but prosecution transcripts now available confirm that significant details were kept from O'Dea.

The police statements of Rogers, Gordon and the other boys who admitted being subjected to Nana's sexual approaches were not made public before or during the hearing. In fact, only Rogers, Gordon and Evans were summonsed to appear, and only to give evidence about events of 31 January. This suggests O'Dea was unaware of their stories.

The Lower Court Hearing opened at Hawera Magistrates Court on Thursday 2 July 1931, before Mr JH Salmon SM and Mr RS Sage JP, the district coroner. It had been decided to run the coronial inquiry with the hearing of the charge. Mr Weston, crown prosecutor from Wellington, represented the Crown. He was assisted by Senior Detective Quirke. Mr O'Dea was assisted by Hugh Biss, lawyer from Wellington. Interest was high and the Hawera courthouse was packed.

The Crown indicated they would be calling 41 witnesses. The case was expected to last until Saturday. Senior Detective Quirke was the first witness and he provided an outline of the facts. Under cross-examination O'Dea asked him why he had been unable to trace Craigie's Rangoon Indian, implying police had not done enough to find him. Quirke said he did not believe the Rangoon Indian existed. He conceded Craigie may have seen an Indian, but was probably mistaken about the date.

Quirke gave an account of the money Tinsley earned while in Hawera. O'Dea skilfully pushed Quirke to admit police were happy with Tinsley's account of his income and spending, and everything was satisfactorily accounted for.

Then O'Dea asked if police had considered the bloodstains found in Nana's trouser pocket may not be the result of the assailant looking for money. He suggested it was more likely someone trying to locate a letter the deceased had in his possession. Quirke replied he had no knowledge of any letter and it was hearsay, but, in fact, they both knew exactly what letter O'Dea was referring to. Still, no letter has ever been found and, even today, it is not certain how or from whom this information originated.

Rogers, Gordon and Evans were next and they simply gave accounts of 31 January. The boys were not cross-examined, which, once again, lends weight to the idea that O'Dea was unaware of their full statements to police.

Edgar Wilton who worked at Masterton Freezing Works testified he had known the accused for a number of years. He recalled Tinsley visiting the plant some time in the middle of January and he had given him a piece of lamb's liver wrapped in newspaper. Under cross-examination by Wilton he did not recognise Tinsley's coat when it was produced in court. Neither did his workmate Cecil McCormack, when asked.

Mention was made of Tinsley telling various witnesses of attending the first day of the Egmont Races on Sunday 1 February, which was also Cup Day. Evidence was introduced proving Cup Day was actually six days later—on Saturday 7 February.

O'Dea did a superb job of deflecting blame from his client and undermining the police case. As he said, it was unlikely a killer would stay at the same hotel as detectives for 10 weeks after the murder.

The tenants in the rooms adjacent to Tinsley's at the Royal Hotel testified. They had gone to a dance at the Savoy tea rooms on the night of 31 January. They returned around 12.30pm, getting to their rooms via the fire escape. They recalled passing Tinsley's room, and noticing the windows were closed. Both men testified the window had been shut fast when they got back, suggesting nobody else had come in that way before them that night. Furthermore, neither of them heard any noises from Tinsley's room or the sound of anybody else coming in via the fire escape after them that night.

Other tenants testified about sitting with Tinsley at meal times in the days following the murder. The brutal death of the Hindu provided a popular topic for discussion, but none of the men heard Tinsley comment about it, nor did they notice anything unusual in his demeanour.

Chhiba Panchia testified in Tinsley's defence, saying he was a pleasant customer who regularly bought fruit and cigarettes from him, and they occasionally played cards together. Panchia stated he had been worried because there was a strange Indian in town asking about Nana and him, and now Nana was dead. He was disappointed police could not trace this strange Indian because he feared the man would return.

The hearing closed on Saturday 4 July, after 34 witnesses had given evidence. O'Dea protested that Mr Pivac should have been called because his testimony about Tinsley's movements was material. He accused police of wanting a conviction more than they wanted to elicit the truth. This earned a mild rebuke from the magistrate who committed Tinsley to stand trial at the New Plymouth Supreme Court. No application for bail was lodged.

Then the coroner returned his verdict: 'Nana Chhiba, a native of Bombay, met his death on the night of January 31/ February 1 at his shop in High Street, Hawera, through being struck repeatedly on the head with a hammer by some person or persons unknown.'

The same teams represented the Crown and Tinsley when the trial proper opened on 17 August 1931, before Mr Justice Blair. Justice Blair outlined the Crown case for the jury and explained that it hinged largely on Tinsley's movements. It had been proved Tinsley worked between 4.30pm and 5pm on Sunday 1 February, and was seen by Healey at 8.15pm. Therefore, it was possible for him to go to the Hindu's shop in between these times, and to be there when Mrs Pickett called in. Blair noted Mrs Gibson was never questioned about whether Tinsley dined in on the evening of 1 February and whether or not he was about the hotel that night, which was a vital omission.

He went on to question whether or not a motive had been proven. Tinsley had been in town for a fortnight before the murder, but had only been into David's store twice. He did not have a score to settle with Nana—he barely knew the man. The Crown would introduce the motive of robbery, but if this was true, why were there large sums of money found stashed upstairs, with minimal effort to hide them? Besides, Tinsley had satisfactorily accounted for the money he earned and spent—his outgoings never exceeded his income during the period in question.

Justice Blair went even further and hinted to the jury that the Crown argument of the way blood was distributed on the coat and walls was inconsistent with explanations from medical experts. That the splashes of blood on the coat corresponded with splashes on wall constituted the main evidence for the Crown, and this really depended on Tinsley being in Nana's shop at 11pm on that Saturday.

A judge is supposed to give a summary of facts for the jury to consider. Blair was going too far, blatantly picking holes in the Crown case. Justice Blair appeared to be biased towards Tinsley, before he had heard the Crown's arguments. He was trying to convince the jury there was reasonable doubt before the hearing had even begun. Mr Weston and Chief Detective Quirke were unimpressed.

Blair continued, asking the jury to place themselves in the murderer's shoes. Would they remain lodging at the same hotel as the two detectives for 10 weeks?

It was the duty of the jury to consider the whole of the Crown case, which meant hearing all 40 witnesses. It was clearly going to be a lengthy affair, if the jury felt there was a case to answer. Blair allowed the jury freedom to regulate its own procedure and adjourn and resume when it saw fit. They retired at 11.40am and deliberated long into the afternoon. Crowds packed the court and street outside well into the evening waiting for a verdict.

Early the next morning when the Court resumed, the jury decided there was no case to answer. Tinsley looked bewildered as he listened carefully to the verdict. When he understood he declared, 'I am an innocent man sir!' He was free to go without any evidence being heard.

There was stunned silence in the courtroom. Outside, a number of supporters, including Chhiba Panchia, had waited through the night. They cheered and celebrated. Few appeared to spare a thought for Nana Chhiba, and the fact his killer had not been found and brought to justice.

Within days of his release, Tinsley returned to Masterton and laid low, but not for long. He and his wife were destitute. While he languished in prison, Julia Tinsley had to raise £300 for her husband's defence, including payment to expert witnesses hired to contradict evidence given by doctors Lynch and Sinclair. She borrowed £70 from family, and drew on £175 of unsettled inheritance from her father's estate—to the detriment of her siblings.

On 25 May 1932, Mrs Tinsley wrote to the Governor General complaining her husband had been wrongfully arrested, and had languished in prison for four months for a crime he hadn't committed. The family had lost out on wages he could have been earning. The police had taken his clothing and had not returned it. The coat and grey trousers had been destroyed when they were tested. Now he was proven innocent, there should be some compensation for the damaged clothing. Further, he was unable to find a job because of his damaged reputation. He had been earning £6 a week at Cleaver's but now was lucky to get relief work at £1.5s a week. He was a 'marked man' and the whole ordeal had caused them much mental anguish.

The Tinsleys felt their only option was to live abroad, but they had no money to travel. They were also in debt to the tune of £280.10s.2d. They were asking for £2000 compensation for wrongful imprisonment and arrest.

In August 1932, Tinsley's local MP demanded answers. The Commissioner responded saying police had returned the blue serge suit, but he conceded nothing had been done about the damaged clothing and he was prepared to compensate for the coat and grey trousers. However, he pointed out a clear inconsistency in Mrs Tinsley's letter. The family could not have missed out on Tinsley's wages while he was in prison—he had left his job in April, and had been unemployed up until the time of his arrest on 12 May.

There was also some uncertainty about claims they had been unable to pay for their legal counsel—under the Justice of Peace Act (1927) the Crown had paid all Tinsley's legal expenses as well as those of his expert witnesses.

Nevertheless, the Tinsleys persevered with their petition and this was heard by the House of Representatives on 7 November 1932. The response from the Solicitor General was it would set a precedent for every criminal if they were awarded compensation. This was usually only considered in cases where there was police misconduct or malicious treatment. In this case, the police had cause to charge and arrest Tinsley, and he was properly committed for trial by a magistrate. Their petition was unanimously rejected.

At the beginning of November, Tinsley was arrested, once again, and charged with theft. There were rumours Tinsley had targeted a Chinese businessman, but details were suppressed. On 11 December he was convicted and fined £5.

In terms of Nana Chhiba's life, money was the cause of many problems. Throughout his life he felt as if his brothers were swindling him with every deal, and in death his estate valued at just £3000—far less than anybody expected—proved difficult to settle. He had given power of attorney to his brother Bhana. Sadly, within months of Nana's untimely death and before the settlement of his estate, Bhana drowned in a steamship accident overseas. This caused the process to drag on for years. Eventually the estate was divided between his surviving brothers.

The investigation into the murder of Nana Chhiba was never reopened, and nobody has ever been held accountable.

8. The Riccarton Racecourse Hotel Murder

Like many classic detective novels, this story begins on a cold, gloomy night, with the sound of a single gunshot reverberating through a hotel. Then the piercing screams of a woman, 'He's dead, he's dead!'

The noise roused people from their sleep.

An hour later, police are called and Constable Murphy arrives at the scene. Pacing back and forth in front of a shocked group of hotel guests in the lounge bar, he may have felt like he was in a scene from an Agatha Christie novel. Murphy surveyed the people in the room and wondered if there was a killer was among them.

The hotel in question was the Riccarton Racecourse Hotel located across the road from the main racecourse gates. The establishment offered meals and accommodation as well as the usual liquid refreshments. By far the busiest week in the hotel's calendar was during the New Zealand Cup Derby, which in 1933 was held between 4 and 11 November. The hotel's 16 guest rooms had been full since the beginning of the month, and each day of the meeting plenty of punters came across the road to have a meal and sink a few ales.

Over the last few years, the hotel had been a bit quiet due to the Depression, but finally things were starting to look up as the number of racegoers swelled to a record number. Maybe this was the sign that the economy was improving.

After the derby, a small number of guests stayed on at the hotel until 16 November. The hotel's proprietor, Donald Fraser and his crew were looking forward to a well-deserved rest. It was not to be.

At 2.20am on the morning of 17 November 1933, Constable Murphy was on duty at Christchurch's Upper Riccarton Police Station when he received a telephone call informing him that a man had just been shot at the Riccarton Racecourse Hotel. In the dark of night, it took Constable Murphy 15 minutes to cycle to the hotel. When he arrived he was met by Elizabeth Fraser, the publican's wife. She was visibly shaken and was being supported by Jack Wilson, the hotel's caretaker, who also looked to be struggling to stay strong.

Elizabeth took a deep breath and calmly told Murphy, 'Don has been shot.'

The three made their way upstairs and walked along the main corridor until they came to the door of a bedroom. Murphy peered into the room. On the floor beside the bed lay Donald Fraser.

Murphy called out to the man and when he received no response, knelt to check whether Fraser was breathing. He wasn't. A pool of blood was slowly spreading beneath him.

Constable Murphy was stunned. He knew Donald Fraser well and not all of is dealings with him had been positive. Even though Fraser had probably accumulated a number of enemies, Murphy had to rack his brain for any one who would have wanted to put a bullet through Fraser's heart.

Donald Fraser had been the publican of the Riccarton Racecourse Hotel for the past five years. Born in Queensland in 1892, he trained as a draper before emigrating to Greymouth with his parents and brother Richard in 1909. There he worked at Despath Foundry, before joining the railways as an engine driver.

In 1914, Fraser was charged with the indecent assault of a teenage girl. He protested his innocence. The girl came from a highly respected family and many locals presumed Fraser's guilt before the case came to court. Fraser was sacked from his job in what he saw as a conspiracy, stemming from the assault charge.

Two days before the trial was due to start, the charges against Fraser were dropped. He might have escaped a conviction but he remained the most despised young man in Greymouth. He couldn't continue living there so he left town.

The following year, Fraser became reacquainted with an old girlfriend named Elizabeth Walton. The pair married in Wanganui and over the next few years, they moved around the North Island working in various draperies. Their first child,

Joyce, was born in 1917.

In 1918, 26-year-old Fraser was conscripted to the Featherston Military Camp. At the end of the war, the Frasers drifted between Palmerston North, Hokitika, Hawera and Wellington. They found it difficult to settle.

With the birth of their son Clutha in 1926 the couple decided on a change of lifestyle, and bought the licence for the Doncaster Hotel in Washdyke, near Timaru. Despite the onset of the Depression, the Frasers' hard work meant they consistently made a profit.

Donald Fraser loved horse racing and dreamed of one day owning a champion race horse. In 1929, he heard that the licence for the Riccarton Racecourse Hotel was up for grabs. Running the hotel would be hard work but he couldn't resist the opportunity. The hotel was a step up from the Doncaster and would afford him some insider knowledge into the racing industry. Fraser's application was successful and on 27 June 1929 the family moved to Riccarton.

Fraser quickly established himself within racing circles. As a landlord, he was tough and no nonsense. He drank but never to excess. He was a generous host but did not tolerate loutish or drunken behaviour. He had a reputation for forcibly removing any patron showing the first signs of trouble. Gruff and taciturn, he was unpopular among the heavy drinkers of the Riccarton set and made a number of enemies. The local police were used to receiving complaints from patrons saying Don had assaulted them for no particular reason. When asked for an explanation, Fraser would merely shrug and say all he wanted to do was run a respectable establishment and could not afford to have drunkards wrecking the joint and spoiling his reputation. But it went much further than that. Fraser had a violent streak and some of his ejections were unnecessarily forceful. More than one man complained of being beaten beyond submission.

In 1931, one man told police he had urinated against the wall of the hotel as Fraser walked outside. Upon catching him, Fraser administered a ferocious beating which left the man requiring hospital attention. Fraser offered a very different explanation, saying the man was disturbing other patrons and had objected to being asked to keep quiet. No witnesses were willing to come forward so Fraser escaped punishment.

Fraser's ferocious reputation was countered by the fact that he employed one of the most popular and friendly barmen in Christchurch, Fred Douglas. It was said that Douglas never forgot a customer's name or order.

The hotel was a two-storey concrete brick building. Half the ground floor was taken up by the public bar and lounge bars. In the other half were an office, the dining room and the kitchen. A passage led through the private section of the ground floor to the back door, which opened into a closed-in porch and backyard.

Outside the office was a staircase that led to the second storey, which was largely taken up with hotel accommodation. Upstairs there were 16 private rooms and two sitting rooms. The Frasers had a small bedroom in the centre of the hotel, which opened out onto a balcony.

The hotel had only one long-term resident, Alfred Higgs, a studmaster who worked at the racecourse. He occupied a room two doors along from the couple. Joyce Fraser had her own room at the end of the passageway and eight-year-old Clutha slept in a room near his parents.

Constable Murphy and Jack Wilson helped Elizabeth Fraser back downstairs where several people milled about helping themselves to drinks at the bar.

Dr Hall arrived on the scene at 3.05am. Constable Murphy ushered him into the small bedroom where Fraser's body lay. The dead man was dressed in socks, a shirt and a singlet. He was lying on the floor beside the bed with his arms and legs outstretched. There was a widening pool of blood beneath the body. The sheet and two blankets that Fraser had been sleeping under were pierced with a bullet hole.

By this time, Chief Detective Dunlop had arrived at the hotel and he assisted Murphy in turning the body over. There was a considerable amount of blood on Fraser's neck and face and his body was still warm. He had been shot point blank in the chest with a double-barrel shotgun while he lay in bed and had probably been killed instantly. The policemen arranged for Fraser's body to be taken to the Christchurch morgue before conducting a search of the room.

It was 4am before Inspector Cameron arrived. He began to interview the people in the bar downstairs about the events leading up to the discovery of the body.

Elizabeth Fraser appeared calmer than she had been when Murphy first arrived. Cameron found her sitting in a chair in the corner of the lounge bar, sipping a glass of brandy, and being comforted by her daughter and another woman.

She told Cameron that the hotel had closed the previous afternoon as was customary. Don had remained in the office to take care of paperwork. Mrs Fraser stayed on in the upstairs lounge for a few drinks with local bookie Edward Russell, who was known as Ted, Alfred Higgs who lived at the hotel, and Jack Wilson. She admitted that she knew this was against the law.

Just as the pub had been about to shut, George Welsh had called in and was invited upstairs. Soon after, Elizabeth Fraser's good friend Marion Wood arrived and was let in by Donald Fraser.

The group partied in the upstairs lounge listening to records and drinking. At around 5pm, they went downstairs for tea. Fraser joined them just as they were finishing their meal. Higgs and Welsh remained downstairs talking with him while he ate.

Mrs Fraser told police that she thought her husband had been drinking in the office, as he was unsteady and his speech was slurred.

According to Elizabeth, Wilson returned downstairs to the bar to clean up at about 8pm. At about the same time Higgs had gone to his bedroom to write letters and listen to the radio and Welsh had popped upstairs to say goodnight to him before heading home. She said she didn't know where her husband was at that stage but she assumed he had returned to the office.

When Edward Russell said he was going home, Elizabeth and her friend Marion had persuaded him to stay on. Another friend, Elizabeth Thompson arrived to pay the Frasers money she owed them for drinks and was invited to join her friends upstairs. Fraser joined the group soon after. He suggested they all go halves in a bottle of champagne, offering 10 shillings himself. The others agreed and made up the cost of the bottle.

The Fraser's daughter, 16-year-old Joyce also joined the group, drinking half a glass of champagne before going to bed at around 9.30pm. Marion Wood left shortly after.

Ted Russell and Elizabeth Thompson stayed for another hour. Both were extremely intoxicated when they left the hotel. Before long, Russell returned saying he'd had trouble navigating his bike and that he was hungry. Donald Fraser laughed and helped him into the kitchen, where he asked Jack Wilson to make sandwiches for them all.

Russell finally left at about 11.15pm. Fraser then told his wife he was going to lock up and go to bed. Elizabeth Fraser said she stayed downstairs and counted the rest of the days' takings and then went upstairs to bed at about 11.45pm.

Don was sitting in bed reading and the couple talked for about ten minutes until they heard the sound of a car pulling up outside. Someone then rang the doorbell. Mrs Fraser said the couple ignored it as they thought it was probably a drunken patron wanting an after-hours drink. But the ringing persisted so Donald pulled on his pants and went out onto the balcony.

According to his wife, he didn't turn on the bedroom light as he went out the French doors onto the balcony. She then heard him call out asking who was there. There was no response so he grumbled and went downstairs.

Elizabeth said she heard low voices for about 20 minutes before she drifted off to sleep. She didn't hear him return to bed but she claimed that soon afterwards she had heard her husband snoring by her side. What seemed to be moments later, she told the inspector, an explosion woke her.

Mrs Fraser could not recall if she had switched on the light but said she had jumped out of bed and ran along the corridor yelling 'Higgs! Don has been shot!'

At this point she raced back to the bedroom and was met by her daughter Joyce. The two then went and banged loudly on the door of Alf Higgs' room. Higgs stumbled out and sleepily staggered into the Frasers' bedroom where he found Donald Fraser's body. According to Elizabeth, Higgs then ushered them downstairs where he telephoned for police and a doctor. Mrs Fraser then asked Higgs to call Marion Wood.

Elizabeth Fraser told Inspector Cameron that she didn't know who would want to kill her husband. She said he had made many enemies over the years but she could think of only one who had actually threatened to kill him.

According to Mrs Fraser, in 1930 her husband had alerted police to a drunken patron passing false cheques. William Thomas was arrested at the hotel. He threatened to shoot Fraser for dobbing him in. Fraser had been shaken by the threat but he hadn't seen Thomas since.

Inspector Cameron then interviewed Joyce Fraser. She said she had been in her bedroom sewing most of the evening before going to say goodnight to her parents and their friends. They had invited her to join them for half a glass of champagne, which she drank before she returned to her room at about 9.30pm. She said she read for an hour before falling asleep. Some time later she was woken by the sound of her mother screaming for Higgs.

Jack Wilson, the hotel's porter and caretaker was 48-years-old, but due to years of alcohol abuse looked much older. In exchange for his work, he lived rent-free in a detached room at the rear of the hotel. He worked hard for the Frasers, grateful to them for putting him up. He was clearly upset over the death of his boss and appeared to be taking the news very badly.

When interviewed, Wilson corroborated Elizabeth Fraser's version of the evening's events. Wilson agreed with that Donald Fraser had been quite drunk when he came to eat his tea but had sobered up after eating his meal.

Wilson said he stayed downstairs to clean up in the bar. While he was doing that, he said Fraser divided his time between the kitchen, bar and office.

According to Wilson, Mr Welsh had left at about 8pm and Mrs Thompson had arrived soon after. He believed Mrs Thompson spent a few minutes with Donald Fraser in the office before joining the party upstairs. His account of the rest of the evening matched Elizabeth Fraser's.

Towards the end of the night, Wilson saw Fraser sitting on the stairs and asked him if he was all right. According to Wilson, the publican had replied, 'I am feeling a bit merry, Jack, not feeling too good.'

Wilson said Fraser often drank whisky alone in his office when he worked late at night. When Wilson went out to his room, he waited a few minutes outside the kitchen door to ensure Fraser would lock it. He heard the key turn in the lock and he went to bed.

Wilson said he was in bed by about 11.10pm. He thought it was about 30 minutes later that he heard a car pull up outside the hotel. The next sound he heard was a loud bump coming from inside the hotel. At the time he thought it sounded like someone falling out of bed.

He fell asleep a few minutes later and was woken when he heard Mrs Fraser banging on his door, screaming 'Jack, Jack, come quick! Don has been shot.'

Wilson said he had hurriedly dressed and ran inside. There he found Mrs Fraser and Joyce standing outside the office while Higgs was speaking on the telephone. He said Elizabeth had followed him upstairs. When he looked into the Frasers' room, he said it appeared that Don had fallen out of bed taking the sheet and blankets with him as he fell. Wilson said he had noticed the bloodstains on the sheet before bending down to check whether Fraser was breathing. He then closed the door and went back downstairs.

Cameron went upstairs to examine the crime scene. Dr Hall, who was arranging the removal of the body, pointed out a thin cartridge wad on the floor between the wardrobe and bed. Later, another wad was found on Fraser's pillow.

Cameron stepped through the French doors onto the balcony. This was the likely point of entry for the assailant having climbed up the fire escape. On the iron grating at the top of the fire escape the inspector found a footprint. Further investigation found that it was the print of a serrated soled rubber shoe, possibly a size eight. Did this belong to the killer?

To test whether it was possible for the assailant to have got away down the fire escape, Cameron climbed down the ladder. The bottom of the ladder reached the backyard. At the foot of the ladder, Cameron noticed some loose shingle corresponding to the gravel on the road. If this shingle came from the boots of the assailant, then it is likely they had arrived by road.

Directly across the road were the vast paddocks of Riccarton racecourse. Beyond the racecourse was forest and farmland. If the killer had run across the racecourse, any tracks would be impossible to determine.

Acting Detective Edwards sealed off the balcony and set about checking for forensic evidence stemming from the theory that the killer had escaped by this route.

Cameron informed Wilson and Elizabeth Fraser about the discovery of the boot print on the fire escape. Elizabeth told him that they were regularly disturbed by drunken patrons attempting to procure liquor after hours. This had not occurred for several months but she thought it might account for the bootprint.

In any case, police ruled this out as a likely escape route. The killer would have had to negotiate his way down the ladder in darkness carrying a heavy shotgun. This would have been extremely difficult unless the killer had an accomplice.

If the assailant had escaped on foot, the racecourse was the perfect place to run to. There were plenty of high hedges, bushes and ponds and it would be the perfect place to dump the murder weapon.

At first light, a number of uniformed police from all areas of Christchurch were bussed in and began searching the entire area. Specialist equipment was ordered to drain the ponds and lakes.

Meanwhile police had ruled out robbery as a motive for the killing when £7.18s.6d in notes and change was found in a locker in Fraser's wardrobe. A gold watch and some coins were found on the mantelpiece. When Fraser's clothing was stripped at the Christchurch mortuary, his pockets contained more money.

A post mortem was conducted by pathologist Dr Arthur Pearson at 7.15 that morning. He found that the cause of death was due to a very severe mechanical injury to the heart. The injuries had destroyed the base of the heart almost entirely on the left side. There would have been no spurting of blood. It would merely have welled up into the wound and overflowed.

The wounds were produced by the discharge of a shotgun. The two charges entered the heart side by side with a thin strip of skin separating the two entrance wounds. The two felt wads from the cartridge were found embedded in shattered muscle tissue. The charges finally lodged in Fraser's back muscles and did not produce an exit wound. Death would have been instantaneous. The time of death was estimated to have been between 1am and 2am.

Pearson believed that the muzzle of the gun must have been very close to the victim. There was only a small amount of gunpowder blackening around the external wound, suggesting the powder was a smokeless brand.

The murderer stood near the right side of the bed on which the victim was lying. According to Pearson's report, the victim had probably been asleep when he was shot and the killer had fired downwards. He said that as there was no lighting from street or from the landing if the bedroom door was closed, the killer would have needed either the light in the bedroom or the one on the balcony to be on. Another possibility was that the killer had an accomplice who had held a torch.

Sergeant Harrison was placed in charge of checking through the list of all persons who had registered shotguns and immediately found a person of interest.

Both Elizabeth Fraser and Jack Wilson had told police that Ted Russell had been at the hotel after closing. According to them he had left an hour before Fraser was shot. Harrison soon found that Russell was the registered owner of a single barrel shotgun.

Chief Detective Dunlop called to see him at McLean's boarding house, along the road from the racecourse, and Russell seemed nervous. He worked at the local freezing works and was rumoured to be operating an illegal bookies out of the hotel. Russell emphatically denied this allegation during his interview.

Russell admitted to having known the Frasers for about two or three years. He was a regular at the racecourse and had an encyclopaedic knowledge of the local racing scene. Russell boasted that the previous year he had recommended the two-year-old gelding Silver Ring to Fraser. On Russell's recommendation, Fraser invested in the horse, which was ridden by one of New Zealand's top jockeys, George Humphries. It soon proved successful and Fraser began reaping the rewards. Silver Ring's success meant that by August, Fraser was confident enough to risk taking the gelding to Australia to race.

For the six week tour, Edward Russell had accompanied Donald and Elizabeth Fraser along with Cyril McCarthy, Silver Ring's trainer, the jockey, George Humphries, and Alfred Higgs. In its first race, Silver Ring came second. The New Zealand contingent made plenty of money and celebrations continued for two days.

They all bet big money on the next race but Silver Ring was not up to pace. Between them, the horse's backers lost hundreds of pounds. Unbeknownst to them, the horse had caught a virus. The Frasers borrowed money from Russell to help cover veterinary expenses.

Russell admitted that after returning to New Zealand he and Don had fallen out over the debt but said that they had patched up their differences and had even talked about investing in another racehorse.

Dunlop asked Russell to account for what occurred during the evening at the hotel. He said he had popped over to the hotel for a drink in the afternoon and was invited back after closing by Mrs Fraser. The rest of the evening was spent drinking upstairs in the company of Mrs Fraser and Mrs Wood. Russell said other people dropped in but never stayed too long. He said that Joyce had joined the group for an hour at 10pm—this varied quite markedly from Joyce's statement that she had been in bed by 9.30pm.

Russell stressed that there was nothing untoward going on between him and the ladies but he agreed that he had been quite drunk and had found it difficult to get on his bicycle to ride home. He thought he'd left just after midnight and he'd cycled straight home. Mrs McLean, who ran the boarding house, said she had heard Russell stumble in at around 12.20am. She also said she'd heard him snoring soon afterwards. He admitted owing a single-barrel shotgun but said that he'd lent it to a farmer a year earlier and it had not been returned.

Word of the murder quickly spread throughout Christchurch. Outside the hotel, a crowd of about 50 people jostled to peer in the windows. Cameron instructed his officers to direct the morbid onlookers across the road. The case continued to fascinate and for the first week of the investigation the crowd remained across the road hoping for some action.

When Fred Douglas, the barman, arrived for work he hadn't heard about Fraser's death. He couldn't work out why there were so many people milling around outside the hotel. He received the shock of his life when he was told his employer had been shot dead.

With the bar closed, Douglas busied himself in the office trying to get the paperwork into some kind of order.

Douglas asked Inspector Cameron to come into the office, closing the door after him. He told the policeman that after he'd arrived that morning, he'd noticed that the fire screen had been removed from in front of the fireplace. Douglas said he found this odd as the fire had not been used for over a month. He also noticed a spent match on the floor and a new box of matches, like the brand sold at the bar, on the mantelpiece. Douglas said he then looked inside the grate and saw a couple of pieces paper that had been burned.

Cameron returned to the office and on searching it, he retrieved something from the wastepaper basket. It appeared to be a letter that had been started then ripped up.

He also found a parcel that had been posted from the North Island several days earlier. Inside was a pair of men's pyjamas and a scarf. The attached card read: *To Don, with Love, EH.*

It didn't take long to find the identity of EH as a letter addressed to Donald Fraser arrived at the hotel the same day. The handwriting on the envelope matched the writing on the card that had been signed *EH.*

Meanwhile, attempts were made to interview the other people who had been present at the illicit party the evening of Donald Fraser's death.

Marion Wood was unco-operative and refused to make a statement. She admitted spending the evening drinking with Mrs Fraser. She told police that the Frasers had been a very happy couple and she had no idea who would want to hurt Don.

Elizabeth Thompson was more forthcoming. She said she and her husband, Alec, were good friends of the Frasers and that they regularly went to the hotel for an after-hours drink. She said Alec had not been with her that evening as he and Don had fallen out three weeks earlier.

She said she had gone to the hotel by herself and had popped into the office to repay Don the money she owed him. He invited her to have a glass of whisky with him, which she did before joining the rest of the party upstairs. She spent several hours with her friends before leaving at about 10.30pm.

Mrs Thompson was reluctant to say why her husband had fallen out with Fraser but eventually admitted that Donald Fraser had caught Alec Thompson kissing his wife. Elizabeth Thompson claimed it had all been a misunderstanding. She told police that she and Alec had been having marital problems and he had sought advice from Mrs Fraser. He thanked her by giving her a friendly kiss. At that moment Fraser had walked in and jumped to the wrong conclusion. He gave Thompson a beating and kicked him out of the pub.

Alec Thompson was the Riccarton milkman and local police knew him well. He was a pitiful man, fond of alcohol and dominated by his overbearing wife. He had a reputation for being sleazy and they thought it likely that he would have made a pass at Mrs Fraser. Even so, he was never seriously considered a suspect.

Alfred Higgs was also very forthcoming when interviewed by Inspector Cameron. He had been present on the night of the murder and he was also a close friend of Don Fraser. As a part owner of Silver Ring, Higgs had accompanied the Frasers to Australia in August 1932. He lost money. Despite this, he and Fraser had been talking about investing in another racehorse.

Higgs told police that the Australia trip had tainted his friendship with Elizabeth Fraser. He said that, in spite of the Frasers' heavy losses, Mrs Fraser had continued to recklessly spend Don's money, drink to excess and openly flirt with other men. After they returned to New Zealand, Higgs said that her behaviour worsened.

Despite admitting to having a few drinks with Don after hours, Higgs said he never drank with Mrs Fraser and her friends. According to him, Mrs Fraser operated a scam where she would invite wealthy male guests to join her upstairs for drinks and then hint of further delights. On these occasions, Mrs Woods and Mrs Thompson would soon arrive. The men would pay to keep the women's glasses filled all night expecting—and sometimes receiving—sexual favours.

Over the past few weeks, Higgs had witnessed the Frasers' relationship deteriorate. They were constantly bickering, most recently arguing over their daughter, Joyce. The 16-year-old was rebellious and wanted to attend socials and dances most evenings.

Fraser was strict and forbade his daughter from going out. Her mother, on the other hand, encouraged her to go out. The couple argued with Joyce frequently siding with her mother against her father.

A week before the murder, according to Higgs, Fraser had refused his daughter's request to attend a dance. She was furious and, encouraged by her mother, she went anyway. The next day Fraser had grounded his daughter and suspended her allowance. She had retaliated by cursing him and scratching his face.

Alf Higgs could not bear to see his friend suffer this indignation and decided to move out of the hotel. The day before the murder he had secured lodgings at a nearby boarding house. He hadn't had the chance to tell the Frasers that he was going to move out.

On the evening before the murder, Higgs said he and Welsh had been in the kitchen when Don came in for tea. The publican seemed to have had a bit to drink. He said Don had gone upstairs to join his wife and her friends, coming back down briefly to grab a bottle of champagne. Higgs told police that his friend had invited him to join the group upstairs but he declined and went to bed. He also said that he didn't get along with Russell and he suspected the man was carrying on with one of the married women.

Higgs couldn't remember what time he went to sleep. Despite his room being two doors away from the Frasers, he said he didn't hear a gunshot but was instead woken by Mrs Fraser calling for him. When he opened the door, Elizabeth Fraser was yelling that Don had been shot. She asked him, 'Didn't you hear the row? Didn't you hear the doorbell ring?'

When Higgs went out into the hallway he said both the hall light and the Frasers' bedroom light were on. He said he struggled to work out what was going on. Joyce had been standing outside her parents' bedroom and her mother stood behind him as he looked into the room. She asked him if he could see any blood and he told her he couldn't. According to Higgs, she then pointed to the pillow where he saw a small dark patch. Looking down at the body, he said he thought he saw Don open and shut his mouth twice.

Higgs said he then guided Elizabeth and Joyce downstairs before calling the police and a doctor. While he was on the phone, Higgs had noticed Elizabeth pick something up from the floor. It appeared to be a white triangle, which she placed in her pocket. He said he thought it could have been a letter. Elizabeth Fraser then asked Higgs to telephone Marion Wood, but he said that he'd refused as there was no reason to involve her.

The pair then walked out into the hallway and Higgs said he noticed that the back door was open. This was highly unusual as the Frasers were meticulous about securing all the doors. Higgs was worried that the killer was still in the hotel but when he mentioned it to Elizabeth, she just walked over and closed the door before going out to wake Wilson.

Higgs said neither Elizabeth nor Joyce had been hysterical but that they had showed signs of being in shock. Elizabeth repeatedly asked him if he could take a drink to Don or help him back into bed. She then asked Wilson to phone Mrs Wood but he said he was so shocked he couldn't do it. Mrs Fraser made the call instead.

Higgs had been present when Constable Murphy first questioned the pair. He thought they had been evasive in their responses, which made him suspect that they may have been involved in Fraser's killing. When Dr Hall arrived, Higgs had shown him upstairs to the Frasers' room. It was then that he noticed the blankets and sheets were all doubled up and twisted at the foot of the bed. He was positive they hadn't been like that when he first went into the room. Then it had appeared that Don had fallen out of bed taking some of the bedclothes with him. Higgs thought that the other side of the bed looked as it hadn't been slept in. From what he saw, Higgs was convinced that Don had been the only person in bed when he was shot. When he went into the room later with Dr Hall, the bedclothes were bunched up giving the impression that both sides of the bed had been occupied.

Higgs also thought that the body had been moved as the lower half of his body was now covered by the sheets when it definitely had not been before.

Inspector Cameron asked Higgs who he thought had killed Donald Fraser. He responded saying that believed either one or both the Fraser women were responsible. Certainly there were some inconsistencies in their stories but Cameron wanted to know why Fraser's wife and daughter would want to kill him. The answer lay in the mysterious EH. When police tracked her down, the dead man's story began to unfold.

Donald Fraser's life had changed on 9 July 1933 when he left Christchurch for a 12-day holiday in Wellington. He left his wife and Jack Wilson in charge of the hotel.

On 12 July, he headed to the races at Trentham. He was happy to be back among the racing fraternity but outside the Riccarton set. During the afternoon, he met up with some friends and they introduced him to a young lady called Eileen Hardcastle. The 22-year-old had recently moved to Wellington from the Hawke's Bay. She seemed to have been charmed by the polite confidence of this handsome older man. Fraser could not keep his eyes of her, offering to escort her around the stables. At the end of the afternoon, he kissed her hand and said he hoped he would see her again. Eileen blushed, and said she hoped they would.

Fraser made sure he would see Miss Hardcastle again. Three days later he took Eileen and a chaperone out to lunch. Over champagne, he charmed both women with his stories. Following lunch, Fraser caught the ferry south bound for home.

On returning to Christchurch he found the hotel in disarray. Elizabeth was drunk and abusive. Fred Douglas had tried to keep on top of the orders and other paperwork but Elizabeth tried to take over and hadn't completed any of it. Liquor had not been ordered, creditors had not been paid and the takings had not been counted or banked. It was impossible for him to work out how much of the takings Elizabeth and Joyce had pocketed.

Donald Fraser had to spend a few late nights in the office before the books were balanced. One night, while he was working in the office, he had put aside his paperwork and penned a letter of thanks to his friends and asked to be remembered to Miss Hardcastle.

A few days later, Fraser received a letter addressed in unfamiliar handwriting. He opened the letter and his heart warmed. It was a letter from Eileen Hardcastle thanking him for his kind thoughts. She also thanked him for taking the time to show her around Trentham before saying that she had enjoyed his company.

Fraser immediately penned a reply asking if he could correspond with Miss Hardcastle. She consented and her eloquently composed letters became a welcome respite from his domestic situation for Donald Fraser.

For her part, Eileen Hardcastle was charmed by Donald Fraser's impeccable manners and she saw him as an intelligent, experienced older man.

As their correspondence continued, Fraser planned to travel north as soon as possible. A three-day trotting meet at Trentham in early September provided the perfect excuse. He booked his passage and told his wife he was off to Wellington.

Eileen Hardcastle was waiting for him at the Wellington ferry terminal. They embraced and he promised that they would have a lovely time together. Over the next few days, they spent all their time together. It was scandalous behaviour but surviving letters reveal that Fraser had openly poured his heart out to Miss Hardcastle, explaining how unhappy his marriage was and hinting that he was in the process of leaving the marriage. A day after he got back from Wellington, he wrote:

At home I was told it was much better without me and wished I would go away every weekend. I had an understanding yesterday. I was told I was hated and we had a mutual agreement to finish and she said she would go at anytime. I am to go my way. I was absolutely no use going on. She seemed very keen to get away from me. That is final. No more of that dear, that wears me out. I do not want any conversation with her whatsoever. When she goes out it is "goodbye" with her, no return. She has got somebody dear and not far away. They are welcome.

From the content of this letter, it was clear that Elizabeth Fraser had admitted to her husband that she was having an affair. However, her husband may have exaggerated the impending end of their marriage in order to keep Miss Hardcastle happy.

Jack Wilson confirmed that he had overheard an argument in which Elizabeth told her husband she had been out with a lover. When asked about this, Mrs Fraser downplayed the explanation by saying she had told Don she was going to the pictures that day and when she returned in the evening, he had complained that he hadn't known where she was. According to Elizabeth, she had responded mockingly, 'Oh Don, if you must know, I was out with my lover'.

Fraser must have known it would not be simple or straightforward to end his marriage. Elizabeth Fraser's name was alongside his on the hotel's lease and she was a part-owner of Silver Ring. She was also reliant on her husband to fund her lifestyle. There was no way Elizabeth Fraser would give up without a fight.

Eileen must have assumed the couple was leading separate lives, and Elizabeth would not care whether or not she addressed her correspondence to the hotel. If Donald Fraser had told Eileen the truth, she might not have been prepared to wait around for him.

On 19 September, soon after his return to Christchurch, Fraser overheard Elizabeth booking passage for her and the children to Sydney for a holiday. Later that afternoon, he telephoned Eileen to tell her that his wife was going on holiday and they made plans for him to go to Wellington while she was away. Elizabeth overheard this conversation and became suspicious. She demanded to know who her husband was talking but Fraser refused to tell her. When he got off the phone, he realised that she could thwart his plans. To appease his wife he told her that he planned to go to Trentham and he thought he'd take the car with him so he could spend a week driving around a few stables to look for a new racehorse. He then added that the people he had been talking to on the phone were potential business partners.

Later that night, he wrote a letter to Eileen:

She wanted to tell me, sweetheart, she has got a lover and had him for two years. A widower for seven years, and she's very much in love with him. She said she would go very soon within a week or two. She felt she would not like to leave me on my own in the hotel, she did not want to be mean with me. She was calm and asked for a divorce and has asked me four times since Friday to go in and sign a mutual separation order.

The next day, Fred Douglas took Don Fraser aside and told him that Elizabeth had been in the office moving papers around as if she was trying to find something specific. Fraser didn't say much except that she would not find what she was looking for.

On 29 September, Fraser left for Wellington. After a night with his mother in Owhiro Bay, he picked up Eileen Hardcastle. The pair spent the next two weeks touring the North Island, staying in hotels as man and wife.

After they returned to Wellington, Fraser called to see his mother. She was visibly upset. Elizabeth had been telephoning three times a day demanding to know where Donald was and threatening to leave him. Mrs Fraser assured Elizabeth that she didn't know where Donald was but Elizabeth did not believe her. Fraser was surprised as he thought his wife was in Sydney. He was alarmed to find out that she had cancelled the trip and was on her way to Wellington.

Fraser collected Elizabeth from the ferry on 18 October. The pair drove her directly to the Royal Oak Hotel, where Fraser rented his wife a room. An argument ensued and Donald left saying that he was busy and she would have to make do by herself but he would lend her the car when he could.

Elizabeth telephoned a friend, Mrs Clarke, who came and picked her up. Together they drove around all the likely racing haunts in Wellington to try and catch her husband. She knew he was up to something but she didn't know what.

21 October was Cup Day at Trentham and Elizabeth knew her husband would not be able to resist the draw of a day's racing. Through her binoculars, she spotted Fraser standing in the Trentham Stand on the arm of a young woman. Elizabeth stormed over to the couple and confronted her husband yelling, 'I know now why you took the car!'

Fraser was embarrassed but grabbed Eileen's hand and walked away leaving his wife standing in the middle of the crowd.

Elizabeth visited her mother-in-law and broke down. She demanded to know who the girl was but Donald's mother said he had not told her anything. All she knew was that he had gone to Palmerston North to look at a horse. Elizabeth begged Mrs Fraser to find out what Don was up to and asked her to write immediately, sending her letters care of Marion Wood.

Don Fraser was booked on a ferry south on 24 October, so his wife and her friend, Mrs Clarke waited at the terminal hoping to catch Fraser with the girl. They were disappointed to see him patiently waiting to board the ferry alone.

A few days later, Fraser posted Eileen a letter:

Your ring on Wednesday night—they were listening in and I have had a bad time since. It has been quiet since this morning and I can't understand it. She is waiting to get something on me. She made trouble in Wellington. This playing up is unsettling me. I asked her to leave the place but she would not. My brown coat is cut to ribbons and my pyjamas have met the same fate. I saved a squirrel coat from the scissors. I have refused her all drink. She got a wire from Wellington signed "Micky".

The daughter scratched my face and made quite a nice job of it. I have cut her allowance completely now. I feel quite worn out and gladly lose four figures to get clear. I don't know what will happen next. Their behaviour is shocking. She says she will divorce me in six months as this can't go on.

Fraser sounded weary but his letter greatly understated actual events.

One day, the hotel cook, Pat Dore, had been playing cards with Jack Wilson in his room. Joyce Fraser had burst in saying that her parents were having a blazing row and her mother was cutting up all her father's clothes. Wilson and Dore raced in and separated the pair. On the floor were Fraser's suit jacket, several shirts and pyjamas cut and torn in a pile on the floor.

A few nights later, Don Fraser was putting out the rubbish and he saw Elizabeth with Alec Thompson, the husband of her best friend. He believed that he'd seen them kissing passionately and proceeded to give Thompson a beating, before barring him from ever setting foot in the hotel again. He then stormed upstairs and cut up several of his wife's dresses in retaliation.

Fraser's relationship with his daughter Joyce had also disintegrated over the past few months. At 16, Joyce Fraser was an attractive young lady and definitely not 'Daddy's Little Girl' anymore. She had grown up stubborn and headstrong like both of her parents.

She enjoyed the attention she received from many of the young men in the racing industry as jockeys and stable boys vied for her attention. Her mother encouraged her to go out and enjoy her life, eagerly listening to Joyce's stories of the clumsy attempts at courtship by the young men.

Fraser believed Joyce was too young to attend socials and go on dates. He thought she should be concentrating on her education. Whenever a potential suitor called, Fraser would intimidate them as much as he could.

Late one night, Fraser was in his office when he heard a bump upstairs. He crept up and opened the door to Joyce's room and found a young jockey climbing through her window from the fire escape. Without a word, Fraser walked over, picked up the boy and manhandled him down the stairs before hurling him out onto the street. All the while Joyce was hitting and spitting at her father.

By the beginning of November 1933, the relationship between Donald and Elizabeth Fraser had become openly hostile but all that had to be put aside for the sake of the business. The New Zealand Derby meant that the hotel would be really busy and even in the leanest of years, the hotel made a huge profit during the race meeting. With all the rooms booked and plenty of people coming across to the hotel to eat and drink, Elizabeth Fraser toned down her behaviour and appeared to do some work. She might not have enjoyed it but she knew the financial benefits would be worth it.

On the evening of 2 November, two days before the racing carnival was due to start, Elizabeth received a telegram from Greymouth that said her mother had suffered a stroke and she was needed immediately. She left at once and her mother died the next day.

Elizabeth returned home on 4 November to help out at the hotel for the first day of the race meeting before returning to the West Coast for her mother's funeral the following day. She returned to Christchurch on 10 November.

Don Fraser may have seemed unsympathetic to the loss of his mother-in-law but he was rushed off his feet at the hotel. But he did himself no favours—he accused the hotel cleaner of being drunk on duty, and decided that Pat Dore, the cook, was just plain lazy, so he sacked them both immediately.

On Elizabeth's return, she worked hard during the day, but immersed herself into nights of hard partying. After all, she felt she deserved it. Joining her each night were her friends, Elizabeth Thompson and Marion Wood.

Meanwhile, Don Fraser would lock himself away in the office at night. He telephoned Eileen regularly and wrote her long, heartfelt letters. On the night of 14 November he started a letter, which read:

Been away, back doing nothing and talk of moving to Greymouth but would keep coming back to torment me. Fired cook and maid last week.

He then tore the sheet up and threw it in the wastepaper basket. On another piece of paper he wrote:

I placed the profit for the week away in my private account for a rainy day. I will show you the slip one day. Almost £6 a week for the whole year. I am getting thrifty, dear. I am saving hard. All out again tonight. I am off to bed early say 10.15pm. I sleep on the balcony. I am feeling quite myself. Still a little bit tired but recovering fast.

This letter was also torn up and thrown in the bin. These were the letters that Inspector Cameron found in Donald Fraser's rubbish bin.

Eileen Hardcastle was devastated when she learned of Don Fraser's death. At the request of the police, she travelled to Christchurch, where she attended Fraser's funeral incognito. After the funeral she was interviewed by police, describing at length Fraser's visits to Wellington and the telephone conversations she'd had with him. She gave them the letters that Donald had sent her in hope that they might provide some clues as to the identity of his killer.

As police continued interviewing hotel regulars, they came across several other people who had visited the hotel the night Fraser was killed. Cyril McCarthy, the trainer of Silver Ring said that he had popped in at the hotel between 7pm and 7.30pm. He wanted to talk to Fraser about the improving condition of the racehorse and its anticipated return to the racetrack. McCarthy said he'd found Fraser in his office, reeking of booze and barely coherent.

James Campbell hesitatingly came forward admitting that he was a regular patron buying liquor illegally after hours. He said he'd popped in to the pub at 8pm and bought some beer off Fraser. When he arrived, Fraser had been sitting alone in the office. He heard noises upstairs and assumed there was a party in full swing.

George Humphries, the jockey, said he'd arrived at 8.30pm and immediately noticed the backdoor wide open but nobody in the bar. He said Fraser was in his office talking on the telephone so he waited outside. While there he caught a small snippet of the conversation:

'I do not know what the devil will do next. The only way she could do anything is by creeping in on me at night.'

Humphries said that Fraser hung up the phone when he realised the jockey was outside. He too believed Fraser was showing signs drunkenness.

There were a number of inconsistencies between some of the statements. In one interview, Elizabeth Fraser told police that she and her husband enjoyed a loving relationship and that they had planned the trip to Wellington together. She said she could not recall confronting her husband in the company of another woman and denied knowing that he was having an affair. She told Cameron that she had seen the parcel containing the pyjamas and scarf but that her husband had said he'd bought them himself. Perhaps in order to divert police attention she also claimed that Fraser had been a nervy for the past two months. Elizabeth remained cool and collected throughout the interview and this did not go unnoticed.

Police were also unhappy with Joyce Fraser's account of her relationship with her father and of her movements on the night of the murder. It was clear that Joyce had lied in her statement and withheld information. She told police she never heard her parents argue but Pat Dore said Joyce had pleaded with her and Jack Wilson to break up a fight between them. Joyce also said that she enjoyed a great relationship with her father. This was contradicted in the statement given by Alf Higgs as well as the letters from Don to Eileen. In her first interview, she said she had gone to bed at 9.30pm and read for an hour but Russell had inadvertently told police that she had been present throughout the evening.

Police found that Joyce herself wasn't as squeaky clean as she liked to make out. It transpired a steady number of jockeys and stable boys were regular visitors to her bedroom, making their clandestine entrances via the fire escape. Given that the scuff mark police had found on the fire escape did not match any of the boots belonging to the men at the hotel, it seemed likely that it had been made by one of Joyce's lovers.

Meanwhile, Ted Russell had something on his mind. Several days after the funeral, he called in to see Detective Dunlop. Russell told the officer that he'd been to the hotel after the funeral to pay his respects when he'd had an unusual conversation with Mrs Fraser that he thought police should know about. It was the first time he'd returned to the hotel since the night of the murder. Elizabeth Fraser had ushered him upstairs and demanded to know why he had not been in before.

He told her that he thought it was best to stay away under the circumstances. Russell said that she then asked him if he thought Don had seemed a little queer lately. Russell felt that she'd been trying to infer that her husband had been suicidal. He had been unnerved by her style of questioning and thought police needed to know lest suspicion be cast on him.

Dunlop then took the opportunity to question Russell about his original statement, in which he had said that Joyce had been with the group all evening. Ted Russell was certain that when he'd returned to the hotel for a sandwich at about 10.30pm, Joyce had been with her parents and Jack Wilson while Wilson made the sandwiches.

Russell then recounted a conversation he'd overhead that evening. He heard Joyce say to her mother, 'We have got him just where we want him.'

We have got him just where we want him.

Russell was certain these were her exact words. At the time he had no idea what they meant, but he had been mulling it over and wondered whether or not Joyce and Elizabeth had ensured that Don was drunk and therefore easier to shoot.

Dunlop asked Russell why he had failed to disclose this potentially vital pierce of information earlier. Russell could not explain himself.

Donald Fraser's mother also came forward after the funeral. She told police that Elizabeth Fraser had allegedly whispered, 'They will never find the gun. It is at the bottom of the sea. The gun is now in the fathoms of the sea.'

Police suspected that Elizabeth and Joyce Fraser had more of a part to play in the crime than was first thought. But there must have been a third person involved because somebody must have disposed of the murder weapon.

By the end of 1933, police were no closer to making an arrest for the killing of Donald Fraser despite the fact that the case was still attracting front-page media attention. This vexed the police commissioner who called in two of the most experienced and revered detectives in the country: Chief Detective JB Young of Dunedin was called in because of his familiarity with Christchurch's criminal underworld and Detective Sergeant Jarrold from Wellington was regarded as possessing one of the best investigative minds in the police force. The Commissioner was so confident that this pair would soon get a breakthrough in the case, he put them in charge of the investigation. The presence of the outsiders did not go down well with local police or, indeed, local papers. As one journalist wrote:

> *It is well known now that these two imported detectives are in sole charge and the Christchurch public is asking if it was altogether a wise step. The man in the street is quite aware of the ability of Young and Jarrold but despite this, he seriously questions the advisability of excluding the skilled men of the Christchurch detective force even from consultation.*

Reading over the case notes and the witness statements, Young and Jarrold soon came to the conclusion the killer could not have been an outsider.

Mrs Fraser said she'd woken to the sound of her husband snoring. Why did she not wake at someone entering her bedroom?

She also claimed that she woke to the sound of the explosion but did not see or hear a figure leaving. How could someone have got out of her bedroom without being seen?

The balcony door was closed and had to be forced open by police. Fraser had been meticulous in locking the front and back doors of the hotel before he went to bed. Yet when Alf Higgs called police at 2am, he noticed that the back door was open. It could only have been unlocked from inside. If the assailant had escaped out the back door, who had unlocked the door?

Dr Pearson's report pointed out that 'in the bedroom there was no good lighting from the street or from the landing if the bedroom door was open. The killer would have needed good visibility as if the light in the bedroom was on or the killer had an accomplice holding a torch'. If the Frasers were both asleep the bedroom light would have been switched off so how would the assailant have known which side of the bed Donald Fraser slept in or if he was actually in bed at the time of the shooting?

Even if the assailant did know which side of the bed Donald Fraser slept in, what were the chances that their bullet would find its target right in the centre of his chest given that the shots were being fired in pitch dark?

Elizabeth Fraser claimed that her husband was in bed when he was shot. Why weren't the blood spatters spread evenly across the whole bed?

She also claimed that she had been in bed with him at the time. Why weren't there any blood spatters on Elizabeth who had been mere inches away when the shooting took place?

Elizabeth Fraser said she was woken by a loud explosion before jumping out of bed, running down the passage yelling, 'Don has been shot!' It was dark. How did she know he'd been shot?

Given that she knew he'd been shot and she claimed she was next to him in bed at the time, wouldn't she have been afraid that the killer was still in the building—or indeed, in the room?

When she was examined by a doctor the morning after the shooting, he reported that there were 'no ill effects such like deafness injury which would be evident if she was in the bed beside him.' Why not?

Constable Murphy said that the other side of the bed didn't look as though it had been slept in. This was backed up by a forensic scene examination. When questioned Elizabeth said that she slept very low on the pillow with her head barely touching it. But if she'd leapt out of bed quickly wouldn't she have disturbed the pillow as she got out?

Alec Higgs said that when he first saw Donald Fraser's body, it appeared as though it had fallen out of bed pulling over the sheet and blanket. Yet when he returned with Constable Murphy, the bedclothes had been rearranged. Had Elizabeth tampered with the scene to try and make it look like she had in bed when she hadn't?

The one piece of evidence working in Elizabeth Fraser's favour also came from her medical examination. The doctor said that if she had fired two barrels of a gun at once, there would be bruising to her shoulder and arm. No such bruising was evident when she was examined.

Having worked out that the likely assailant was a hotel insider, Young and Jarrold examined possible motives.

Elizabeth Fraser certainly had sufficient reason to want to kill her husband. She knew that Donald Fraser was in love with someone else and had been talking about divorcing her. The financial and social implications of this would have been devastating for her. On the morning before Fraser died, he received a gift of pyjamas and a scarf from the 'other woman'—this could have tipped Elizabeth Fraser over the edge.

The couple had also been fighting regularly over the raising of their daughter Joyce and over Elizabeth's drinking and socialising.

The inconsistencies in Elizabeth Fraser's statements only served to cast further suspicion on the woman. If she hadn't killed her husband, it was likely she knew who did.

Elizabeth told police that Donald had been very drunk on the night he was killed, yet she also claimed that when she went to bed, he'd been sitting in bed reading and that they'd had a ten-minute conversation before they were disturbed by the ringing doorbell.

There was some suggestion that Elizabeth had tried to plant the idea that her husband had been suicidal. If he had shot himself, where was the gun?

Another theory that had been raised with police was the question of the burned documents in the fireplace. Donald Fraser had a packet of matches in his pocket when he died. Was he the one who had burned the pages? There was some suggestion that Donald Fraser had changed his will the evening of his death but then changed his mind and burned the new will. The remains of which were the documents the police found in the fireplace. If it was Donald Fraser that had burned the documents, why did he go and get a new packet of matches from the bar when he had a packet of matches in his pocket?

Joyce Fraser also came under suspicion as having a motive for killing her father. Their relationship had soured over recent months and his strict parenting style didn't sit well with the headstrong young woman. Her mother let her do what she wanted so with her father out of the way, Joyce would always have been able to have her own way. She had also clearly lied about her movements on the night of her father's death. Then there was the snippet of conversation that Russell overheard, 'We have got him just where we want him.'

If Elizabeth or Joyce had shot Donald Fraser, the question of the murder weapon and its whereabouts completely vexed police. They believed that Elizabeth had procured a gun a few months earlier for the purpose of protection while Fraser was away. It is unknown whether Fraser knew his wife had a gun.

The forensic test on the ammunition gave police an interesting lead. The type of cartridge that was used had only been sold in limited amounts in the South Island. There had only been 1000 rounds sent to Christchurch by the manufacturers, the Colonial Ammunition Company. Of these, there were still 950 rounds in stock. The 50 rounds that had been sold were traced. The person who bought them had legitimately used 23 of the rounds and still had the other 27. This ruled out the possibility that the ammunition had been bought in Christchurch. The cartridges had only been supplied to two other towns in the South Island—Dunedin and Greymouth. Elizabeth Fraser had been in Greymouth one week prior to the murder.

That still left the question of what had happened to the murder weapon. A search of the premises was carried out just before first light, mere hours after the killing. If it had been Fraser's wife or daughter that killed him, they would have needed an accomplice to discard the weapon while they played the role of bereaved family members for the police.

Dr Pearson estimated the time of death to have been between 1am and 2am. Elizabeth Fraser woke everyone up at 2am and the police didn't arrive for another 20 minutes. This would have given the killer and an accomplice enough time to dispose of the gun. Who would have wanted to help them cover up such a dreadful deed?

The obvious suspects were the men who had been in the hotel the night of the shooting. Police quickly ruled out Alf Higgs as he was a close friend of Donald Fraser and he clearly held Elizabeth Fraser in disdain.

Jack Wilson was one of Elizabeth Fraser's drinking partners and he had downplayed the fight between the Frasers that ended when Joyce asked him and Pat Dore to intervene. But was that enough to make him want to protect Don Fraser's killer? After Fraser's death Wilson had gone on a drinking spree. The police, who were watching him closely, believed that if he had been guilty, the drink would have loosened his tongue and he would have confessed. It didn't and he didn't. Unable to cope with staying at the hotel after Fraser's death, Wilson left his job at the pub and moved away from the area.

Could Ted Russell have helped the killer? Police received a number of anonymous letters accusing him of being involved. Russell said he had left the hotel at midnight and he was heard returning to his boarding house twenty minutes later by his landlady. Although he was reportedly having an affair with his landlady, she had no reason to lie to police. Russell was also able to produce his only registered firearm and, on examination, it was found not to have been shot for some time.

Having largely ruled out the obvious suspects, police considered the possibility that someone else had been hiding near the scene on the night of the murder and had taken the gun and disposed of it.

After Wilson left the hotel, his room and job were taken over by Charles Chaney. He had worked at the hotel on-and-off helping out behind the bar and chauffeuring Mrs Fraser. Chaney was also thought to be a close confidante of Mrs Fraser. Like Wilson, Charles Chaney enjoyed his grog and occasionally attended Elizabeth Fraser's illicit parties. He had, however, been noticeably absent the night of the murder.

Not long after Don Fraser's funeral, rumours began circulating about Chaney and Mrs Fraser. People thought it distasteful that he had moved into the hotel and seemed to have assumed the position of landlord so soon after Fraser's death. When challenged, Chaney said he was merely helping out during what was a painful period.

Was it possible that Chaney had kept a low profile on the night of the killing and then, at a pre-arranged signal from Elizabeth, snuck into the hotel to dispose of the gun without being seen?

Young and Jarrold were contacted by a Mr Sollitt who was a self-proclaimed private investigator. He was well known to local police as he was always willing to offer his opinion on serious cases and he was usually way off the mark. He had offered the benefit of his skills and knowledge to Inspector Dunlop but had been dismissed. Detective Young, however, hadn't been so hasty.

From 24 December 1933 to 9 January 1934, Sollitt was installed undercover at the hotel posing as a travelling salesman. Each day he would loiter in the bar drinking and trying to make conversation with staff.

After completing his assignment, Sollitt provided a full report to Young. According to the report, Charlie Chaney was running the bar. Most evenings Elizabeth, Joyce, Chaney and various other guests would adjourn upstairs to party. In the whole time he was there, Sollitt never heard any mention of Don Fraser.

On 24 January 1934, Young and Jarrold went to the hotel to re-interview Elizabeth Fraser. On arrival, she told them she was sick and to come back at 3pm. On returning to the police station, Young received a call from Charles S Thomas, top Christchurch barrister and a long-time police adversary. He said he had been instructed to act for Elizabeth Fraser and he had told her not to make a statement. Undeterred, the officers returned to the hotel. Elizabeth was white with rage and refused to speak to them.

At the end of January, a rejuvenated Silver Ring won the James Hazlett Gold Cup at a race meeting near Dunedin. Elizabeth, in the company of Joyce and Chaney, accepted the cup, making only a passing reference to her husband in her speech.

In early April, the police commissioner offered a reward of £300 and indemnity against prosecution for any information leading to the conviction of the offender or offenders in the case. Three days later he added a clause that a free pardon would be granted to any person implicated who becomes an informant, he or she not being the actual killer. On 30 June, the reward was increased to £600. But there were no takers and no advances were made in the case.

By the time the inquest opened to a packed Christchurch Magistrates Court on Thursday 28 June 1934, the police were no closer to catching Donald Fraser's killer. Presiding over the inquest was senior magistrate, Mr ED Mosley. Representing police was Chief Detective Dunlop, who had been one of the first officers on the scene. Detective Sergeant Jarrold supported Dunlop at the hearing. Charles Thomas represented Mrs Fraser and Mr M J Burns represented witness Alfred Higgs.

Elizabeth Fraser took the stand on the first morning. She remained cool and frank under intense cross examination by Dunlop. She consistently denied that she and her husband had any marital problems. She also denied having ever suspected her husband of having an affair or that they had ever disagreed over how to raise their children. Dunlop then raised the incident with Alec Thompson asking, 'Can you tell us what was the difference between you that caused you to cut up some of his clothes?'

Elizabeth Fraser corrected him saying that the clothes hadn't been cut up but they had been torn. She then attempted to explain what happened, 'One night I was in the office and Mr Thompson came in. He had been living apart from his wife. He started telling me his troubles. We were drinking and I advised him to make it up with his wife. He talked to me for awhile and thanked me for the good advice. Then he kissed me. My husband asked me, and I said he kissed me about half a dozen times.'

Details followed of Elizabeth Fraser tearing up her husband's coat and Don Fraser tearing up a dress belonging to his wife. The magistrate weighed in with a question for the woman on the stand.

'How does that accord with your statement that you were on perfectly good terms with him?'

She responded, 'We were on good terms. We had only one row.'

Dunlop then veered the cross examination towards Fraser's relationship with Eileen Hardcastle. 'Have you ever complained to other persons about the conduct of your husband with other women?'

Mrs Fraser replied in the negative.

'Up until the time of the tragedy had you any knowledge that he was intimate with any other women?'

Again the response was negative.

Dunlop then told the court about Fraser's trip around the North Island with the young woman and that Elizabeth Fraser had cancelled a trip to Sydney to travel to Wellington to confront him about his affair.

Elizabeth denied ever having planned a trip to Sydney, saying that she and her husband had planned the Wellington trip together.

Dunlop was stunned at this response but continued, 'When you were at the Trentham Races in October 1933, do you remember meeting your husband in company with a young woman?'

For once, Mrs Fraser responded positively.

Dunlop continued, 'And that was one of the days you were not with your husband?'

Elizabeth Fraser said that she had gone with her husband to the races that day but that he had not been with her all day. Dunlop then asked whether she had been suspicious about the nature of her husband's relationship with the woman. She said she wasn't.

Elizabeth Fraser's visit to her mother-in-law then came under scrutiny. 'Did you ask Mrs Clark to call at Mrs Fraser's to see if he was there because you were worried about his movements?'

She said she had been worried and when Dunlop asked why, Elizabeth Fraser became evasive. 'That's what I have been waiting for you to ask me.'

Dunlop encouraged her to answer the question. She continued, 'The day after I arrived there he said he was going to commit suicide as he was sick of life, and I could not understand why. He was all right for a couple of days. He asked me for some money. I opened my purse and when he saw how much I had, he said it was too much for me to have in a hotel, and took it from me.'

When Dunlop produced the letters that Donald Fraser had written to Eileen Hardcastle, Elizabeth Fraser's lawyer, Charles Thomas strenuously objected.

Dunlop read, '*I had an understanding yesterday. I was told I was hated, and we had a mutual understanding to finish. She said she was ready to go at any time. I to go my way. She said it was no use in going on.*'

Thomas responded, 'Is that to his wife or another mistress? It is most unfair. He was writing to mistresses making excuses.'

Not to be put off, Dunlop went on, 'The letter continues "*that is final. When she goes it is no return. She has got somebody dear and not far away. They are welcome*".'

The lawyer leapt in, 'What question is going to be asked?'

Dunlop responded that he was going to ask Mrs Fraser what she had to say about the letter. Finally Elizabeth Fraser answered, 'I am surprised if those words are intended to refer to me.' She then went on to say that not one word of the letter was true.

If Elizabeth Fraser's testimony defied belief, it was nothing on her daughter's. Joyce Fraser insisted that she had only had half a glass of champagne before kissing her beloved Daddy goodnight and heading for bed around 9.30pm.

Dunlop then asked her what she had done in the hours before she went to bed. She told him that about half an hour before she joined her parents for a drink, she'd gone outside to get a towel and book she'd left outside earlier.

Asked if that was the only time she went outside, Joyce said it was, before adding, 'Except for a short time talking. It was after I went down again. I was talking to two boys.'

There had been no mention of this second trip outside in her original statement. Dunlop quickly recovered, asking who the men were.

Joyce said she didn't know who the lads were but that she'd met them recently at a dance at the racecourse. She denied having arranged to meet them in the backyard of the hotel and said she didn't know why they were there but she thought they might have wanted to come in for a drink. It was before dark when they arrived and Joyce said she spent about 20 minutes talking to them before sneaking back inside.

When Dunlop challenged Joyce as to why she'd never mentioned this before, she said she hadn't thought it was necessary to mention them. She then continued to deny knowing who they were, what they looked like or where they were from.

Exasperated, Dunlop decided to change tack and ask her about her relationship with her father. Joyce told him that they got on well. He then asked if she had ever seen her parents quarrel. She said she was only aware of one fight between them, but said that she'd been out when it happened.

Asked for more detail, Joyce said, 'I had been down to the club. It was on a Thursday night. When I came inside I went straight upstairs. I heard a noise in Mother's bedroom. I heard Father's voice. He seemed to be very angry. As I came in he went to tear up her coat, and I went to take it from him.'

Dunlop then asked Joyce if she'd ever scratched her father's face. She said she hadn't.

'In a letter he said that he had not spoken to you since he had received that scratch,' he continued.

Again Joyce Fraser denied it. But Dunlop wasn't letting her off that easily, 'Do you remember when a servant Pat Dore was sitting on the old porter's bed when you went across and called out that you wanted her because your father and mother were quarrelling.'

'I remember going downstairs to her. But don't remember where she was. I might have said it. That was the same incident,' she responded.

Both Elizabeth and Joyce Fraser's testimonies were completely at odds with what Alfred Higgs had to say. He was open about the state of the Frasers' relationship, saying that it had seriously deteriorated in the two months leading up to his death. He told the court that Elizabeth and Joyce regularly took sides against Donald Fraser.

Another piece of Higgs' testimony caused a stir. He told the court that when he'd gone into the Frasers' bedroom after the shooting, he'd noticed something unusual. He said that he believed that if Elizabeth Fraser had been in bed beside her husband, her pillow would have been indented and there would have been blood on her side of the sheets.

He continued, 'The doctor and I were standing looking over the bed. I said in a quiet voice, "Look at the pillows doctor". The doctor walked around the bed and examined the pillows thoroughly. He said, "There are no traces here", and then commenced to examine the bed on the same side as I was. When he got near the bottom he said, "There is a mark here". He said no more. The bed gave the appearance of having been slept in only on the side occupied by the murdered man.'

Dunlop asked Higgs what state the bed had been in when he'd first seen it.

Higgs replied, 'I was surprised to see the clothes all disarranged at the foot of the bed. I did not notice this when I first entered the room.'

He then went on to say that there was no indication that anyone had got of bed in a hurry, saying, 'It gave the impression that it had not been slept in.'

Ted Russell was next on the stand, giving an account of his movements on the night of the murder. He told the court that he'd left the hotel but then returned to get something to eat, going straight into the kitchen when he arrived. Dunlop asked him who else was in the kitchen when he got there.

Russell was quite sure in his reply, 'Wilson the porter, Mrs Fraser and Joyce.'

Dunlop leapt on the suggestion that Joyce Fraser had not gone to bed as she'd said. 'We have been told by other witnesses that Joyce's last appearance downstairs was at 10 o'clock. Can that be true?'

Russell said it couldn't so Dunlop asked the question again. 'Do you swear on your oath that around about midnight, you saw Joyce in the kitchen?'

Unwavering, Russell responded, 'I do.'

Asked if he'd heard Joyce say anything, Russell said he had. When asked to elaborate, he said, 'Really I didn't quite get what she said. It was something like this, "We have got him just where we want him" or something like that.'

During his testimony, Russell made it clear that Donald Fraser had made no secret of the fact he had a lover, adding that the publican regularly read Eileen's letter aloud in the bar, which made Elizabeth angry.

Jack Wilson was next to be questioned. It was clear that his recent drinking binges had taken their toll on him. He said he could not recall seeing Joyce in the kitchen the night her father was killed but then added that there was a great deal he could not remember.

When asked questions about what had happened that night, he either could not recall or would answer with something entirely different to what he had said in his original statement. The magistrate became frustrated with Wilson and challenged him.

Wilson replied that whatever he said in his original statement was true.

At the completion of the evidence, the magistrate Mosley concluded, 'I have listened to a great deal of evidence and I have listened to it carefully too, over a period of four days, and I am pleased to be able to say that there are certain witnesses, apart from the technical and official witnesses, who could be looked upon as being truthful. I have pleasure in saying that these are Alfred Higgs, Mrs Thompson, James Campbell, Cyril McCarthy and George Humphries. I leave to the public the estimation of the other evidence that has been brought before this court.

'Unfortunately, the evidence does not reveal the perpetrator of this crime, horrible and shocking as it is to any respectable citizen that the crime has not been solved. I trust that the efforts of the police will yet lead to the discovery of the perpetrator or perpetrators, and to their due punishment.

'I therefore return a verdict that Donald Fraser died at the Racecourse Hotel Riccarton on November 17 1933, and that his death was due to murder by some person or persons whose identity has not been disclosed, the murder being done by a double-barrelled shotgun, such gun evidently being held at point blank range.'

At the close of the inquest, the police were no closer to catching their killer, and came in for some heavy criticism from the media and the Christchurch public. It was frustrating as they were sure that Elizabeth Fraser knew who had killed her husband but she was never going to tell. Why would she? She was living at the hotel with Charles Chaney. It seemed that they were running the business together while continuing their after-hours antics. However, Elizabeth's drinking was no longer restricted to the evenings. She was often seen drunk in public and her behaviour was becoming quite outlandish.

There was no movement on the case until the beginning of September 1935, when an anonymous letter was sent to the police commissioner, which alleged that Elizabeth had closed her savings account withdrawing the staggering sum of £3000—the equivalent of about $300,000 today.

Two weeks later, Elizabeth Fraser left the country along with her son Clutha, her brother Allan and Charlie Chaney. They said they were taking Silver Ring to Australia to race. Police suspected she wouldn't come back and wrote to the Commissioner of Police in Sydney warning him that she might try to buy a hotel licence and that she was not a fit person to hold a licence. There is no record of her returning to New Zealand.

Today, the Riccarton Racecourse Hotel is still operating. The main hotel building remains as it was in 1934 but has undergone many renovations over the years. In 1996, the first floor was closed to guests and it has been reported that some staff members have been afraid to go upstairs. Owners and staff report hearing doors slam, lights being switched on and off and taps being turned on and off when there has been no one upstairs and when the doors have been locked. These supernatural occurrences are attributed to the restless ghost of Donald Fraser pacing the upstairs corridors waiting for the justice he never received.

9. An Unusual Arrangement

Waihou Valley is a fertile valley in the Hokianga region of Northland. Despite its isolated location, being 22 kilometres from Kaikohe, early farmers quickly recognised the potential offered by the valley's rich soil.

In 1936, numerous small Maori settlements were scattered throughout the region, and residents eked out a simple existence but they were content in their lifestyle and isolation, casting wary disdain on Pakeha society. The clash between Pakeha progress and traditional Maori life was one that both sides struggled to accept. A police report at the time described local residents as, 'being of Hau Hau origin and it is stated many of them are the descendents of slaves. They habitually break the law and many of them have come into contact with the police and have served terms of imprisonment. They are of a low standard of mentality, but possess a great deal of native cunning.'

This is completely untrue but highly indicative of Pakeha opinion at the time. Local Maori lived off the land and their concept of 'ownership' differed from that of Pakeha settlers. The majority of arrests in the area at the time were on account of conservation offences. Kereru, the fat native wood pigeon, were a local delicacy and they inhabited the Puketi and Omahutu State Forests in large numbers. Many Maori in the area would go into the forest and shoot kereru in order to eat them. The fact that Pakeha had declared the birds a protected species was of little concern to them.

Northland police regularly enforced conservation laws with vigour. As a result, many local Maori were suspicious of the police and authority. As a result of their negative experiences at the hands of police, they responded by lying or withholding information when questioned.

The relationship between local Maori and settler farmers was a more positive one. The farmers relied on Maori manpower, employing them to work on their farms and in bush gangs. As a result of these economic interactions, Maori cautiously accepted the presence of the farmers and both cultures lived in relative harmony.

Ernest Severin Nelson was been born in Sweden in 1881 and his family emigrated to New Zealand three years later. They settled in Hawke's Bay where Nelson attended school and began his working life.

In 1912, he purchased a 480-hectare block of land in the Waihou Valley between Okaihau and Rangiahua. The land was covered in scrub and he toiled hard clearing his land before building it into a viable holding.

When he moved to the area he was quickly accepted by local residents. He was friendly, generous and eager to learn the ways of the Maori. Nobody had a bad word to say about Nelson. He preferred employing Maori labourers and paid more in wages than any other farmer in the region, and did not charge them rent when they lived on his property. Nelson saw this as an ideal way to retain employees. Many farmers complained they would employ a Maori and he would work for a week or two before disappearing without warning. This was another sign of the clash between Pakeha and Maori culture—for local Maori, life had its seasons and they were not used to being tied down to working when they were told to. Nelson's generosity and flexibility meant that some local Maori realised that being loyal to Nelson was quite profitable.

In 1920, Nelson fell on hard economic times, and sold the farm to his brother, William Siegfried Nelson. Despite no longer owning the farm, Ernest stayed on as manager.

During the 1920s, the Nelson brothers built a number of dwellings on the farm. There was a large six-bedroomed house occupied by Ernest; a sharemilker's cottage with four rooms; and a smaller cottage with four rooms occupied by farmhands. There was also a garage and implement shed.

The homestead was about 800 metres from the main road. Visitors had to travel along a private road to reach the gate to the main house. About halfway along the track was a creek that couldn't be forded by motor vehicles in heavy rain. A small plank bridge across the creek meant that the only access to the house was on foot if the creek was in flood.

By 1932, Ernest Nelson was once again in a sound financial position and he bought the farm back from his brother, who then bought a farm at Pakaraka, 26 kilometres away.

When he bought the farm back, Nelson was running 140 dairy cows and 1500 sheep on his 480 hectares. He was also a well known breeder of Red Poll cattle. Part of his success was down to his openness to new technology. He was an early advocate of top-dressing, for which he paid exorbitant prices, but which also yielded profitable results. Many believed Nelson to be the richest man in Northland. He had lived frugally since he moved to the district 23 years earlier, and his house contained the most basic of items. People thought the farmer must be sitting on a goldmine.

By 1935, Nelson was 55 years old and unmarried. He had toiled hard for years so was physically fit but his hearing had deteriorated so that he was completely deaf in his right ear and had only partial hearing in his left ear.

At the end of the year he weighed up his life achievements and decided he lacked two important things in life: a wife and family. He had tried, without success, to seduce his live-in housekeeper, 21-year-old Ellen Dargaville. The young Maori woman had been working for Nelson since April 1934. Ellen soon tired of Nelson's infatuation with her, complaining to her boyfriend that the farmer would open the door to her bedroom and invite her to sleep with him, but she always feigned sleep and he would leave. Eventually she installed a lock and bolt in order to discourage her boss. This proved no deterrent. Nelson would persist with knocking until she opened the door and told him to go away. Nelson made it clear he wished to marry the girl but she repeatedly turned him down before finally leaving his employment in August 1935.

Despite his attempts to ingratiate himself with his housekeeper, Nelson was usually shy and reserved. He was also self conscious about his hearing. He regularly socialised with local Maori and he was always invited to hangi and socials where he would sit and talk happily with his hosts and their guests but was always the first to leave.

One settlement where Nelson was a regular visitor was Rahiri, six kilometres west of where he lived. Rahiri was the family home of the proud kuia, Ringa Henare. Ringa was a sprightly 86 year old who had reared her children and was still bringing up many of her grandchildren. The Henare whanau lived a fairly traditional life in a small collection of whare clustered around a small marae.

Many of the older Maori women in Rahiri joked they should find a wife for Nelson from among the younger generation. He would smile shyly, joking that nobody would have him because he was too old and deaf.

Some of the women schemed to match Nelson with one of Ringa Henare's granddaughters, who were all very beautiful. They reckoned that Nelson was an old man and would not last too long. All the girl needed to do was marry the man and bear him some children. When he died, the inheritance would be theirs.

Old Ringa Henare was not interested in such scheming. In her mind, Mr Nelson had been good to her whanau and he deserved their respect. Ringa also knew that arranged marriages were no longer an accepted norm and her granddaughters would never accept being dutiful to a husband they had been made to marry. A match like this would not work.

Before Christmas 1935, Nelson met Ringa's 16-year-old granddaughter, Mary Henare at the local Rangiahua Sports Day. It became immediately clear he was taken with her. At the end of the day, he invited her to tea. She accepted and the following day, the pair enjoyed a picnic lunch and then he took her for a ride in his car. They then arranged a trip to Kaikohe the following week.

On the day of the planned trip to Kaikohe, Nelson finished his farm duties and wore his best suit when he called for Mary. She giggled at his awkward gentlemanly attention. In Kaikohe, Nelson asked if there was anything she wanted. By the end of the excursion, he had purchased clothes, a silver watch and face powder for her. Mary had never been spoiled like this before, and when he dropped her home, she allowed him to kiss her on the cheek and hold her hand as he walked her to her door.

When Mary arrived home, her bounty had not gone unnoticed. Her whanau crowded around telling her she was lucky, and would get more gifts if she were 'to be with the old man'. Mary laughed and was aloof at questions as to whether she would court Nelson. Her granddaughter's behaviour disturbed Ringa, who admonished the girl for accepting the gifts if she didn't love Nelson.

By the beginning of 1936, Mary was a frequent guest at the Nelson farm. Nelson would call for her several times a week. Winifred Woodgate had replaced Ellen Dargaville as housekeeper, and she lived in Nelson's house with her husband Bill, who was employed as a handyman. According to Mrs Woodgate, Nelson was like a love struck teenager around Mary. He began to take pride in his appearance and sought her advice as to how to make his meagre furniture seem modern.

One day, Nelson took Mary horse-riding. While showing her around the farm, he turned to her and proposed marriage. She declined but did not reject him outright.

Nelson thought he had made Mary uncomfortable with his directness and felt that perhaps it had been too soon to ask. He continued to pursue her despite her refusal.

One day not long after the failed proposal, Nelson called to visit Mary, but she was not there. As he left her whare, he paused on the deck and spied an attractive girl he had not met before. She gave him a wide smile, before skipping off with a bunch of girls.

Nelson was loyal to Mary, but he had to know the name of the girl who had caught his eye. She was Jane Smith, the 18-year-old granddaughter of Ringa Henare, and therefore, Mary's cousin.

Jane Smith was born in 1918, the first child of Jack and Mihi Smith. Within two months of Jane's birth, Mihi succumbed to influenza as the epidemic spread mercilessly throughout the country. Jack was grief-stricken and incapable of caring for his newborn daughter so she was raised by his wife's mother, Ringa Henare.

Eventually, Jack took Maud Henare, Mihi's younger sister, as his common-law wife. Jane was bright and fun-loving but she clashed badly with her stepmother. Despite this, she enjoyed a loving relationship with her father but Jack spent months at a time working in the bush and rarely saw his daughter.

Ringa may have been a woman of an older generation but she recognised the value of a solid Pakeha education, and ensured all her mokopuna attended school. Janie and her cousins attended Rangiahua Public School. She was an average student and was regularly punished for speaking Maori in class or in the playground. However she excelled at sports and was naturally athletic. She left school at the age of 14, as was usual for the time.

By the time Jane left school she was quite physically mature. Despite her young age, she was regularly sought out by older men. When she left school she drifted into a cycle of seasonal work when it suited. She held various housekeeping or farmhand positions, which she would keep until she got bored and she would simply walk off whenever something else took her fancy.

By the time she made Nelson's acquaintance, Jane had been living at Huatau with her aunt and uncle, Lena and Noka Rawiri. There she was paid 10 shillings a week to milk the cows and look after the children. Jane seemed happy with this arrangement as she had no real prospects and she was not an ambitious girl.

Word of Nelson's interest in Jane spread around the small community like wildfire. Jane's paternal grandmother, Takapehi Smith, took it upon herself to ride to Nelson's farm for a korero. She asked him outright which of the two girls he wanted, telling him it was not good to keep two on the go. Nelson was taken aback with her forthrightness, and stammered his reply. He told the kuia that he liked them both, but only wanted to be with the one who loved him best. The woman rode away without proffering a response.

A whanau hui was called and the two girls were summoned. Ringa, who was in control of proceedings, asked both girls about their feelings for Nelson.

Mary told the gathering that Nelson had proposed marriage, but she was not interested because he was too old.

Ringa angrily asked the young girl why she had accepted Nelson's expensive gifts if she hadn't loved him. Mary responded that the gifts had been given in exchange for her time and friendship. This response met with jeers and laughter.

Furious, Ringa ordered Mary to immediately return all of the gifts Nelson had given her.

Next, Jane was asked about her feelings for the farmer. She told the group that she liked Nelson, causing Mary to snort, 'Well, you can have him!'

At the conclusion of the hui, Ringa Henare rode up to Nelson's farm with Jane's father, Jack. The pair told Nelson of their decision.

Until now, Nelson had barely spoken a word to Jane, but seemed pleased to be given the blessing to court her. He began taking Jane on daytime excursions. Like her cousin before her, he drove Jane to Kaikohe and bought her the latest fashions, gramophone records and jewellery.

Two weeks after the pair's courtship began, Nelson attended a hui at Rahiri, where he stood up in front of the elders and formally asked for Jane's hand in marriage.

Ringa gave her approval as long as Jane understood marriage was considered a serious commitment. Jane was simple but headstrong, and Ringa needed some assurance that the girl realised what she was doing. Jane's stepmother, Maud stood up and gave her vocal support to the union.

Jane's father, Jack, had been silent until now. He stood up and asked his daughter in Maori. 'Is it true you want this old man, true or humbug? I leave it up to you.'

Jane replied in English, 'Yes I am going to marry this fellow.'

Nelson was crowded with well-wishers and people patting him on the back. He could scarcely believe he was engaged to this beautiful girl. He announced that they should celebrate with a big party the following day. Nelson asked Jane to accompany him to town where he planned to buy an engagement ring and provisions for the party. Maud Smith hugged Nelson and would not to let him go. She clambered into the car insisting she chaperone the couple.

In Kaikohe, Nelson bought Jane a beautiful wedding dress and several other outfits. He also traded in his old car and paid cash for a brand new 1936 V8 Ford.

The trio then drove to Nelson's farm. On arrival there, he handed the car keys to his new fiancée, telling her the car was at her disposal. The two women had never seen such generosity before.

As the pair drove away from the farm, Maud leaned over to kiss her stepdaughter, the only gesture of affection the woman had ever shown, and congratulated her on having snared the wealthy farmer. 'See girl, you did good. Think of all the good things you'll get; the car, money, the farm after he dies.'

The following day, everyone celebrated the engagement at a party held at the marae in the couple's honour. Nelson put on an elaborate hangi and plenty to drink.

Before long, Maud was drunkenly pressuring Janie to consummate her relationship with Nelson. Jane was embarrassed by her stepmother's behaviour, so Nelson reassured her it was not necessary. He was happy to wait until they were married. However, Jane did retire to Nelson's room and they spent the night together, although both later said Nelson slept in an armchair.

Wedding preparations then began in earnest. The Kaikohe Registry Office was booked for 26 February, a mere fortnight after the engagement. Nelson paid for catering and accommodation at Waihou Hotel in Rangiahua was arranged.

Maud became a daily visitor to the farm, helping to organise the wedding and making suggestions on modernising the house for the new bride. Nelson listened patiently and ordered a new lounge and bedroom suite from a department store catalogue. These new articles were due to arrive the day before the wedding.

Having been assured of her continuing employment, Winifred Woodgate was thrilled to see Nelson so happy. She set about spring cleaning the house in preparation for Jane's arrival.

While preparations for the wedding were in full swing, Jane moved back to her grandmother's house in Rahiri. But after a few days there, she decided to go back to live with her former employers, the Rawiri family. She was very close to her aunt Lena and wanted to spend her last days as a single woman with her family.

Maud Smith was concerned at the influence Lena Rawiri seemed to be exerting over Jane, and hoped this would not continue after the girl was married.

Meanwhile, Nelson's brother William heard about the engagement and was not happy. What on earth was his brother doing marrying a native girl?

On 24 February, William went to the farm to talk to his brother but was told that Ernest was at the Hukerenui Hotel. William drove directly to the hotel where a pre-wedding party was in full swing. He took his brother aside and asked him if the rumours were true. Nelson confirmed that he was to be married.

William grabbed his brother by the shoulders, shaking him. 'What on earth are you doing? Can you not find a proper kind of a girl?'

Ernest Nelson began to cry. He understood what his brother meant but he was happy with Jane. He told his brother that he would go through with the wedding but probably would not sign. The expression 'sign' was commonly used amongst the Maori when a legal marriage was intended. There was no formal or written record if there was no sign. If all parties were in agreement the partnership was accepted. William Nelson left content in thinking that the couple would have a ceremony but this would be a pretence because his brother would not sign the register.

On 26 February 1936, Ernest Severin Nelson and Jane Smith were formally married at the registry office in Kaikohe. The vows were heard in front of Jane's family who also witnessed the signatures on the marriage certificate. The bride was said to look radiant in her white wedding dress.

After the ceremony, a reception was held at Rangiahua Hall, where the men from Rahiri had laid down an elaborate hangi. The wedding dance was attended by many Maori from around the district and celebrations continued long into the night. None of Nelson's relatives attended.

After a long and enjoyable night, Nelson and his bride retired to a room at the nearby Waihou Hotel.

In the morning, the couple rose late and had breakfast before checking out of the hotel and driving to Nelson's farm.

Winifred Woodgate had foregone the wedding celebrations to carry out last minute preparations for the bride's imminent arrival. The new furniture had arrived and the house was in immaculate order. Nelson proudly showed Jane her new home. The young woman seemed unfazed by her new surroundings.

Having seen the house, Jane decided to return to the Rawiris to collect the last of her belongings. She drove off leaving Nelson and Woodgates awaiting her return.

As the day drew on, Nelson began to worry when Jane did not return. When she was still not back at 10pm, Nelson rode over to the Smiths to see if Jane was there. Jack and Maud were surprised to see him. They hadn't seen Jane but made excuses that the girl had probably been caught up in some emergency at the Rawiris. Maud agreed to accompany Nelson to the Rawiris' house.

The pair arrived in Huatau at midnight and found Nelson's car parked outside the Rawiris' whare. Maud led the way, knocking loudly on the door. Noka Rawiri answered and Maud marched straight in.

Once inside, she found Jane lying in the middle of the bed beside Lena. The children were all asleep on the floor of the two-roomed whare. Maud asked her stepdaughter what the hell she was doing. She told her that she had to return with her husband immediately.

Jane replied that she would not.

On hearing this, Maud told Nelson to return to the Smiths' whare to wait for Jane there. Nelson replied, 'There are only two words I want to hear from Jane. Will she come back to me or stay here?'

Jane responded that she was going to stay with the Rawiris, before hiding her head beneath the covers. Broken-hearted, Nelson took the keys to the car and drove away.

Once he had gone, Maud grabbed Jane by the hair, and set about thrashing her violently. Lena screamed at her husband telling him to remove Maud from the whare, but Noka Rawiri sat frozen staring in disbelief.

Eventually, Lena managed to reach over and push Maud out the door. Maud stormed off, threatening the Rawiris that this was not over and they would all pay for what they had done.

The next day an emergency hui was called at the marae in Rahiri. Jane was supported by Lena Rawiri, who opted to represent her young friend. Maud was furious and said that Lena had no right to speak at this hui, before demanding that she be ejected.

The whole affair was humiliating for Ringa Henare. She opened the hui by formally apologising to Nelson, and saying that Janie had understood the obligations that came with the vows she had taken. She also said that she would ensure Jane returned to her matrimonial home.

There was a great deal of discussion and debate, which concluded with Jane agreeing to return to Nelson's house accompanied by her grandmother, Ringa, who would help would stay for three days to help the young woman settle in.

When presented with the plan, Nelson said he would do anything to make his wife happy and comfortable. He was in full agreement with the plan so the pair moved into his house.

Over the next three days, Ringa did what she could to ensure Jane would settle in her new surroundings. The housekeeper, Mrs Woodgate, believed Jane was unaccustomed to Pakeha ways and offered to show the Maori women how to operate appliances and generally keep house. Both Ringa and Jane appeared grateful for the assistance offered.

Ringa would sleep on the couch while Jane occupied the marital bed. Nelson rose early to tend to his farm, returned briefly for lunch and finished work at around 6pm each day so the couple didn't spend much time together.

After three days, Ringa announced it was time or her to leave as sufficient time had passed for her granddaughter to settle in. Nelson dutifully drove her home.

Jane quickly got bored with being at the house because there was nothing for her to do—all the housework was done by Winifred Woodgate.

Two nights after her grandmother left, Jane announced that she was going out. It was raining heavily and Nelson told her she should not leave because the car may not be able to cross the creek. Jane ignored him and got in the car. Nelson chased after her carrying her coat. The pair argued in the car until Nelson gave up. He hopped out of the car and Jane roared off down the road at top speed.

Two days later, Jane telephoned Mrs Woodgate to say that her grandmother was very ill and she had decided to stay with her and nurse her. Jane told the housekeeper that she thought she would be able to return to the farm the following week.

In Okaihau the following day, Nelson met Jane's grandmother, Takapehi Smith. Seeing the old woman was fit and well, he asked after Ringa Henare. Takapehi was surprised by his concern and assured him that the kuia was fit and healthy. Nelson was devastated that Jane had lied to him and was unable to hide his disappointment from Takapehi.

Determined to find out what was going on Takapehi tracked Jane down. The young woman told her that she had been mistreated by Nelson's housekeeper.

The next day Takapehi rode to the farm and told Nelson that Jane would not return as long as the Woodgates were living there. He was shocked to hear his wife's accusations against Winifred Woodgate.

Winifred and William Woodgate had been hard-working and loyal employees since their tenure began in August 1935. Winifred was at a loss to explain what she had done to upset the girl, telling Nelson that she had gone out her way to make Jane feel at home.

Nevertheless Jane would never return to the farm while the Woodgates were still in residence. Takapehi told Nelson there was a possibility that the Rawiris might return with Jane.

'I don't want them. I can't keep them. I've not got much more money than anyone else,' he replied.

Nelson reluctantly agreed to acquiesce to Jane's desires and, with a heavy heart, he handed the Woodgates their notice. They were astounded but agreed to move out on 30 May. Until then, Nelson had to accept Jane was not returning home, so a routine was established whereby Nelson would finish work early on Fridays. Jane would then collect him from the farm and drive to the Waihou Hotel where they would reserve a room for the weekend. Sometimes she would stay with him, but she usually returned to the Rawiris, leaving her husband to sleep alone in the hotel. Nelson would often spend Saturday and Sunday nights with the Rawiris before Jane drove him home early on Monday morning. On these weekend visits Nelson would often to accompany Jane and the Rawiris to Kaikohe where he would buy groceries, clothing and furniture for the Rawiris, stocking their small two-roomed whare.

Word of Nelson's generosity towards the Rawiris spread, irking Jack and Maud Smith. When they heard Nelson had purchased an expensive gramophone player for the family, Maud almost exploded. She stormed off to the Rangihaua sports ground, where the local community had gathered to watch a game of rugby.

Just after the match finished, Maud spotted Jane, Lena and Noka Rawiri and several of their children making their way towards Nelson's car. Jane had no sooner opened the door to allow Lena to climb in, when the pair were suddenly attacked by Maud Smith. In front of about 100 spectators, Maud grabbed Jane by the hair, pulled her out of the car, and forced her to the ground.

A shocked Noka Rawiri attempted to intervene as he saw Maud lunge for his wife, but the furious woman slapped him hard in the face, sending him reeling to the ground.

'You should give your wife a hiding, or leave her or kill her!' Maud spat. She then reached into the car and pulled the stunned woman out of the car.

Maud accused Lena of being 'a rogue bastard' and 'a freeloader' before screaming that 'she should be chopped up.'

Lena threatened utu or revenge on Maud but after things had calmed down a bit, the Rawiris decided on a more straightforward form of retribution. Lena got Jane to drive her to Kaikohe, where she instructed a solicitor, Mr Guy, to initiate proceedings against Maud Smith. While they were there, Lena prompted Jane to ask the lawyer what benefits she would receive if Nelson divorced her or if he died. Mr Guy told the pair that he was unable to answer their questions as he did not know the Nelsons' history.

Meanwhile, Maud Smith soon realised that she had overreacted and disappeared deep in the forest to Omahutu, where her husband Jack was working in a bush gang. She decided to stay there until things calmed down a bit.

It's hard to know what Nelson made of the exchange—the combination of his deafness and the fact that he didn't speak Maori meant that he may not have been aware of exactly what the fight was over. Besides which, he was counting the days until the Woodgates left and his wife returned to the farm.

On the morning of Saturday 30 May, the Woodgates finally left the farm that had been their home for the past year. Nelson gave them generous bonuses and was extremely upset to see them go. However, he knew that if his marriage was to work then they had to go. Winifred Woodgate understood Nelson's position but her husband was less forgiving, believing the farmer to be a fool.

On the afternoon of 30 May, with the Woodgates safely gone, Jane Nelson moved back to the farm escorted by both of her grandmothers, her father and various aunts and uncles. Jane gave a verbal undertaking that she was going to stay and live as a dutiful wife.

That same day, Kato and Miriam Hapeta moved in as replacement housekeepers. Jane and the couple were distantly related and Nelson hoped their presence would make his wife more comfortable at the farm.

The next morning, Nelson accompanied Jane to basketball practice in town. When the practice was finished Jane drove to Huatau and picked up the Rawiris and a young fellow named Pape Eruera. Together, they all went to a wedding in Taheke.

Celebrations went on late into the night. Despite being oblivious to the conversation around him, Nelson seemed to enjoy himself. Other guests kept him well supplied with drinks to the point that he was quite inebriated when Jane drove back to the farm.

The following Saturday, Jane drove Nelson and the Rawiris to Rangiahua to watch a rugby game. In the car park they met Pape Eruera and invited him to join them for lunch, which he did. That night the group went to see a western, *Tom Kean*, at the movies. Pape decided not to go with them, choosing to play billiards instead.

As they were driving home they came across Pape walking along the road. It was late so Pape reluctantly agreed to accompany the group to Nelson's farm, where they would spend the night.

Pape, Lena, Noka and the children slept in the lounge, and woke early the next morning. Lena and Pape went for a walk around the farm. The Nelsons got up a bit later than their guests and Jane prepared breakfast for everybody. Afterwards, Nelson went to work on the farm and Jane drove everyone to their respective homes before returning to the farm.

On Monday morning, Jane asked Nelson to accompany her into Okaihau as Noka Rawiri wanted Nelson to pay for a gun that he was getting repaired. While his own gun was being repaired Noka had the use of a double-barrel shotgun that belonged to Nelson but that Jane kept at the Rawiris' house.

Meanwhile, Maud Smith had come back from Omahutu. On her return, she was served a summons to appear at the Rawene District Court on 10 June to answer a charge of common assault against Lena Rawiri. Maud was furious that Lena had reported her to the police and returned to Omahutu to tell Jack what had happened.

On the morning of Tuesday 9 June, Nelson went to work on the farm, putting the car keys in his pocket as he went. When Jane started to look for the keys, Miriam Hapeta told her Nelson had them. Jane then walked out to the cowshed and returned a few minutes later with the car keys. After breakfast, she drove off without saying another word to Miriam.

Later in the day, Jack and Maud Smith arrived back at Rahiri. They were both worried about Maud's court appearance the following day and they spent a long time discussing what they should do. Maud planned to defend the charge vigorously believing her actions had been justified. On a more practical note, they realised that they had no way of getting to Rawene for the hearing so they decided to enlist Ernest Nelson's assistance.

At about 4.30pm, Jack Smith telephoned the farm and spoke to Kato Hapeta. Smith asked Hapeta to pass on an urgent message ensuring requesting the use of the car the following day.

Kato Hapeta went out to tell Nelson and found him repairing a fence. Nelson told Hapeta to call Jack Smith to telling him he could use the car, but that he would have to retrieve it from Jane.

Having received Nelson's permission to use the car, Smith arrived at the Rawiris at 6pm. He knew that if he told Jane the truth about wanting the car to take Maud to court the next day, Jane would refuse to hand over the keys.

Instead, Smith told his daughter that Nelson had given him permission to take the car into Kaikohe to run an errand. Jane reluctantly handed over the keys on the assurance that her father would return the car later that evening.

Smith drove home and collected his wife and infant son, then drove to the Nelson farm. It was 6.30pm when they arrived. The day's rain had subsided to a drizzle and visibility was poor. Smith drove cautiously along the track to the house, passing 14-year-old Jimmy Hapeta along the way. The son of the housekeepers, Jimmy had been dispatched to collect the newspaper from the letterbox. The boy told Smith that the river was flooded and it was not safe to cross so Smith drove as far as he could, before parking up and walking the rest of the way to the house.

When they arrived, Miriam Hapeta was washing the dishes so Maud grabbed a tea towel and helped her finish up. Jack Smith joined Ernest Nelson and Kato Hapeta by the fire in the lounge. Once the dishes were finished, Maud joined the men to talk about the court hearing. Nelson knew nothing about it and was surprised that Jane had never mentioned it. Smith told Nelson that he would ask the magistrate if he could order Jane to cease her association with Lena Rawiri. Nelson lit his pipe and nodded his approval.

Just before seven o'clock, Ken Howe arrived at the backdoor to collect the day's mail and newspaper. Ken was the eldest son of Edwin Howe who, along with his wife and seven children, had arrived at the farm two days earlier to work as a sharemilker. Miriam Hapeta gave Ken the newspaper but told the boy to wait as Nelson would go to get the mail shortly. Howe waited outside talking with Jimmy Hapeta.

A couple of minutes later, the telephone rang and Miriam answered it. The caller was Jane Nelson. She'd realised what her father's plan was and raced to Rangihaua Hotel to phone her husband.

Jane asked Miriam whether Nelson had given her father permission to use the car, before asking whether Jack was planning to use the car to take Maud to court the next day. Miriam lied and said she was unaware of any court case. She told Jane that Smith had mentioned something about going to Rawene.

Jane then demanded to know where Nelson was. Miriam told her he was speaking to some people about business but did not tell her that her father and stepmother were at the house. Jane then told Miriam that said she would go over to her father's place and take the car from him.

As Miriam Hapeta hung up, she looked at the clock. It was 7.10pm. The housekeeper then called out to remind Nelson that it was time he collected the mail. Nelson told his guests he would be back shortly and walked out into the night, passing Ken Howe and Jimmy Hapeta as he went.

The pair watched Nelson head over to the dog kennels before he returned to the house and looked in the back door without a word. He then wandered down the driveway in the direction of the letterbox. The mist hung low and there was no moonlight so they quickly lost sight of him.

A few minutes later, Miriam Hapeta poked her head out the backdoor and asked where Nelson had got to. The boys pointed to the track. She went back inside and joined her husband and Jack and Maud Smith sitting in the lounge by the fire. Only now did Miriam tell them about the telephone call.

At around 7.20pm, Jimmy Hapeta and Ken Howe were still outside, but Howe was growing cold and impatient. There was no sign of Nelson so Howe decided to go home.

It took him about five minutes to walk back to the sharemilker's cottage. He had almost reached the door when he heard a gunshot reverberate through the night. He went inside and gave the newspaper to his father, asking whether he had heard the gunshot. Ed Howe said he hadn't heard it but that it was probably duck shooters.

Meanwhile, Robert and Mary Martin, Colin Martin and Wi Kaira, who lived in one of the workers' cottages, also heard the shot. Robert Martin went outside to investigate but it was so dark he couldn't see anything. Martin told the others he thought the noise was a truck backfiring.

Back at Nelson's house, the guests were starting to wonder where he was. Kato Hapeta said he thought Nelson was probably delivering the post to the Howes and the other workers.

The Smiths decided to leave at about 7.45pm. Jack Smith asked Miriam Hapeta to phone Jane Nelson at the hotel to tell her that they had just left Nelson's house. Maud then lit a torch and led the way along the track to the car, while Jack followed behind carrying their son who was fast asleep.

Kato Hapeta stood on the porch and could barely make out the lights of the car as it left the property in the direction of Rangiahua. He then went inside and put another log on the fire in Nelson's bedroom while Miriam phoned the Waihou Hotel looking for Jane. The phone was handed to Lena Rawiri who told Miriam that Jane had convinced Bill Land, the publican, to give her a lift to her father's place leaving the Rawiris at the hotel. Lena asked where Ernest Nelson was and Miriam told her that he was out getting the mail.

Miriam and Kato then sat out on the verandah to wait for Nelson. When he hadn't returned by 8.15pm, they decided to go to bed.

When Jane left with Land, they drove straight to the Smiths, which was roughly a kilometre and a half from the hotel. Finding nobody home, Jane asked Land to drive her to Rahiri in case Jack was at his mother's place.

There was no sign of the car there either so Land drove them back to the hotel. When they got there, Lena told Jane that Jack was on his way home with the car. Jane telephoned for a taxi to take her to back to her father's house. When they arrived there was still no one home.

Jane instructed the driver to head towards Nelson's farm but a few minutes later Jane saw the Ford drive past them. She told the taxi driver to turn around, and they followed the car. On arrival at the Smiths' place, the taxi driver asked if he should wait but Jane told him not to. He switched off his meter at 8.15pm.

As Jane jumped out of the taxi, Maud Smith, who was in no mood for a confrontation, quickly carried her child inside. Jane squared up to her father, who stood defensively guarding the car. The stand-off was tense. Jane demanded the car keys from her father. Smith refused.

He told his daughter that he would be using the car to take Maud to court the next day. He told Jane he was happy to give her a lift to Rawene but that he would not be taking 'that rabble'.

Jane told him that she had promised to take the Rawiris to Rawene but that she would be happy to drop Maud at Horeke in time to get a ferry to town. Smith knew his daughter would not do as she said so he refused her offer.

Eventually, Jane realised that her father was not going to give her the car keys so she asked him if he would drive her back to the hotel.

At the hotel, Jane asked her father to wait while she phoned to book a taxi to take her to Rawene the following day. He agreed but his daughter only pretended to make the call before going back outside and telling Smith that there were no taxis available the following day and she didn't know what to do. Smith decided to avoid rehashing the argument and excused himself, saying he needed to get home.

Once her father had left, Jane booked a taxi to go to Rawene the next day and then caught a taxi back to the Rawiris' place.

After leaving his daughter at the hotel, Smith returned home. He and Maud were concerned that Jane might try to convince Nelson to allow her to use the car the following day. They decided to drive over to Nelson's farm to ensure that he didn't change his mind. Jack and Maud reached the farm at about 10pm. They drove carefully along the track to the creek. The mist had lifted, making the track more negotiable. On arrival at the creek, they agreed that Maud should go and talk to Nelson, while Smith stayed in the car with their sleeping son.

Maud took a torch and walked along the track. She had only walked about 100 metres when she came across the body of a man lying just off the path. Frightened, she raced back to the car to tell Jack of her discovery.

Smith drove carefully along the track. Shining the headlights to where the body was lying, he could see that it was Nelson. He took off at top speed driving through the swollen creek to the farmhouse, sounding the horn as he went. Soon the Hapetas, the Martins and Wi Kaira were gathered out the front of the house to find out what the commotion was about. Maud told them that she'd found Nelson dead—probably from heart failure—on the track up to the house.

It was 10.28pm when Kato Hapeta telephoned police. He was told not to touch the body and that police were on their way. Kato Hapeta, Jack Smith and Robert Martin drove back down the track to wait for the police.

Miriam Hapeta then telephoned William Land at the Waihou Hotel. She asked the publican to tell Jane that her husband had died of heart failure. Land quickly dressed and drove to the Rawiris. He knocked loudly on the whare door waking Noka Rawiri. When Land went inside he saw the children asleep on the floor and Janie lying in Noka and Lena's bed.

When Land told them that Nelson had died of a heart attack, Noka started yelling at his wife in Maori. From the smattering of Maori he knew, Land thought that Noka was blaming his wife for causing the stress in Nelson's life thereby causing the heart attack. Jane appeared to take the news coolly. She quietly dressed and Land drove them to the farm.

An hour later, Constable Robertson and Dr McLean arrived at Nelson's farm. There they met Hapeta, Smith and Martin who led them to Nelson's body. The farmer was lying on his back with his left arm across his chest. In his right hand, he was still clutching the day's mail. A partly-smoked cigarette was lying on his chest. There appeared to be patches of blood bedside the body and the pool of water he was lying in was also stained with blood.

Robertson carefully pulled the body over at which point Dr McLean noticed a gunshot wound below the man's left shoulder. Nelson had been shot at close range from behind. It was pitch black so Nelson would not have seen the assailant and due to his deafness he would not have heard any movement.

Constable Robertson left Dr McLean with the body while he went to the house to call Inspector O'Hara in Kaikohe to tell him that they were now dealing with a murder.

As soon as Robertson returned to the scene, he saw the headlights of a car drive slowly along the track. As the car approached, Constable Robertson told the driver to turn back. Land told the officer that he had Nelson's wife with him. Robertson told them that there was nothing they could do and that they should return in the morning. Land obeyed and drove Jane and the Rawiris home in silence.

At 3.30am, Inspector O'Hara and Senior Sergeant Finch arrived, soon followed by Dr Buckley and Detective Nalder who had come from Whangarei. They carried out an immediate inspection of the body and removed it to a nearby shed. They then searched the area where Nelson had been shot but they found no footprints leading to or from where the body had fallen.

Once it was light enough, they undertook another scene search and found two fresh cartridge wads in patches of blood to the right of where the body lay, but there was no sign of a cartridge or of the murder weapon.

Dr Buckley carried out an examination of Nelson's body. He found a wound of about 4.5 centimetres in the left side of Nelson's chest. No singeing or powder marks could be seen on Nelson's clothing or on the wound. There were also two small puncture wounds at the back of Nelson's left arm. From one of these a shotgun pellet was recovered. A number of pellets were also found embedded in Nelson's pectoral muscles.

Buckley found that a hole had been blown into Nelson's left lung and both auricles of the heart had been lacerated by the bullet. He also believed the wound could not have been self-inflicted, and Nelson would have died instantly.

At 9am, Jane Nelson returned to the farm with Ed Land. She told Detective Nalder that she didn't know who would want to murder her husband. When questioned as to her movements the previous day, Jane told him that she had left the farm in the morning and had been with the Rawiris ever since. Land confirmed that she had been at the hotel between 7pm and 8pm which eliminated Jane as a suspect in her husband's killing. When asked about her husband's plans the previous day, she told police that he had mentioned meeting a man who owed him money. She said she didn't know who the man was or how much he owed. Jane also told police that Nelson had purchased a double-barrel shotgun two weeks previously but that he'd never used it and it was stored at the Rawiris' whare.

Detective Nalder and Senior Sergeant Finch drove to the Rawiris to interview them, and uplift Jane's gun as well as Noka Rawiri's newly repaired weapon along with a box of CAC No.5 shot cartridges. Noka Rawiri told them that he had cleaned his rifle the previous night when he got back from the hotel.

Uniformed constables arrived at Nelson's farm mid-morning and were immediately dispatched to collect guns from neighbouring farms. Many of the local Maori denied owning guns as they had hidden their guns in the bush to avoid getting in trouble for shooting kereru. They feared that they would be punished for illegally shooting the birds if they handed over their guns. Police didn't see it this way, however, and were immediately suspicious when locals claimed not to own any weapons.

Noka Rawiri was frightened. Five years earlier, his gun had been stolen by Karney Smith who used it to shoot a love rival, Muka Smith. Karney had then returned the gun to Noka, thereby casting suspicion on the Rawiris. Noka worried that he was being framed again. In front of police, he loudly blamed his wife for her part in the mess. He told Lena she should have released her hold on Jane and made her return to Nelson where she belonged.

Lena Rawiri denied having any hold over Jane. Lena explained that Jane did not get along with her stepmother and that whenever they rowed, Maud would tell lies about Jane to her husband. He would then choose his wife over his daughter. As a result, Smith used to regularly beat Jane, often for things she had not done. Lena pointed out that it was no wonder Jane enjoyed the freedom afforded to her by the family.

Lena told police that she had overheard Maud complain that she had no money and that she wished Jane would agree to marry Nelson, as he would provide them with anything they wanted.

Jane had laughed at the suggestion, while Lena interjected saying he was far too old for her. Maud replied, 'Yes, but look at the house and the beautiful farm we would have if she married Nelson.'

Lena went on to say that Maud seemed obsessed with the idea of Jane's marriage. She accused Maud of having schemed up ways to drive Nelson and Mary Henare apart in favour of Jane. Lena also said that Maud had spread a rumour that Nelson had slept with Jane and therefore could not marry Mary. She believed that it was this rumour that caused the hui to be called at which Jane's marriage to Nelson was arranged. Lena felt sorry for the girl and agreed to let Jane stay. Jane soon broke down crying saying that she never wanted to be married.

Maud Smith told a different version of the story. She said that Jane had wanted to marry Nelson but Lena had persuaded her to stay with her family in order to get Nelson to give them gifts, groceries and money.

Various people gave differing versions of events contradicting each other. Investigating police officers found this extremely frustrating as this internal report shows:

All of the Maoris in the locality are related to each other and it seems that it is a very difficult matter to get a truthful statement from any one of them. Many of the statements made by the same person are contradictory in their essential features. On occasions deliberate lies have been told, sometimes for the purpose of misleading police and at the other times false information was supplied with a view of pleasing the interviewing officer.

Inspector O'Hara—who had established an inquiry base at the Waihou Hotel—decided to bring in some Maori police officers to assist with interviewing and translation. He also hoped that the people being interviewed might be more at ease speaking their own language. It didn't provide the breakthrough that O'Hara had hoped it would.

While these interviews took place, officers continued to comb Nelson's farm for clues. But the breakthrough they were looking wasn't made by a police officer. On 20 June, ten days after Nelson's death, a *Truth* photographer, Powell discovered the overshot wad embedded in the mud. Both wads found came from a case made from felt, which was commonly used to keep the powder and shot in place in a shotgun cartridge.

Mr W.C Whitney of Colonial Arms Ammunition Co inspected the wad and determined that it came from a CAC long range 2½ inch No.4 shot cartridge. However, to find the killer, the police really needed to find the gun.

When a foot search of Nelson's farm failed to deliver a weapon, the focus shifted to the river. Divers covered ten kilometres of water checking all of the holes where a gun could have been trapped. The river banks were also meticulously searched and nothing was found.

After carrying out searches on Nelson's property, police moved to neighbouring properties and later, other farms in the valley. Most of the farms had high grasses, raupo and rushes and were covered in thick scrub making for slow and painstaking work.

With no murder weapon, police focused on possible suspects. Initial suspicion fell on Jack and Maud Smith. The fact neither the Smiths nor the Hapetas claimed they had heard the fatal shot was thought to be suspicious, particularly when others on the property had heard it. This theory was tested when an officer fired a shot at the same spot the killer had been standing, and no one inside Nelson's house heard it thereby proving their claim. Police also found the Hapetas to be honest, upright people and believed them when they said that the Smiths had been with them when Nelson was shot.

Police then questioned how the Smiths had managed to leave the property without seeing Nelson's body. Why didn't they raise the alarm? The fact is they did not see him. His body was just off the track so he would not have obstructed their path. It was dark well before 8pm and there was a low mist. The car windows were thick with condensation and only one windscreen wiper was working.

The Smiths' return to Nelson's farm at 10pm was also viewed with suspicion. What was the reason for their return? Why did they not merely telephone? Jack and Maud independently told police that they did not trust Janie and that a few choice sweet words from her could change Nelson's mind.

With the Smiths out of the picture, police sought out other possible suspects. Nohe Henare said she had seen a man on a black horse riding near Sam Henare's place on the morning of 10 July. She thought the horse belonged to one of the Erueras, but did not recognise the rider. Later, she saw the horse grazing in the Wheokis' paddock. The horse did not have saddle marks but it was sweaty and covered in mud, as if it had been ridden hard and long.

Stella Howe, the sharemilker's wife, told police that when they had moved into the farm cottage on 8 June, she had seen a strange man dressed in worker's clothes and a grey coat sneaking around Nelson's home and peeping in the windows before running off along the driveway. She thought she saw Jane talk to the same man later that day behind the dog kennels.

The descriptions of the man and the horse were circulated and it didn't take long before the man was identified. William Eruera, known as Pape, was a dapper 22-year-old man who worked sporadically on farms and in the bush, but was mostly unemployed. For a young man without steady employment, he always seemed to be flush with money. Nobody asked where he got the money and he never said. One employer described Pape as a 'Lazy Maori who always seemed to have money and flash clothes.' The black horse seen by Nohe Rawiri was Pape's horse, Queenie.

Pape was popular with the district girls. He had many relationships but the one girl he loved he could not have. Jane was four years younger than Pape. They attended the same school and had grown up together. Pape paid no attention to Jane until he left school. By that time Jane was blossoming into an attractive young woman.

In Jane's final year at school, Pape was working on a nearby farm. They began exchanging glances and having flirtatious conversations. Soon Pape was walking Jane home from school. The pair began dating and they attended dances and socials together. Despite Jane's young age, the pair became lovers and they often talked of marriage. But theirs was a forbidden love. Pape and Jane were first cousins. Sophia, Pape's mother, was the sister of Jane's mother, Mihi, and her stepmother, Maud.

Initially their companionship caused no alarm. The elders believed Pape was chaperoning his younger cousin in a protective, almost brotherly manner. When word reached Ringa Henare of the true position, she resolved to put a stop to it immediately.

In October 1934, Jane and Pape were summoned to attend a hui. All of their whanau was present. Ringa told the pair she knew what was going on and asked them to explain themselves. Jane looked at the ground in shame, and admitted that she and Pape were lovers. Ringa nodded and said this had to stop. It was immoral because they were cousins. Jane started crying and agreed it would stop.

Pape looked at Jane in stunned disbelief and shook his head. He expected Jane to defy their elders and declare her love for him. In that brief moment, she had dismissed their relationship ignoring the commitment they made to each other every day.

Ringa looked to her grandson and expected him also to acquiesce. But he refused to give Jane up, and said he would rather die.

Over the next few months the pair seemed to keep their distance. After a period of moping, Pape disappeared from the settlement and went to work in the bush. When he emerged a month later, he seemed happier and was soon dating a local girl called Daisy Heperi. He only saw Jane at local sporting events and they seemed to keep their distance from each other.

Pape usually lived at Kapakapa, near Rahiri, with his mother, younger sister, and cousin, Dick Otene. Police interviewed Sophia and Otene and they independently said that Pape and Otene had spent the day of 9 June fishing on the Waipapa River before returning home at about 4pm. They then chopped wood and ate dinner before sitting outside singing and playing mandolin until they went to bed at about 9pm. They never left the whare all night.

Police located Pape on a farm twenty kilometres away in Utakura. He seemed surprised that they wanted to talk to him. He told Inspector O'Hara that he had gone to Utakura on 11 June to talk with the farmer who owned the land his family leased in Kapakapa. Pape's mother had sent him to see the farmer as she thought they were about to be evicted. Pape said he'd stayed in Utakura to work for the farmer in lieu of unpaid rent.

Of his alleged relationship with Jane, Pape admitted that they had been lovers until the hui called by their grandmother and elders in 1934. Pape admitted he had been hurt by Jane's decision to finish with him, but said if that was what she wanted then ending was the best thing to do.

Pape worked in a bush gang with Jack Smith during February and heard about Jane's impending marriage from Maud Smith when she visited. He recalled attending the wedding in Taheke and seeing Nelson and Jane there but said that soon after that he moved back to Kapakapa and only saw Jane at sports events.

Pape was unable to produce the single-barrel 12-bore rifle registered in his name. He said it was in the possession of his 17-year-old brother, Wati, who resided with the Wheokis at Rahiri.

Of all the Eruera's, Wati, the second youngest, was regarded by local police as the most troublesome. In a report at the time he was described as, 'Unreliable. A bad type of Maori and a notorious liar.'

Wati told police that he had come back from working in the bush on the morning of 9 June and that he didn't have his brother's gun. He said he had tea at about 6.30pm that night with his brother Manu before riding back to the Wheokis' place sometime during the evening. Wati admitted riding his brother's black horse, Queenie, on the morning of 10 June.

Doubt was soon cast on Wati's story when his brother Manu told police that he had seen Wati carry a gun out of the bush that day while witnesses at Rahiri said he didn't have it with him when he came home that night.

A further interview was conducted with Wati Eruera in which he admitted to using Pape's gun to shoot pigeons. He told police that he had hidden the gun in the lagoon because he did not want to be caught shooting pigeons. He said he had retrieved it from the lagoon the next morning and was sure nobody had used it. He did not tell police because he was worried he would be blamed for the murder.

Meanwhile at the Eruera whanau whare, police found a rusty double-barrel shotgun with a broken breach. It had clearly not been used for some time. They also located two packets of CAC No.5 cartridges.

When asked to explain why they had cartridges and no fireable gun, Dick Otene—a cousin of Pape's who lived with the family—said that he had borrowed a gun from another Eruera brother, Hina, and taken the cartridges at the same time. He told police that he had returned the gun to Hina.

Manu Eruera arrived in time to hear his cousin's explanation. He furiously accused Otene of lying to the police. Manu said he had just come from Hina's whare and Hina had complained to him that Otene had not returned his gun.

Otene hung his head and admitted that he had taken Hina's gun pigeon shooting and had left it in the bush with the intention of retrieving it the following day. When he heard about the murder he didn't produce the gun as he was scared he'd be arrested for shooting pigeons. Otene then led police to the spot where he'd hidden the gun and a box of cartridges.

At the same time as the Erueras were being interviewed, their neighbours Pai and Huia Clark were also talking to police. They could not account for Pape or Otene's movements but said they had heard people singing and playing mandolins until about 9pm. Initially, they said that it was nine-year-old Noble Eruera they could hear singing.

Several days later, the Clarks changed their statement saying they had definitely heard Otene and Pape singing. This change of heart came as rumours of Pape's involvement in Nelson's death began to spread. The Clarks, like the Erueras and the Rawiris were firmly on Jane's side of the rift between her and her father and stepmother. Ringa Henare and Manu Eruera, however, sided with the Smiths.

Everyone who supported Jane and the Rawiris remained firm on their alibis making it difficult for the police to prove a case against Pape Eruera.

Having gathered a number of 25 possible murder weapons from around the Waihou Valley, police sent the guns to the Arms Bureau in Wellington for forensic testing. The testing was carried out by Senior Sergeant GG Kelly.

Of the weapons, Kelly found that nine had been fired recently and four of these could have caused the wound pattern found on Nelson's body. These guns were the ones belonging to Hina Eruera, Noka Rawiri, Pape Eruera and Ernest Nelson himself.

The greatest similarity was produced from the left barrel of Nelson's gun—a Louis de Brus DB Hammer—which was stored at Rawiris. Kelly also found that the barrels had been cleaned since it had been fired. Both Nelson's gun and Noka Rawiri's gun were stored quite openly. This complicated things for police as it meant that anyone could have taken the guns and used them before returning them.

By the end of July, Detective Nalder was replaced with Detective Sergeant John Walsh. Based in Auckland, Walsh was a cop revered by police and criminals alike. It wasn't long before Walsh got what he hoped would be an important breakthrough in the case.

Dick Heperi, a local Mormon elder, approached police to report a conversation he'd just had with Jane Nelson. According to Heperi, Jane had said she knew who killed her husband but that it wasn't her place to tell the police. Adding somewhat cryptically, 'If they are not smart enough to catch him he will get two more. If he walks up now with a double-barrel shot gun he might get three. He is pretty shrewd.'

Heperi asked Jane to name the killer but she refused.

Walsh knew that Jane held the key to the mystery of who murdered her husband. Jane Nelson's behaviour after Ernest Nelson's death seemed to prove this. She was often seen driving to Kaikohe accompanied by Lena Rawiri. The pair would then return with newly-bought furniture, gramophone records and children's clothes. To other locals, it seemed as though Jane didn't have a care in the world and she certainly wasn't behaving like a grieving widow.

Detective Walsh and Detective Sergeant McHugh took turns to interview Jane. Although she seemed willing to co-operate with police, each statement she made seemed to conflict with the last. McHugh, a veteran of many murder investigations, said that Jane Nelson was one of the most frustrating people he had ever had to interview in his entire policing career. In a report, he wrote it 'had been necessary to interview Jane Nelson twelve times over, and unfortunately she did not disclose all the information contained in her various statements in the first instance. During the progress of the inquiry it was necessary to see her repeatedly for further questioning. It was found impossible to get a statement giving full details at any one interview.'

Detective Walsh could not work out whether Jane was just simple or whether she was deliberately being evasive. He was determined to find out.

Walsh arranged for several plainclothes Auckland constables, including a Constable Duddy, to spend a few weeks among the community in Waihou Valley attending sports days, drinking in the hotel and loitering around town hoping to overhear conversations.

Within days the men reported that most of the locals seemed to think Pape

Eruera had killed Ernest Nelson, and that Jane knew about it. Frustratingly, there was no evidence to substantiate this.

A travelling circus arrived in town drawing out all the local residents. While there, two constables observed Noka and Lena Rawiri and Jane Nelson meet Pape Eruera and Dick Otene. They reported that Otene shook hands with Noka, Lena and Jane but Pape thrust his hands in his pockets and refused to acknowledge them. Despite this Pape Eruera was later seen paying for Jane at various sideshows.

McHugh interviewed Jane once more asking about her unfaithfulness to her husband. Unwavering, Jane told the officer that she had never been attracted to Nelson and never wanted to marry him. She had been forced to marry him by Maud Smith, who convinced her of the good things Nelson would provide.

She told him that as soon as they were engaged, various members of her family started pressuring her for loans, sheep, cattle and general goods. At first she conceded and Nelson always happily complied expecting Jane to sleep with him in return. As word spread of Nelson's generosity, more demands by family were made. Jane said she could no longer bear it and sought refuge with Lena Rawiri although police believed the only reason she remained living with the Rawiris was because they would tolerate Pape's visits.

Jane also admitted that she had had a number of sexual partners over the years including an elderly Pakeha farmer she had worked for. But she also told McHugh that her consistent lover was Pape Eruera.

While everybody had assumed Jane and Pape's relationship had ended after the hui in 1934, they had only cut contact for a few months before resuming their relationship in secret. Jane told McHugh that all she ever wanted to do was marry Pape, but she knew their marriage would never be accepted.

He asked outright if Pape shot Nelson out of jealousy. Jane denied it.

Walsh then paid a visit to Pape. He stuck to his story until he was told Jane admitted the ongoing relationship. Pape blushed and admitted he told lies because he did not want to get Jane in trouble. He confirmed that they had stopped seeing each other after the hui but when he ran into Jane at a function a few months later, they snuck off to have sex and resumed their relationship from then on.

Pape admitted he and Jane continued having sex before and after the marriage, with the last time being on the day before Nelson was murdered.

Pape said he did not know Nelson well. He told Walsh that he'd accompanied

Nelson, Jane and the Rawiris into Okaihau, but he spent the evening playing billiards while the others went to the pictures. He also said that he'd been uncomfortable about staying at Nelson's farm that night because he had never stayed the night in a Pakeha house before.

The next day, Jane and Lena visited DS McHugh and asked him to accompany them to visit an elderly farmer who was reputed to have second sight. They were convinced he would tell them who had killed Nelson. McHugh was cynical but reluctantly agreed to accompany them.

The farmer carried out a private reading for the women without McHugh present. He later told the inspector that he believed the killer was a young man Jane had been joyriding with. The farmer also said that he'd told Jane to tell the truth.

This was enough to spook Jane into agreeing to tell McHugh what she knew. In the interview, Jane told him that Pape Eruera was extremely jealous of her relationship with Nelson, so much so that he told her he was planning to shoot her husband.

Jane said she went along with the plan and told Pape that her husband left the house to collect the mail about 7pm on Tuesday, Thursday and Saturday nights. Pape had also taken the opportunity to recce the farm when he stayed there the night.

She also told McHugh that she had agreed to stay away from the farm for the week so that suspicion didn't fall on her.

The couple decided that they would marry nine months after Nelson's death and live on the proceeds of his estate.

Following this admission from Jane, O'Hara reviewed some of the other statements that had been taken from locals.

One man, Jock Anderson told police that a week before the murder Pape Eruera had said to him, 'One of these days I will get you to work for me.'

Anderson did not know what he meant at the time but he now interpreted it to mean that Pape would marry Jane after the old man died and she would inherit the farm. Anderson also said that he regularly saw Pape leave the Rawiris whare in the morning. He also reckoned it was common knowledge that the Rawiris had encouraged the relationship between the pair.

In another statement, a patron at the Waihou Hotel said they'd heard Pape drunkenly abusing Jack Smith for blaming him for the murder. Pape had then boasted that he would kill the Smiths in revenge.

Pape was also heard saying, 'I had a rough time up at Nelson's homestead with police. The rope was about half an inch off my neck.'

Despite all the evidence mounting against Pape Eruera, he had an alibi. His mother, Sophia, was adamant that her son and Dick Otene had not left their whare after dinner. This was backed up by the Clark family who stuck to their amended statements saying that they heard Pape and Otene singing and playing mandolins on the night of the murder.

O'Hara clearly had a suspect in the frame but he needed an ace in the pack.

James Cummings was the man who could change the course of an investigation overnight. He arrived at the behest of his old friend and student, John Walsh. Chief Inspector of Palmerston North, Cummings set a day aside to read the contradictory statements. He then recommended Walsh interview Pape Eruera and Dick Otene separately.

Inspector O'Hara and Detective Aplin interviewed Otene, and Inspector Cummings and Detective Walsh spoke to Eruera.

During the interview Pape admitted his ongoing sexual relationship with Jane. He denied ever threatening to kill Nelson and when the murder was discussed he said, 'I don't know who did it, but good luck to the bugger that shot him.'

Throughout the interview, Pape was sweating and defensive. He accused Jane of being a liar and said he felt nothing for her and was now in love with Daisy Heperi.

After about eight hours of interrogation, Cummings and Walsh left Pape in the interview room. A few minutes later, Jane walked in and began to address Pape in English. He was confused by this as they usually spoke Maori. He should have worked out that it was all part of Cummings' plan and that the conversation was being listened to.

The two lovers looked helplessly at each other until Jane told Pape exactly what she had told police: that they had planned Nelson's murder and that he had carried out the crime. Pape started shaking, asking Jane if she wanted to see him hang. She responded, 'You know what I told the police is true.'

Pape looked disgusted and accused her of being a liar.

Jane responded by saying she was telling the truth and that she would testify accordingly.

Despite Jane's threats, Pape Eruera admitted nothing and the police had no choice but to free him. The following day an urgent hui was held at Rahiri and all whanau were required to attend. Old Ringa stood up saying she was unhappy at what she had heard and was humiliated by accusations against her mokopuna. She demanded to know if the rumours were true. The old woman addressed her grandchildren, 'Did you have anything to do with the killing of Mr Nelson? If so you tell me now!'

The pair shook their heads.

Ringa then told them to be careful, truthful and respectful of police and whanau.

As time wore on, the investigation team saw some more changes in personnel. Inspector O'Hara remained in charge while Cummings and Walsh returned to their own posts in Palmerston North and Auckland respectively. Percy Nalder was recalled to assist O'Hara. Having re-interviewed Pape Eruera, Dick Otene and Jane Nelson there was little more the police could do but wait for the inquest.

Before long, a new development in the case became apparent. Jane Nelson was clearly pregnant. The police asked Jane about her pregnancy and she consented to an examination. In early September she was found to be six or seven months pregnant.

Jane told them that after her last period she had had sex with a local man called Muka Marsh prior to her marriage and that she had also slept with her husband. She denied having intercourse with Pape during this time, and despite the multitude of lies she had told, this appeared to be true as Pape was working away in a bush gang when conception was thought to have occurred. Jane was certain it was her husband's child.

The district coroner, Mr TJV Dunlop was in charge of the inquest into Ernest Nelson's death when it opened at Nelson's Farm on 22 October 1936.

Having read all the various statements, Mr Dunlop said he thought it was clear that many of the Maori witnesses were unlikely to give verbal evidence that matched the statements they had given. He also said he believed it was not safe to continue a hearing without a qualified Maori interpreter so the hearing was adjourned for a later date.

Commissioner Denis Cummings read the notes from the coroner and believed the evidence set out in the briefs was sufficient for the coroner's purposes, although he had grave doubts; 'it is perhaps inadvisable to bring out evidence by the woman, Nelson regarding her intimacy with Mr Pape Eruera, which does not concern the real issue.'

There was no actual evidence to connect Pape Eruera with the murder other than the widow's allegations, and he was able to supply an alibi to the contrary. Inspector O'Hara urged the Commissioner, 'You may consider it would not perhaps be wise to abandon the very possible theory that some other person may have committed this crime, for instance the Smiths—Jack and Maud were very closely associated with Nelson before he was killed and afterwards. They also had alibis supplied. I am afraid evidence of Jane Nelson could be viewed with grave doubts, but her statement of course may be true.'

The accusations hit Jack and Maud Smith hard. They decided they could no longer live in the area they had both grown up in and moved to Piha. They were followed by Manu Eruera and his family as they had been ostracised from the rest of the Eruera s for taking the side of the Smiths.

Lena and Noka Rawiri were not considered suspects as they had been at the Waihou Hotel when the murder was committed. However they could not bear the accusations from the Smith supporters so they too uprooted and moved to Rawene.

Pape Eruera was still firmly in police sights. Their suspicions were bolstered when Wati Eruera told a relative that Pape had asked him for his shotgun back two days before the murder. He also said that he'd concealed the gun at a designated spot near where his brother and Dick Otene were fishing. They could easily have retrieved the gun on their way back to Kapakapa.

The police believed Pape had planned the murder with Jane's help. They thought that Pape had made his way from his whare, either alone or with Dick Otene, to Nelson's farm. He is thought to have followed the course of the Puketi railway line and then gone cross-country six kilometres to Nelson's farm. Knowing the area well, he or they could easily escape undetected back the way they had travelled.

The alibi provided by Sophia Eruera and the Clarks meant that police had no way of getting a conviction against Pape Eruera.

On 10 November 1936, Jane gave birth to a healthy baby boy, whom she named Ernest Severin Nelson. Their first visitor was Inspector O'Hara, who on seeing the dark-skinned baby commented that Jane should now be satisfied as to who the father was.

Jane maintained that Nelson was the father and instructed her lawyer to ensure Nelson's estate pass either to her or to Nelson's newborn son. When Nelson's brother, William, heard of her intentions, he immediately applied a claim as beneficiary of the estate and set about contesting the legitimacy of the child. His case was supported by Dr Frengley of Bay of Islands Hospital who signed an affidavit stating that Ernest Nelson underwent an operation on an enlarged prostate gland in April 1934. The operation rendered him sterile and therefore unable to father a child.

Jane was shocked at this revelation and chose not to pursue the child's claim on the estate. She then quickly discharged herself and her baby from hospital. She was collected by Lena Rawiri and joined the family at their new home in Rawene.

Police continued to monitor the movements of Pape and Jane, keen to see whether they would quietly reunite. Restricting their movements was the fact that the police had impounded Jane's car until the completion of the inquest into her husband's death. Whenever she wanted to use the car, Jane had to apply to police with an explanation.

Pape remained in the valley and was spotted with several different girls. He was a social pariah and was blamed for the rift in the family caused by Nelson's death. The only time he was reported to have left the valley was when he went to Rawene to spend Christmas with Jane and the Rawiris.

Other than this there were no reports of continuing contact between the pair.

In March 1937, Constable Butler was called to a domestic dispute at a farm on Mataura Road. As he attempted to calm the farmer, he noticed the remains of a shotgun that appeared to have been burned recently. The gun's single barrel was badly dented and the wooden stock was missing. The farmer told the constable that he had only taken up tenancy recently and the gun was there when he arrived.

Butler set about trying to work out whether the gun could possibly be linked to the Nelson killing. What he found out surprised him. The farmhouse near which the gun had been found had previously been tenanted by Edwin Howe and his family.

Howe had started work for Nelson two days before the shooting. On the night of the murder, Ken Howe waited at the backdoor of Nelson's house while Ernest

Nelson went to get the mail. He claimed to have heard a gunshot as he walked home.

After Nelson's death, the Howes offered to stay and help run the farm but William Nelson installed temporary managers and the Howes had to leave.

The Howes were never considered suspects. They barely knew Nelson and had no reason to kill him. According to police notes at the time, they had been irritated at being asked for their guns and had to be reminded before they begrudgingly complied.

After the burnt gun was found, Ken Howe was interviewed by police. He said that the broken gun had been left by the previous tenant named O'Meara. The Howes, according to Ken, had added it to the scrap pile and burnt it before the family left the Mataura Road property.

Mr O'Meara had been asked by police to hand over his gun at the time of the murder but he had told police that he did not have one. He was not considered a suspect because he did not know Nelson and he had been at home on the night of the murder. Police were convinced that Ken Howe was telling the truth.

Police also investigated other possible leads. In one of Jane's early statements, she said that Nelson had mentioned catching up with someone who owed him money. Jane said that she thought this could have been a Maori man from a neighbouring farm who asked Nelson for a loan of £15 to pay a fine for theft of kauri gum. The man provided Nelson with a letter purportedly signed by his employer, Alf Faithfull, guaranteeing repayment of the money. Nelson trusted him and wrote a cheque.

Repayment was not forthcoming, which irked Nelson. On the morning of the day he was killed, Nelson told Jane and the Hapetas that he was going to have it out with Faithfull. However none of them ever found out whether he had the chance to speak to Faithfull.

When interviewed by police, Alf Faithfull he could not remember ever asking for a loan from Nelson. When shown the letter, Faithfull went out the back and dragged his teenage son in by the ear. Young Faithfull had forged his father's signature on behalf of the worker. Faithfull and his son had both been at home on the night of the murder so they were crossed off the list of suspects.

When the date for the inquest was finally announced, it aroused great interest from all over Northland. All of the hotels and guest houses in the area were quickly booked out. Nelson's family, who had travelled from Hawke's Bay, were unable to get a bed in a hotel and had to be billeted by locals.

The inquest opened at Kaikohe District Court on Wednesday 19 May 1937, before the district coroner, Mr TJV Dunlop. Mr Wylie of Kaikohe appeared for Jane Nelson, Mr Johnson of Whangarei represented Nelson's three brothers, and Mr Gray represented the Public Trustee. Detective Sergeant Walsh from Auckland represented the police.

On the morning of the inquest, the tiny courthouse was packed with spectators and people jostled for position outside the building, craning their heads in to listen to proceedings through open windows.

The first day a number of witnesses came forward, but it was the merry widow that the crowd was waiting anxiously to see. When Jane Nelson's name was called early on the second day, all eyes went to the back of the court room.

Ron Ablett, of *Truth*, described the scene:

> *When her name was called, there was a hush among the crowded gallery. Dressed in a smart grey tailored suit and fawn coat, her luxuriant black bobbed hair curled beneath the latest grey felt hat. Mrs Nelson walked deliberately to the witness stand.*

Detective Sergeant Walsh was quick on the attack, quizzing her about her relationship with Pape Eruera, in particular contact they had together in the days leading up to the murder. This line of questioning was vigorously opposed by Jane's lawyer, Mr Wylie.

Walsh: What did Pape tell you about Nelson during that drive?

Jane: He asked if I was happy with him and I said no.

Walsh: What did Pape say to that?

Jane: He told me he was going to shoot Mr Nelson. He asked me who goes down for the mail, and I said sometimes the sharemilker and sometimes himself.

Walsh: When was all this to happen?

Jane: Sometime that week. I did not think Pape would carry it out. I did not think he was game enough to do it. I never told my husband or anybody else about Pape saying he would shoot my husband.

The Nelson brothers' lawyer, Mr Johnson, was not as interested in finding Nelson's killer as he was in securing Ernest Nelson's estate for his brothers. The estate was worth about £20,000.

Jane, who had been composed and calm for most of the day, found Johnson's questioning hard going. He asked her questions about her relationship with Pape. Jane had already all but named Pape Eruera as the murderer so his line of questioning seemed a little odd. But Johnson knew something not many other people did.

Johnson: I take it you and Pape were lovers?

Jane: Yes.

Johnson: And you still are?

Jane: (pause) Yes.

Johnson: You denied after Mr Nelson's death that you were going to have a baby when you were questioned by the public trustee.

Jane: Yes.

Johnson: Why did you conceal it from your husband and others?

Jane: I was frightened that was all.

Wylie: This is getting onto something that may incriminate the witness.

Johnson: Not at all.

Coroner: She need not say if it will incriminate her.

Johnson: Did your lover Pape know?

Wylie: I object! That is incriminating.

Johnson: Why?

Wylie: Because you are making allegations which may involve my client in the crime.

Johnson: Just you wait. I have not begun yet.

Jane: I refuse to answer.

Although Jane had earlier named Pape as her husband's killer, she now admitted that they were still lovers and refused to incriminate him further. The rest of the questions put to Jane were answered with denials or objections from Wylie.

After the medical and firearm evidence was heard, Mr Dunlop concluded:

'This is a very cruel fate for a white man to meet with, especially one who had been such a good friend and Good Samaritan to the natives of the district. The evidence disclosed at this inquiry shows that the police have pursued their efforts untiringly and unceasingly to unravel a mystery which presents very great difficulties, in view of the fact the perpetrator evidently left no direct evidence at the scene of the crime. The tenacity with which the police continue their investigations in crimes of this kind is well known, and I feel confident that no stone will be left unturned to bring the murderer of Mr Nelson to justice.'

Mr Dunlop returned a verdict by death as the result of a gunshot wound in the back, inflicted by some person unknown.

Acknowledgements

In most old cold cases, the disappearance or murder of a family member was a taboo subject within families. Therefore stories passed down through generations were often only rumours or hushed whispers overheard. This was certainly true for the descendants of the people involved in the cases in this book. To this end, I thank the Dorgan, Jew, Walker, Bayly and Fraser families for taking the time to talk to me, correct misconceptions and answer painful questions from the past. I hope this book assists in answering some of the questions they may have about their ancestors.

Graeme Dunstall's excellent history of New Zealand policing, *A Policeman's Paradise? Policing a Stable Society 1918–1945*, provided excellent references to Bill Bayly and the murders he was alleged to have committed. It was reading Graeme's book that inspired me to research the cases featured here. I thank Graeme for the inspiration, and for allowing me to make reference to his writings throughout the book. Many of the historical statistics on crime during the inter-war years are derived from his meticulous research, and I am very much indebted to him.

This book could not have been written without the cooperation of the New Zealand Police, and I wish to thank staff at the Office of the Commissioner for kindly allowing me access to view these files.

I also wish to thank staff at Archives New Zealand in Wellington, who patiently and promptly assisted me by providing files, advice and service.

I would also like to thank descendants of various police and scientific personnel who provided personal diaries and records from family members who were involved in the investigations. These have been vital in allowing me to accurately convey the thoughts of those involved in the cases presented.

Today, murders occur almost daily but only some make the headlines. The early twentieth century was a time of innocence, and each murder continued to make front-page headlines throughout the subsequent investigation and trial. Much of the publicity stemmed from sensational reporting bordering on the crime fiction made popular by Ngaio Marsh and Agatha Christie. This was largely done in response to a lack of communication by police, some of whom distrusted media. In some chapters I may appear critical towards newspapers such as *Truth* for their style of reporting. However if it wasn't for their doggedness, cases such as Gwen Scarff and Elsie Walker would not have remained in the public eye for so long and, in the latter, would not have resulted in the public outcry that resulted in significant legislative changes. I therefore acknowledge the importance newspapers played in maintaining public interest in cases at the time when newspapers were virtually the only source of media available to all New Zealanders. I wish to thank Dermott Malley, the current *Truth* chief executive officer, for providing some of the images in this book. It is pleasing to see the *Truth*, an independent newspaper again, and I truly hope that it can continue to reclaim the popularity afforded to it during last century.

I wish to thank the staff at Auckland War Memorial Museum and Christchurch Library who were able to reproduce images for the book. Thanks also to Sherwood Young, police historian (retired) and grandson of JB Young who featured throughout the book, for supplying me with a photograph of his grandfather. Similarly, I thank all those who were able to provide me with relevant images.

This book is dedicated to Noel Glamuzina and Ruby for providing much needed inspiration. The bulk of the book was written during my tenure in Auckland when I was assisting with the production of the acclaimed television series, *The Missing*. Noel lovingly accepted me into his palatial 1920s mansion in Orakei, adorned with décor and furniture from the Art Deco period. Each time I walked through the door it was like stepping back through time to the Jazz Age. The sounds of George Gershwin, Noel Coward, Glenn Miller and Josephine Baker playing in the background helped me immerse myself into that era.

Thank you to my wife, Puna and son Raea for their love and patience allowing me to take precious family time away to complete this and my other projects.

Lastly, thanks to Nic McCloy and the team at Allen and Unwin who understood the vision and provided me help and guidance throughout this project. Thanks also to Dorothy Vinicombe for steering me in the right direction.

Bibliography

Books

Bainbridge, Scott, *Still Missing: more unsolved missing person cases in New Zealand,* Penguin, Auckland, 2008

Barnett, Stephen, *Those Were The Days: a nostalgic look at the 1920s from the pages of* The Weekly News, Moa Publications Ltd, Auckland, 1988

Barnett, Stephen, *Those Were The Days: a nostalgic look at the 1930s from the pages of* The Weekly News, Moa Publications Ltd, Auckland, 1987

Bromley, ACP, *Hawera District Centenary,* Central Committee of Hawera District Council, Hawera, 1981

Carr, Margaret, *Policing in the Mountain Shadow: a history of the Taranaki police*, Margaret Carr, New Plymouth, 1989

Cherrett, Owen, *Without Fear or Favour: 150 years of policing Auckland, 1840–1990*, NZ Police and L.Patrick Hunter, Auckland, 1989

Dalley, Bronwyn and McLean, Gavin (ed), *Frontier of Dreams: the story of New Zealand*, Hodder Moa Beckett, Auckland, 2005

Dalley, Bronwyn, 'The Cultural Remains of Elsie Walker', in *Fragments: New Zealand social and cultural history*, Dalley, Bronwyn and Labrum, Bronwyn (eds) Auckland University Press, Auckland, 2000

Dunstall, Graeme, *A Policeman's Paradise? Policing a stable society, 1918–1945,* Dunmore Press, Palmerston North, 1999

Eldred-Grigg, Stevan, *A New History of Canterbury,* (John McIndoe Ltd, Dunedin, 1982

Joseph, George, *By a Person or Persons Unknown: unsolved murders in New Zealand,* The Law Book Company, Sydney, 1982

King, Michael, *The Penguin History of New Zealand*, Penguin, Auckland, 2003

Leary, L.P, *Not Entirely Legal,* Whitcoulls, Christchurch, 1977

Leckie, Jacqueline, *Indian Settlers: the story of a New Zealand South Asian community*, Otago University Press, Dunedin, 2007

Lynch PP, *No Remedy for Death: the memoirs of a pathologist*, John Long Limited, London, 1970

Meredith, Sir Vincent, *Long Brief: recollections of a crown solicitor*, Collins, Auckland, 1966

O'Hara, Charles, *Northland Made to Order, a district police history*, Northland Publications, Whangarei, 1986

Parker JS, *Timaru Centenary, 1868 to 1968*, Christopher E Dawson, Timaru, 1968

Rorke, Jinty, *Policing Two Peoples: a history of police in the Bay of Plenty, 1867–1992*, J Rorke and New Zealand Police, Tauranga, 1993

Rosier-Jones, Joan, *The Murder of Chow Yat,* Stead and Daughters Ltd, Wanganui, 2009

Smart, MJG and Bates, AP, *The Wanganui Story,* Wanganui Newspapers Ltd, Wanganui, 1973

Spicer, Charles E, *Policing the River District: the first 100 years of the Wanganui Police, 1886–1986*, CE Spicer and New Zealand Police, Wanganui, 1988

Stokes, Evelyn, *A History of Tauranga County*, Dunmore Press, Palmerston North, 1980

Swain, Evan, *New Zealand's Unsolved Murders*, Wilson and Horton, Auckland, 1972

Thomson, Barry and Neilson, Robert, *Sharing the Challenge: a social and pictorial history of the Christchurch Police District*, (JC Rowe and the Christchurch Police District History Book Committee, Christchurch, 1989

Williams, Tony, *Unsolved Murders in New Zealand*, Hodder Moa Beckett, Auckland, 1999

Wilson, HJ (ed), *The Bayly Case,* National Magazines Limited, Wellington, 1934

Wises New Zealand Guide, 8th Edition, Wises Publications Limited, Auckland, 1987

Young Sherwood, *Guilty on the Gallows: famous capital crimes of New Zealand*, Grantham House, Wellington, 1998

Archive New Zealand References

Archives New Zealand/ Te Rua Mahara o te Kawanatanga Wellington Office

CW Boakes, Christchurch, murder of EGI Scarff 1927 (P 1 1927/833)

Elsie Walker File (P 1 1928/1724)

Murder of Constable Dorgan, Timaru 1921 (P 1 1921/1274)

Murder of ES Nelson, Waihou Valley (P 1 1936/738)

Murder of Francis Jew 1921 (P 1 1921/1087)

Murder of Margaret Oates, Wanganui 1923 (P 1 1923/1413)

Murder Tinsley/Walter 1931 (AANN W4321 1 31/185)

Rex v/s Bayly

Riccarton Race Course Murder – Donald Fraser 1933 (P 1 1933/1462)

Tinsley WJ, Report upon petition of above for compensation for alleged wrongful arrest and imprisonment on a charge of murder (1933) (J 1 W1190 Bundle 10 1933/31/14)

Articles

Guthrie, Noel, 'Thomas Thomson: more than just a businessman', *Timaru Herald*, 07/08/93

Newspapers

The Auckland Star

The Dominion

The Evening Post

The Hawera Star

The New Zealand Herald

The Northern Advocate

The Press

The Star, Christchurch

The Timaru Herald

Truth

Wanganui Chronicle

Websites

Green, David, 'Bayly, William Alfred 1906–1934', *Dictionary of New Zealand Biography*, updated 22 June 2007. www.dnzb.govt.nz

'Crimes, Unsolved', from *An Encyclopaedia of New Zealand*, edited by A. H. McLintock, 1966. Te Ara—the Encyclopedia of New Zealand, updated 23 April 09. www.TeAra.govt.nz/en/1966/crimes-unsolved/1

http:// paperspast.natlib.govt.nz

www.nzhistory.net.nz

Image credits

Section one

T&J Thomson, Timaru, courtesy of South Canterbury Museum, 2000/218.4

Stafford St, Timaru, courtesy of South Canterbury Museum, 2193

Inspector JB Young, courtesy of Sherwood Young

Francis Edward Jew, courtesy of the *New Zealand Herald*

Vincent Meredith, courtesy of the *New Zealand Free Lance* Collection, Alexander Turnbull Library, Wellington

Gwen Scarff, courtesy of Christchurch Library

The spanner of death, courtesy of *Truth*, reproduced by Auckland War Memorial Museum

Onlookers at Burwood, courtesy of *Truth*, reproduced by Auckland War Memorial Museum

Elsie Walker, courtesy of the *New Zealand Herald*

Evidential photographs from the Elsie Walker case, courtesy of Archives New Zealand

Section two

The lonely mountain road, courtesy of *Truth*, reproduced by Auckland War Memorial Museum

Bill Bayly leaving court, courtesy of the *New Zealand Herald*

Walter Tinsley, courtesy of *Truth*, reproduced by Auckland War Memorial Museum

Crime scene photograph of Donald Fraser, courtesy of Archives New Zealand, P 1 1933/1462

Riccarton Racecourse Hotel, courtesy of Peter Stevenson

The driveway where Ernest Nelson's body was found, courtesy of Archives New Zealand, P 1 1936/738

William Alfred Bayly, courtesy of the *New Zealand Herald*

William McIlveney, courtesy of the *Dominion Post* Collection, Alexander Turnbull Library, Wellington

Ward Wohlmann, courtesy of the SP Andrew Collection, Alexander Turnbull Library, Wellington

Nana Chhiba, courtesy of Archives New Zealand, R22343, AANN W4321 1 31/185

James Cummings, courtesy of the *New Zealand Free Lance* Collection, Alexander Turnbull Library, Wellington